U.S. Markets for Vaccines

Characteristics, Case Studies, and Controversies

Ernst R. Berndt, Rena N. Denoncourt, and Anjli C. Warner

The AEI Press

Publisher for the American Enterprise Institute

WASHINGTON, D.C.

Distributed to the Trade by National Book Network, 15200 NBN Way, Blue Ridge
Summit, PA 17214. To order call toll free 1-800-462-6420 or 1-717-794-3800.
For all other inquiries please contact the AEI Press, 1150 Seventeenth Street, N.W.,
Washington, D.C. 20036 or call 1-800-862-5801.

Library of Congress Cataloging-in-Publication Data

Berndt, Ernst R.
 U.S. markets for vaccines : characteristics, case studies, and controversies / Ernst R.
Berndt, Rena N. Denoncourt, and Anjli C. Warner.
     p. ; cm.
 Includes bibliographical references and index.
 ISBN-13: 978-0-8447-4280-9
 ISBN-10: 0-8447-4280-5
 1. Vaccines industry—United States. 2. Market surveys—United
States. I. Denoncourt, Rena N. II. Warner, Anjli C. III. Title.
 [DNLM: 1. Vaccines—economics—United States. 2. Drug
Discovery—economics—United States. 3. Drug
Industry—economics—United States. QW 805 B524u 2009]

 HD9675.V333.U6 2009
 381'.456153720973—dc22
                                                          2009006713
13 12 11 10 09   1 2 3 4 5 6 7

Printed in the United States of America

U.S. Markets for Vaccines

Contents

LIST OF ILLUSTRATIONS   ix

ACKNOWLEDGMENTS   xi

INTRODUCTION   1

PART I: DIFFERENTIATING CHARACTERISTICS OF VACCINES   5

INTRODUCTION TO PART I   7

1. ENVISAGING AND DEVELOPING A VACCINE   12
   Intellectual Property Protection and Other Barriers to
      Market Entry *12*
   Preclinical and Clinical Development *14*

2. PLANNING FOR VACCINE LAUNCH   26
   Manufacturing Facility Complexity, Scale Economies,
      and Costs *26*
   Coordination with Public Health Officials and Payers *30*
   Distribution and Delivery Channels and Payers *32*

3. ROLLING OUT THE NEW VACCINE   39
   Product Liability Issues *39*
   Pricing, Product Differentiation, and Marketing *42*
   Post-Launch Surveillance *52*
   Industry Structure, Concentration, and Shortages *54*

PART II: FOUR CASE STUDIES   61

INTRODUCTION TO PART II   63

4. **DIPHTHERIA, TETANUS, AND PERTUSSIS AND RELATED**
    COMBINATION VACCINES   66
    Disease Overviews and Treatments 66
    Historical Background and Currently Available
      Formulations 68
    Evolution of More Convenient Combination Formulations 72
    Rationalizing the Bundled-Product Landscape 73
    Manufacturing Issues 75
    Pricing and Marketing 76
    Post-Launch Surveillance 76
    The Long-Term Outlook for the DTP Vaccine Segment 77

5. **SEASONAL INFLUENZA VACCINES**   79
    Influenza Disease and Its Treatments 79
    Vaccine Development Timelines 80
    Thimerosal Preservative Issues 84
    Clinical Development: Testing for Safety and Efficacy 86
    Manufacturing Developments: Egg-Based versus Cell-Based
      Production 87
    Influenza Vaccine Distribution Issues 94
    Extensive Role of Government in Flu Vaccine Supply
      and Demand 95
    Pricing, Marketing, and Nonprice Competition 97
    Post-Launch Surveillance 99
    Pandemic Issues 101
    Future Issues and Challenges 102

6. **PREVNAR—THE SEVEN-VALENT PNEUMOCOCCAL CONJUGATE**
    VACCINE   104
    Disease Background 104
    Preclinical Research and Development 105
    Clinical Development: Testing for Safety and Efficacy 106
    Manufacturing Issues 107
    Securing a Listing on the ACIP Recommended Schedule 109
    Pricing and Marketing 110

Post-Launch Surveillance   *111*
The Evolving Competitive Landscape   *112*
Emerging Challenges: Replacement Phenomena   *114*
Implications for the Developing World   *115*
Conclusion   *117*

7. VARICELLA ZOSTER VACCINES   118
Preclinical Research and Development   *120*
Clinical Development: Testing for Safety and Efficacy   *121*
Manufacturing Issues   *123*
Pricing and Marketing   *124*
Post-Launch Surveillance   *125*
Emerging Challenges and Issues   *126*

PART III: ONGOING AND FUTURE ISSUES IN VACCINE POLICIES
      AND R&D   129

INTRODUCTION TO PART III   131

8. CHALLENGES IN MAINTAINING PUBLIC TRUST IN
      VACCINE SAFETY   132
The Autism "Epidemic"   *132*
The MMR Three-in-One-Jab Panic in the United Kingdom   *135*
Mercury, Vaccines, and Autism   *143*

CONCLUSION: BEYOND THE TURNING POINT—THE EXPANDING
      FOCUS OF VACCINE R&D   156

APPENDIX A: ORGANIZATIONS (AND NUMBER OF INDIVIDUALS)
      INTERVIEWED, FEBRUARY–AUGUST 2007   161

APPENDIX B: THE THREE TRADITIONAL PHASES OF CLINICAL
      DEVELOPMENT FOR VACCINES: A SUMMARY   162

APPENDIX C: ADVISORY COMMITTEE ON IMMUNIZATION PRACTICES
      RECOMMENDED IMMUNIZATION SCHEDULES, 2009   165

APPENDIX D: CDC PEDIATRIC, ADULT, AND INFLUENZA VACCINE
      PRICE LISTS, 2008   176

NOTES   183

References   205

About the Authors   227

Index   229

List of Illustrations

FIGURES

5-1   The Cell-Based Influenza Vaccine Manufacturing Process   *90*
5-2   Technology Shift in Influenza Vaccine Production   *93*

TABLES

I-1   Manufacturers' Revenues from U.S. Sales of Vaccines,
      Other Biologics, and Pharmaceuticals in Billions
      of Dollars, 2001–7   *10*
1-1   Estimates of Transition and Cumulative Success
      Probabilities for Vaccines, Biopharmaceuticals, Biotech,
      and Pharmaceuticals   *17*
1-2   Alternative Estimates of Mean Clinical Development and
      Approval Times, Mean Time Duration in Months   *20*
1-3   1996–2005 Mean Clinical Development and FDA Approval
      Times, Mean Time Duration in Months   *22*
1-4   FDA Approval Times for Innovative and Follow-On
      Vaccines, Mean Time Duration in Months   *24*
3-1   Number of Manufacturers of ACIP-Recommended Vaccines
      Posted on CDC Vaccine Price List, November 5, 2008   *57*
4-1   Selected Vaccines Licensed for Immunization and
      Distribution in the United States, as of October 2008   *69*
5-1   Thimerosal Content in Currently Manufactured
      U.S. Licensed Influenza Vaccines, Updated by the FDA
      March 14, 2008   *85*
5-2   Influenza Vaccine Manufacturers for the 2008–9
      Influenza Season   *98*
7-1   Timeline of Varicella Vaccine Development   *119*

AC-1 Recommended Immunization Schedule for Persons
       Aged 0 through 6 Years—United States, 2009 *166*
AC-2 Recommended Immunization Schedule for Persons
       Aged 7 through 18 Years—United States, 2009 *168*
AC-3 Catch-Up Immunization Schedule for Persons Aged
       4 Months through 18 Years Who Start Late or Who Are
       More Than 1 Month Behind—United States, 2009 *170*
AC-4 Recommended Adult Immunization Schedule: United
       States, October 2007–September 2009 *172*
AD-1 Pediatric/VFC Vaccine Price List, November 5, 2008 *177*
AD-2 Adult Vaccine Price List, November 5, 2008 *179*
AD-3 Influenza Vaccine Price List, November 5, 2008 *181*

Acknowledgments

The research for this book was undertaken and initially written when Rena N. Denoncourt and Anjli C. Warner were second-year MBA students at the MIT Sloan School of Management. Particular thanks are due the numerous individuals who gave us their time to engage in interviews, and who commented on drafts of the manuscript. Research support from Merck & Co. Inc. to the MIT Center for Biomedical Innovation is gratefully acknowledged, as is data support from Murray Aitken at IMS Health. We have benefited from the comments of Henry Grabowski at Duke University and Kenneth Kaitin at the Tufts Center for the Study of Drug Development, and from the editorial staff at the American Enterprise Institute. Any opinions and views expressed herein are those of the authors, and are not necessarily those of the research sponsor or of MIT.

Introduction

The administration of vaccines for the prevention of contagious diseases, particularly in the pediatric population, provides a classic example of what economists call *consumption externalities*—that is, the effects of a decision on parties not directly involved in that decision. Not only does the vaccinated infant gain immunity against the disease and thereby directly benefit from the vaccination, but the increase in that infant's immunity and the prevention of his or her carrying disease strains benefit other nonvaccinated individuals (such as siblings, playmates, and caretakers) by lowering their likelihood of contracting the disease.

Parents are unlikely to take these indirect benefits fully into account when deciding to bear the monetary and nonmonetary costs of vaccinating their children. Alternatively, knowing that most other individuals are vaccinated, an individual may decide not to bother with the inconvenience of becoming vaccinated, reckoning that the chance of getting the disease from any vaccinated individual is close to zero. *Herd immunity*—the relative but not complete immunity in a community of people—can therefore be attained even if somewhat less than 100 percent of individuals in the community are vaccinated, since the probability of a nonvaccinated individual's infecting others decreases as the proportion of the vaccinated population increases.

Because of such positive consumption externalities associated with vaccines to prevent contagious diseases, what economists call a *market failure* emerges (less consumption occurs than is efficient from a societal vantage), creating an economic rationale for some form of government policy intervention. For this and other reasons, governments frequently subsidize early-stage vaccine research and development, and provide many vaccines for free or at nominal price. Most schools and day care centers routinely require

proof of vaccination before children are enrolled, rationalizing this mandatory vaccination in large part as being in the interests of public health.[1]

The consumption externalities of vaccines for prevention of contagious
diseases and their mandated utilization represent one important way in
which vaccines differ from many other medicines, such as small-molecule
pharmaceuticals and (typically larger-protein) biologics. But that is not the
only difference. In the text that follows we will compare markets for vaccines, pharmaceuticals, and other biologics on a number of dimensions.
Although contagious diseases are in many cases global, for reasons of space
limitation, here we will confine our discussion primarily (but not completely) to U.S. markets for vaccines.[2]

Historically, vaccines other than seasonal influenza inoculations have
been targeted primarily to the infant and pediatric populations. Recently,
however, those targeting the adolescent and adult populations have stimu-
lated the emergence of new vaccine markets, and therapeutic vaccines
for the treatment of diseases (rather than their prevention) are now also
under development.

Our goal for this book is to fill what we perceive to be an unmet need—
to provide students in undergraduate and graduate courses in economics,
business, and public health, as well as industry and policy analysts, with a
self-contained overview of the U.S. markets for vaccines. We compare vaccine markets with those for traditional, small-molecule pharmaceuticals
and for nonvaccine biologics by examining the entire life cycle of a typical
medicine, from intellectual property and preclinical development all the
way through to product launch and post-launch surveillance.

The book is organized into three sections. In the first section, we provide an extensive discussion on vaccine markets in general, but focus on the
various stages of the product life cycle. In the second section, we focus on
four vaccine case studies which illustrate the changing dynamics of various
vaccine markets. The case studies are, first, the traditional pediatric combination vaccines for prevention of diphtheria, tetanus, and pertussis, along
with various bundled and unbundled incarnations; second, the seasonal
(annual) influenza vaccines; third, vaccines for creating immunity to various strains of pneumococci that cause pneumonia, otitis media (middle ear
infection), bacterial meningitis (infection of the membranes covering the
brain and spinal cord), and endocarditis (infection of the heart values) in

both pediatric and adult populations; and fourth, vaccines that prevent chickenpox in the pediatric population, as well as the reactivation of a latent form of chickenpox known as shingles (an infection that produces a severely painful skin eruption of fluid-filled blisters) when given again later in life. In the final section of the book, we review the long-running controversies regarding claims that the combination measles, mumps, and rubella vaccine causes autism, and then conclude by commenting on the expanding focus of vaccine research and development (R&D) and issues that will be raised by these efforts in the future.

In carrying out the research for this book, not only have we assembled information from numerous documents, reports, and monographs, but we have also conducted anonymous interviews with thirty-five individuals from fourteen organizations. These organizations include various private-sector vaccine manufacturers and consultants, the Centers for Disease Control and Prevention (CDC), academic institutions, industry trade organizations, medical associations, physician groups, and Blue Cross Blue Shield of Massachusetts. Although the identity of the individual interviewees is confidential, some details regarding their institutional affiliations are provided in appendix A.

PART I

Differentiating Characterisitcs
of Vaccines

Introduction to Part I

Let us begin our discussion of vaccine markets with a few definitions:

A *biologic* is

> any preparation made from living organisms or their products and used as diagnostic, preventive, or therapeutic agents. Kinds of biologics are antigens, antitoxins, serums, and vaccines.[1]

A *vaccine*, as defined historically, is

> a suspension of live (usually attenuated) or inactivated microorganisms (e.g., bacteria or viruses) or fractions thereof administered to induce immunity and prevent infectious disease or its sequelae.[2]

A *vaccine*, as defined more recently, is

> a preventative or therapeutic agent that achieves its desired effect by stimulating the immune system of the individual.[3]

And a *new chemical entity* (or *pharmaceutical*) is

> a novel medicine product where the active ingredient is a chemical substance that has been created or synthesized. Active ingredients which are "chemicals" are created using physical and chemical manufacturing methods which are capable of a high degree of consistency (manufacture is reproducible).[4]

Although many subtle distinctions are present, for our purposes it will be useful to distinguish biologics from new chemical entities, or, more commonly, pharmaceuticals. As the definitions above highlight, biologics are made from living organisms or their products, whereas pharmaceuticals are chemical entities that are created or synthesized. Vaccines are a specific type of biologic. While the traditional role of vaccines has been to prevent disease, currently a number of them are under development to treat disease. Among such therapeutic vaccines are, for example, agents that induce an immune response to specific cancer cells.

One obvious way in which vaccines differ from other biologics and from pharmaceuticals is that, for the most part, vaccines are administered only a handful of times during one's lifetime (first to the healthy child and then as occasional booster shots over the life cycle), whereas most biologics are injected or infused at regular intervals to people with chronic illnesses, perhaps several times a week or month, over the remainder of the individual's life. Self-administered pharmaceuticals are more diverse in their dosing frequency, with some used only occasionally for acute episodes, and others every day or several times a day for maintenance treatment of chronic conditions. As a result— and of importance to their market size—the volume of administrations for vaccines is considerably less than that for other biologics, and much less than the number of pharmaceutical tablets or capsules consumed.

Revenues and profits from vaccines depend not only on volume measures, but also on unit prices and the cost of goods sold. Demand for vaccines is generally thought to be more responsive to prices than demand for other biologics or pharmaceuticals. With the latter two, persons who may benefit from the treatment are to some extent identifiable, allowing manufacturers with market power to take advantage of consumers' willingness to pay by charging high prices, a phenomenon economists call extracting consumers' surplus. For most vaccines, however, such information is less likely to be available, as we cannot know whether a particular child, if not vaccinated, would have contracted the disease. This limited capability to identify specific beneficiaries from preventative vaccinations lessens the ability of vaccine producers to extract consumer surplus in the form of higher prices, thereby reducing their profitability.[5]

As many analysts recognize, reliable data on manufacturers' revenues from vaccine sales in the United States (and globally) are difficult to obtain, since vaccine shipments are difficult to track. Unlike most pharmaceuticals, which are distributed through wholesale and retail channels that can be readily monitored, a substantial portion of vaccines is shipped directly from manufacturers to collection centers and depots at states' departments of public health, which then distribute them to health-care providers. This decentralized distribution makes accurate monitoring and measurement difficult. Moreover, physicians' prescriptions, which in principle could provide an additional tracking record, trigger only a small portion of vaccinations, since numerous clinics administer vaccines without prescription. As a result, data service companies such as IMS Health in Plymouth Meeting, Pennsylvania, are widely viewed as providing lower-bound estimates of revenues from vaccine sales in the United States.[6]

With these caveats noted, in table I-1 we reproduce IMS Health's estimates of manufacturers' revenues from U.S. sales of vaccines, other biologics, and pharmaceuticals for 2001–7.[7] As the table shows, vaccine revenues, although growing at a substantial rate of around 18.5 percent annually, are but a very small proportion of biopharmaceutical sales—at $6.1 billion, they comprised only about 2.2 percent of total biopharmaceutical revenues in 2007. The substantial 25 percent growth in vaccine sales from 2005 to 2006 and the spectacular 74 percent growth from 2006 to 2007 reflect, in large part, the growing success of Wyeth's Prevnar, the first "blockbuster" vaccine, for treatment of pneumococci-related illnesses such as meningitis and otitis media (middle ear infections),[8] and the very successful launch of Merck's Gardasil to prevent cervical cancer.

In comparison, sales of nonvaccine biologics also grew substantially but slightly less rapidly than vaccines, at a 16.2 percent annual rate from 2001 to 2007. In 2007, these biologics had total sales of $35.4 billion, accounting for 12.9 percent of biopharmaceutical revenues. In contrast, sales of pharmaceuticals (small molecules) were much greater, at $233.9 billion. They comprised 84.9 percent of all biopharmaceutical revenues in 2007 and grew at a respectable rate of 6.5 percent annually between 2001 and 2007, but at a considerably lower rate of but 3.5 percent between 2006 and 2007. It is worth noting again, however, that IMS Health likely underestimates actual U.S. sales revenues from vaccines.[9]

An alternative perspective for assessing the relative economic importance of vaccines, other biologics, and pharmaceuticals is provided by the

TABLE I-1

MANUFACTURERS' REVENUES FROM U.S. SALES OF VACCINES, OTHER
BIOLOGICS, AND PHARMACEUTICALS IN BILLIONS OF DOLLARS, 2001–7

Year	Vaccines	Other biologics	Pharma-ceuticals	Total	Vaccines/ total (percent)
2001	2.2	14.4	160.1	176.7	1.25
2002	2.2	18.3	177.1	197.6	1.11
2003	2.7	22.5	196.4	221.6	1.22
2004	2.4	26.7	211.7	240.8	1.00
2005	2.8	31.9	219.4	254.1	1.10
2006	3.5	34.2	225.9	263.6	1.33
2007	6.1	35.4	233.9	275.4	2.21
AAGR[a]	18.5 percent	16.2 percent	6.5 percent	7.7 percent	

SOURCE: Data graciously provided by Murray Aitken, IMS Health.
NOTES: a = Average annual growth rate, 2001–7. Revenues not adjusted for inflation.

2002 U.S. Economic Census, which reports, among other measures, the value of shipments from domestic manufacturing establishments. Two caveats should be borne in mind when interpreting these U.S. Census shipment data. First, to the extent that products are exported and/or imported, census-based production data will differ from domestic consumption data, such as those reported by IMS Health.[10] Second, although considerable pharmaceutical manufacturing has traditionally occurred in Puerto Rico, the Census Bureau does not include Puerto Rico in its total U.S. calculations when counting the value of shipments emanating from domestic manufacturing.[11] Of the estimated $111.4 billion in total biopharmaceutical production in the United States in 2002 (about 56 percent of IMS Health biopharmaceutical sales revenues), vaccines accounted for $3.0 billion (2.7 percent), other biologics $5.5 billion (5.0 percent), and pharmaceutical preparations the remaining $111.4 billion (92.3 percent).[12] Hence, while the IMS Health consumption and U.S. Economic Census domestic production numbers differ, both indicate vaccines are a relatively small player compared with other biologics, and particularly compared with traditional small-molecule pharmaceuticals.

As we noted in the introduction to the book, a useful way to organize the discussion of comparisons among vaccines, biologics, and pharmaceuticals is via the life cycle of a typical therapeutic agent. Accordingly, we begin in chapter 1 with the role of intellectual property protection, then consider preclinical and clinical development issues. In chapter 2 we look at manufacturing and cost characteristics, public–private interactions, and distribution and delivery channels as well as payers. Chapter 3 covers liability issues, along with pricing, product differentiation, and marketing; post-launch surveillance; and industry structure and concentration.

1

Envisaging and Developing a Vaccine

Before a vaccine is approved for administration to humans in the United States, typically many years of research and development will have taken place, during which time the underlying scientific hypotheses are tested, refined, and retested to establish proof of concept. Developers also assess the commercial feasibility of the vaccine, since to be successful, potential vaccines must overcome both scientific and economic hurdles. In this chapter we focus on the earliest stages in vaccine development, examining the role of intellectual property protection and the challenges encountered during the preclinical and clinical development stages. To provide context, we compare vaccines, other biologics, and pharmaceuticals in these early development stages.

Intellectual Property Protection and Other Barriers to Market Entry

Patent protection plays a very important role in many medical product industries. For pharmaceuticals, both product and process patents are common.[1] For biologics, however, obtaining defensible product patents has historically been difficult. According to U.S. patent law, the discoverer of a naturally occurring phenomenon—such as an element, chemical, or mineral—cannot patent the phenomenon, since one prerequisite for patent protection is the "invention" criterion, which states the subject matter must be "a product of human ingenuity." Since the 1980s, however, courts in the United States have ruled that in some cases natural substances are patentable if they are "isolated and purified" or otherwise "insubstantially modified."[2] This and other legal precedents have led to numerous U.S. patents being issued for naturally occurring DNA and protein biomolecules.[3]

In interviews conducted for this book,[4] we learned that product patents generally (but not in all cases) play a smaller role for vaccines than they do for nonvaccine biologics and pharmaceuticals. Patents on manufacturing processes for vaccines, by comparison, are much more common and are applied for and granted about as often as those for nonvaccine biologics.[5] A number of individuals we interviewed stressed that nonpatent barriers to market entry, such as complex manufacturing know-how, substantial scale economies,[6] and understanding of the U.S. Food and Drug Administration (FDA) regulatory process, are just as important—if not more important— than patent protection for vaccine developers. One exception to the typically minor role of patents in vaccine development involves adjuvants—formulated large molecules which, when added to the vaccine antigen (the vaccine component that prompts the generation of antibodies to fight the targeted disease), help stimulate the body's immune system, making the antibody response faster, stronger, and/or longer lasting.[7] Adjuvants are patentable and have become important components of several vaccine companies' patent portfolios.[8]

A recent example of an influenza therapy for which patents played a prominent role is Tamiflu (generic name, oseltamivir), the oral drug for avian flu which is marketed by Roche under an exclusive licensing agreement with Gilead, the patent-holder.[9] In 2005, when concerns about a possible avian flu pandemic arose, Tamiflu was the only medicine shown to be effective in treating human cases of the potentially dangerous H5N1 avian flu strain. Roche's manufacturing capacity, however, was viewed as being woefully inadequate to meet global demands if a pandemic were to emerge. In response, numerous public officials in the United States and elsewhere called for the Gilead/Roche patent to be infringed or invalidated; some also argued that Tamiflu should be manufactured under compulsory licensing to other firms.[10]

Notably, the short-run capacity shortfall would not have been alleviated by such patent annulments, as the shortage was due largely to the scarcity of shikimic acid, the raw ingredient for Tamiflu which is extracted from the pods of the star anise grown in mountain provinces in southwest China. Moreover, although it is a treatment for mitigating the health consequences of flu, Tamiflu is not, in fact, a vaccine, but rather a member of the class of medicines known as neuraminidase inhibitors, which work by limiting the spread of the influenza virus inside the body.[11] Ironically, since 2005, Roche has worked diligently and successfully to increase manufacturing capacity substantially, but with concern over a possible avian flu pandemic waning, the company's 2007 Tamiflu sales were estimated to be only half those of 2006, leaving it with considerable inventory and excess manufacturing capacity.[12]

Preclinical and Clinical Development

Although the available data are meager, evidence suggests that, at least in 2000, vaccine manufacturers spent about 16 percent of the proceeds of sales on research and development, approximately the same proportion as that spent by pharmaceutical manufacturers.[13] Several inherent characteristics of vaccines complicate and differentiate their development paths relative to other biologics and pharmaceuticals.[14]

First, because vaccines generally prevent disease rather than treat it, they are usually administered to healthy individuals, often infants. This distinction implies that the clinical efficacy endpoint of a vaccine—that is, the goal of the treatment—typically cannot be the elimination of disease symptoms and characteristics, but instead may involve a measure of immunologic response, such as a serum antibody level that correlates with protection from disease (often called a biomarker, or a surrogate endpoint). An alternative clinical goal is a difference in disease rates, following the passage of an adequate amount of time, between test subjects receiving the treatment and those given a placebo.

Second, the Hippocratic injunction to "do no harm" is particularly pertinent to such testing, since vaccines are administered to healthy people—disproportionately infants and children. As doing harm to an otherwise healthy child is perceived by many as being more dreadful than worsening the condition of an already disease-stricken individual, safety assessment is particularly intense, and safety requirements are extremely tight. While safety concerns are clearly paramount for other biologics and pharmaceuticals, vaccine manufacturers are now being asked to disprove even very rare adverse effects prior to gaining market approval.

For example, after years of careful development, a rotavirus vaccine licensed in 1998 was withdrawn from the U.S. market in 1999 when it was found to cause a rare but serious intestinal obstruction in 1 in 10,000 recipients.[15] This exceptional caution mandates unusually large phase III trials, as in the case of Merck and GlaxoSmithKline, two competing developers of different rotavirus vaccines, who are reported to have tested their products in preapproval trials with a combined total of more than 140,000 children.[16] Moreover, since many vaccines are designed to have long-lived impacts, their short- and long-term efficacy benefits must be weighed against their short- and long-term risks and costs. This risk–benefit determination entails close monitoring of the trial participants for extended periods of time—longer than with many other biologics and pharmaceuticals.

Third, for some of the combination vaccines that target several different diseases (such as diphtheria, tetanus, and pertussis, or measles, mumps, and rubella), or the conjugated multivalent vaccines that are effective against more than one type of bacterium or virus, the clinical development path requires study designs that compare the treatment group given the new combination vaccine to other treatment groups given vaccines having either single, or at least less numerous, components, rather than to a placebo. Instead of aiming to establish a statistical difference between the placebo and new-treatment groups, these trials (called noninferiority or equivalence trials) are designed to demonstrate no reduction or difference (respectively) in efficacy of the new treatment compared to the other active treatment group or groups. Noninferiority and equivalence trials are not unique to vaccines—they also often occur for other anti-infective therapeutics and oncology products where use of a placebo group would be unethical—but they are relatively common among vaccines. An important economic implication of this type of study design is that since the comparison is with another treatment group rather than a placebo, the absolute magnitude of the difference in the measured clinical endpoint among the various treatment groups (the "effect size") is typically smaller, requiring a larger and more costly sample size to achieve results that are statistically significant.[17]

Two other aspects of clinical development for vaccines are worth mentioning briefly here, although they will be discussed in more detail later. Generally, early in the vaccine development process, considerable discussion takes place among payers for the vaccine (such as the Centers for Disease Control and Prevention), providers of the vaccine (such as the American Academy of Pediatrics and the American Academy of Family Physicians), and vaccine developers regarding dosing schedules and other

desired attributes of a new vaccine product in the context of existing vaccination schedules. The necessity for coordination arises because the payers
for vaccines—particularly for pediatric vaccines—are heavily dominated by
the public sector, and because combination vaccines and coordinated vaccination schedules generate important benefits, such as convenience to
patients (and their parents), which subsequently facilitate adherence to recommended treatment guidelines. Also critical is the assessment of possible
interactions among the existing and candidate vaccines. While discussions
among payers, providers, and developers also take place during the development process for other biologics and pharmaceuticals, for vaccines this
set of interactions is considerably more complex, intense, and lengthy.

Second, like other biologics, vaccines are derived from living organisms
whose manufacturing production can result in product heterogeneity,
reflecting the inherent random nature of their underlying biological activity. One consequence of this, discussed in more detail below, is that regulators such as the FDA typically require vaccine developers to have fully
scaled-up manufacturing facilities qualified considerably before the pivotal
phase III trials begin. This requirement is in contrast to most small-
molecule pharmaceuticals, for which final scale-up of manufacturing facilities can be certified later on in the development process, using traditional
criteria to characterize chemical structure and establish bioequivalence
between molecules produced during the early clinical phases and those
manufactured for sales to the U.S. market

What are the consequences of these differential clinical development
characteristics among vaccines, biologics, and traditional pharmaceuticals
for development times and probabilities of success? While available information is relatively meager and in some cases dated, two published studies
are of particular interest.[18]

A seminal (though now dated) study is by Struck (1996), who looked
at transition and cumulative success probabilities[19] for 266 vaccine development projects conducted between 1983 and 1994 and compared them
to 472 "biopharmaceutical" projects from 1983 to 1991 that he had examined in a previous study (1994). Both studies were based on publicly available data from PharmaProjects, a database that tracks drugs in research and
development. Struck's "biopharmaceutical" data sample consisted only of
biologics, about 10 percent of which were vaccines.[20] Based on these data,

TABLE 1-1
ESTIMATES OF TRANSITION AND CUMULATIVE SUCCESS PROBABILITIES
FOR VACCINES, BIOPHARMACEUTICALS, BIOTECH, AND PHARMACEUTICALS

Conditional transition probability	Struck (1996)		DiMasi and Grabowski (2008)	
	Vaccines	Biopharma-ceuticals	Biotech	Pharma-ceuticals
Preclinical to phase I	0.57	0.57	NA	NA
Phase I to phase II	0.72	0.88	0.837	0.710
Phase II to phase III	0.79	0.86	0.563	0.442
Phase III to preregistration	0.71	0.93		
Registration to launch	0.96	1.00	0.642	0.685
Cumulative launch probability				
Preclinical to launch	0.22	0.40	NA	NA
Phase I to launch	0.39	0.71	0.303	0.215
Phase II to launch	0.64	0.80	0.361	0.303
Phase III to launch	0.68	0.93	–	–
Registration to launch	0.96	1.00	0.642	0.685

NOTES: NA = not available. DiMasi and Grabowski (2008) do not distinguish among end of phase III, preregistration, registration, and review, but only provide data on phase III to launch.

Struck compared conditional transition probabilities (that is, the probabilities of the products under development completing one phase successfully and going on to the next) and cumulative launch probabilities (the probabilities of progressing all the way from phase I to launch) for vaccines and biopharmaceuticals. Results are given in table 1-1.

Although preclinical success probabilities to phase I for vaccines and biopharmaceuticals were identical at 0.57, thereafter these probabilities for vaccines were generally lower than for biopharmaceuticals, with particularly large differences between phase I and phase II (0.72 versus 0.88) and from phase III to preregistration (0.71 versus 0.93).[21] The cumulative vaccine success probability from phase I to launch was 0.39, while that for biopharmaceuticals was 1.8 times larger, at 0.71. Struck interpreted the lower success probability for vaccines going from phase III to preregistration as a reflection of the common decision to put vaccines into phase III studies based on less definitive data, such as surrogate markers, which may be misleading as indicators of the true efficacy of the vaccine.[22] Regarding the much higher cumulative success probability to launch for biopharmaceuticals than for vaccines, Struck was cautious, stating,

> The strikingly high success rate for biopharmaceuticals is explained, partially at least, by the fact that many of the biopharmaceuticals developed and marketed between 1983 and 1991 have been substitutes or replacements for natural molecules in humans—less risky markets. The road ahead for biopharmaceuticals may be rockier.[23]

In interpreting these findings, several individuals we interviewed made a number of qualifying comments, in addition to reinforcing Struck's caution about "low hanging fruit of early biologics."[24] First, pointing to examples such as Merck's refrigerator-stable Varivax-II and Varivax-III vaccines,[25] which were approved by the FDA but never launched, and its combination hepatitis-A and hepatitis-B vaccine development project, which was apparently clinically successful but ultimately abandoned, several interviewees noted that cumulative launch probability calculations tend to confound commercial and clinical phenomena. Vaccine projects can be abandoned for commercial reasons (such as market size judged to be too small to justify huge launch costs), even though the clinical results may be very positive. Although some interviewees believed this to be the case more often for vaccines than for other biologic or traditional pharmaceutical projects, all acknowledged that evidence to support this interpretation is proprietary and not currently available, nor is it likely ever to become available.

A second interpretation of Struck's 1996 findings centers on the heterogeneity of vaccine development projects. Although these projects are generally initiated based on a combination of expectations for both technical and commercial success,[26] exceptions were made during the 1990s when, for humanitarian, public health, and other reasons, a substantial number of HIV vaccine projects were begun in full recognition of likely technical failure. Had these projects been excluded from Struck's analysis, some interviewees argued, the vaccine–biologics comparison would have been more favorable to vaccines. Indeed, some believed that, particularly for those vaccines having blood serum biomarkers and reliable animal models, vaccine development projects were more likely to be clinically successful than pharmaceuticals or other biologic projects at comparable phases of development.[27]

Overall, therefore, on the issue of relative transition and cumulative launch probability success rates among vaccines, other biologics, and pharmaceuticals, we interpret the evidence to be dated, limited, and equivocal.

Turning now to development timelines rather than success probabilities, Struck found in his 1996 study that, as we show in table 1-2, most advantages between vaccines and biopharmaceuticals were reversed—at each transition phase except preclinical and phase I, development took less time for vaccines than for biopharmaceuticals. Excluding preclinical studies, the total development time from phase I through launch was 91.2 months for vaccines and 115.2 months for biopharmaceuticals (7.6 versus 9.6 years).[28] The shorter vaccine development times were particularly substantial (and statistically significant) from phase III to preregistration and from preregistration to registration.

Struck attributed the phase III advantage of vaccines to the relatively high incidence of their targeted diseases (particularly in certain geographic locations and in cases where the vaccine was the first to address an unmet medical need). The perceived urgency facilitated rapid recruitment of test subjects, thereby reducing the length of time for vaccines in phase III. The typical testing of vaccines in healthy individuals meant that the availability of subjects was unconstrained by disease prevalence and incidence, which also facilitated rapid recruitment.[29]

Struck attributed the registration advantage to the fact that, at the time of his study, vaccine developers tended to pursue fewer new disease target indication approvals than did producers of biopharmaceuticals, since a greater number of disease targets typically required additional regulatory data review. This regulatory advantage may no longer be the case, however, particularly for the multivalent vaccines (discussed later in the case studies).[30]

Even though vaccines were excluded from its analysis, a much more recent study published by DiMasi and Grabowski in 2008 is of interest, since it compared success probabilities and development times by trial phase for "biotech" and pharmaceutical products. The DiMasi and Grabowski

TABLE 1-2

ALTERNATIVE ESTIMATES OF MEAN CLINICAL DEVELOPMENT
AND APPROVAL TIMES, MEAN TIME DURATION IN MONTHS

Phase	Struck (1996)		DiMasi and Grabowski (2008)	
	Vaccines	Biopharma-ceuticals	Biotech	Pharma-ceuticals
Preclinical	28.8	27.6	NA	NA
Phase I	24.0	21.6	19.5	12.3
Phase II	21.6	26.4	29.3	26.0
Phase III to preregistration	16.8	24.0	32.9	33.8
Registration, review, and launch	28.8	43.2	16.0	18.2
Total excluding preclinical	91.2	115.2	97.7	90.3

NOTES: NA = not available. Registration, review, and launch time is the sum of Struck's (1996) pre-registration to registration plus registration to launch times. Struck's numbers in years are converted to months by multiplying by twelve.

"biotech" sample was composed entirely of 522 biologics[31] that first entered clinical testing between 1990 and 2003; the data were taken from PharmaProjects, R&D Focus, and iDDb3.[32] The pharmaceutical data covered 534 drugs; detailed results from testing of these products were written up in a previously published study.[33]

As shown in the last two columns of table 1-1, success probabilities in the DiMasi and Grabowski study were greater for biotech than pharmaceutical projects from phase I to phase II (0.837 versus 0.710) and from phase II to phase III (0.563 versus 0.442), but were slightly lower for biotech than pharmaceutical projects in the critical phase III to launch stage (0.642 versus 0.685). When they cumulated their results over all phases by multiplying success probabilities, DiMasi and Grabowski found that those going from phase I to launch were about 1.4 times greater for biotech than for pharmaceutical projects (0.303 versus 0.215).

These findings raise several issues. First, as noted above, Struck conjectured in his 1996 study that the greater success probabilities of biopharmaceutical versus vaccine projects may in part have reflected the fact that the early 1983–91 biopharmaceutical projects in his dataset were relatively low-risk human enzyme replacement studies, and that subsequent bio-pharmaceutical R&D might be more risky. Citing a previous study by Halliday and others which concluded that the cumulative success probability for new chemical entities (pharmaceuticals) from phase I to launch was 0.25, Struck noted in his own 1994 study the analogous cumulative success probability for biopharmaceuticals of 0.71, which was larger than that for pharmaceuticals by a factor of 2.84. In comparison, the DiMasi and Grabowski study, based on more recent 1990–2003 data, still found a larger success probability for biotech than pharmaceutical projects—0.303 versus 0.215—but this relative advantage was now much smaller; at 1.42, it was exactly half as large, consistent with Struck's conjecture.[34]

Turning away once again from success probabilities toward relative total development times, recall from table 1-2 Struck's 1996 finding that mean development time from phase I to launch was 91.2 months for vaccines and 115.2 months for biopharmaceuticals. In their 2007 comparison of biotech products with pharmaceuticals, DiMasi and Grabowski reported that the mean duration of clinical studies between phase I and launch was slightly longer for biotech (97.7 months) than for pharmaceuticals (90.3 months). Although the study methods were not necessarily comparable, one could conjecture by combining the DiMasi and Grabowski results with the previous findings from Struck that cumulative clinical development times for vaccines were likely to be less than those for other biologics, and closer to those for pharmaceuticals.

In a 2006 study, Reichert provided some related evidence on relative development and approval times, limiting her analysis to only those development programs that eventually succeeded in obtaining FDA product approval. More specifically, calling vaccines, biopharmaceuticals, and new chemical entities what we have in this section designated, respectively, as vaccines, other biologics, and pharmaceuticals, Reichert examined clinical development and FDA approval times for 15 vaccines, 65 biopharmaceuticals, and 168 new chemical entities. Reichert excluded the preclinical phase from her analysis and defined the clinical development phase as extending from either the U.S. FDA filing date of the first investigational new drug application or the date that clinical study was initiated (most likely outside the United States)—whichever was earlier—to the date the biologics license application was submitted to the FDA.

TABLE 1-3
1996–2005 MEAN CLINICAL DEVELOPMENT AND FDA APPROVAL TIMES, MEAN TIME DURATION IN MONTHS

Biopharmaceuticals	1996–2000	2001–5	1996–2005
Development time	68.0	83.0	75.6
Approval time	15.9	18.5	17.2
Number	32	33	65
Vaccines	**1996–2000**	**2001–5**	**1996–2005**
Development time	NA	NA	NA
Approval time	27.8	28.6	28.1
Number	8	7	15
New chemical entities	**1996–98**	**2002–4**	**Total**
Development time	70.3	84.0	75.0
Approval time	16.8	18.0	17.2
Number	110	58	168

SOURCE: Reichert 2006.
NOTES: NA = not available (although mean development and approval times for the four innovative vaccines are 80.0 and 13.9 months, respectively).

As shown in table 1-3, over the five-year periods from 1996 to 2000 and from 2001 to 2005, mean development times for biopharmaceuticals increased from 68.0 to 83.0 months (a 22 percent increase), while mean FDA approval times increased from 15.9 to 18.5 months (a 16 percent increase). These development times were in between those reported by Struck for biopharmaceuticals and by DiMasi and Grabowski for biotech products, calculated from the data in table 1-2, at 72.0 and 81.7 months, respectively.[35] The Reichert biopharmaceutical mean review times were much smaller than the 43.2 months reported by Struck, but in line with the DiMasi and Grabowski estimate of 18.2 months.

Reichert did not report comparable 1996–2000 and 2001–5 statistics on development and approval times for new chemical entities (pharmaceuticals), but instead reproduced 1996–98 and 2002–4 values from an earlier study. As seen in the bottom panel of table 1-3, for new chemical entities both mean development times and FDA approval times increased between 1996–98 and 2002–4 (from 70.3 and 84.0 months to 16.8 and 18.0 months, respectively); moreover, at 84.0 months, the 2002–4 development times for new chemical entities were almost identical to the 2001–5 times for biopharmaceuticals (83.0 months). Reichert's mean development times for new chemical entities—70.3 months for 1996–98 and 84.0 months for 2002–4—bracketed the estimate of 78.0 months by DiMasi and Grabowski, while her mean approval times (16.8 and 18.0 months) were slightly less than the 18.2 months reported by DiMasi and Grabowski.

For vaccines, however, the findings were much more intriguing. As shown in table 1-3, Reichert reported mean approval times for vaccines increasing only slightly between 1996–2000 and 2001–5, from 27.8 to 28.6 months—very close to the 28.8 months reported by Struck. Among the fifteen vaccines she examined for the period 1996–2005 overall, however, Reichert distinguished eleven "follow-on" vaccines (representing incremental improvements in previously existing products, such as combination vaccines to reduce the number of injections given to children, or intranasal delivery for influenza vaccine) from four "innovative" vaccines. Notably, of the four innovative approved vaccines (RotaShield for rotavirus, LymeRx for Lyme disease, Prevnar for pneumococcal disease, and Menactra for meningococcal disease), the first two were later withdrawn from the market.[36] Not surprisingly, the mean development time for follow-on vaccines was slightly less than that for innovative vaccines, consistent with benefits gained from the accumulated knowledge regarding the nature of the infectious agents and the accepted desirable outcome measures (for instance, immune response to the vaccine). The mean development time of 80.0 months for innovative vaccines was only about 10 percent longer than the 72.0 months reported by Struck, and closer to the 1996–2005 mean development time for biopharmaceuticals (75.6 months) and the 1996–2004 mean development time for new chemical entities (75.0 months), as reported by Reichert.

However, for vaccines the approval time histories differed sharply from the relatively similar development times. As shown in the far-right column of table 1-4, at 33.3 months the mean approval time over the entire ten-year period for follow-on vaccines was more than twice the 13.9 months for the four innovative vaccines; this more rapid approval of innovative vaccines

TABLE 1-4

**FDA Approval Times for Innovative and Follow-On Vaccines,
Mean Time Duration in Months**

Innovative vaccines	1996–2000	2001–5	1996–2005
Mean approval time	14.3	12.9	13.9
Range approval time	8.6–19.0	12.9	8.6–19.0
Number vaccines	3	1	4
Follow-on vaccines	**1996–2000**	**2001–5**	**1996–2005**
Mean approval time	35.8	31.2	33.3
Range approval time	14.7–97.4	3.2–71.5	3.2–97.4
Number vaccines	5	6	11

Source: Reichert 2006.

persisted through both five-year intervals, at 14.3 versus 35.8 months from 1996 to 2000, and 12.9 versus 31.2 months from 2001 to 2005. These findings suggest that innovative vaccines received much more rapid approval than did the follow-on applications. The mean times for follow-on vaccines, however, masked considerable heterogeneity in FDA approvals; remarkably, for the five follow-on vaccines approved in 1996–2000, approval times ranged from 14.7 to 97.4 months, while for the six vaccines approved between 2001 and 2005 approval times ranged from 3.2 to 71.5 months.

To summarize this section, for a variety of reasons—the considerable variation among therapeutic areas due to the age of some of the data,[37] the incomplete reporting of statistical testing of significant differences, and the confounding of clinical and commercial failures by cumulative launch probabilities—the evidence that success probabilities are lower for vaccines and pharmaceuticals in general than for other biologics is equivocal. Some of the evidence suggests, however, that development times have been shorter for vaccines than for other biologics and pharmaceuticals, while mean FDA approval times have, on average, been longer for vaccines than for other biologics and pharmaceuticals, particularly for follow-on vaccines.

What do these variations imply for economic costs of development, both cumulative out of pocket and when capitalized to reflect opportunity costs (that is, taking into account what could have been earned had these funds been invested elsewhere)? According to DiMasi and Grabowski (2008), out-of-pocket costs per approved biologic have been about 20 percent less than costs per approved pharmaceutical ($559 million versus $672 million in 2005 dollars), but because of longer development times for biologics, capitalized costs have been very similar, with those per approved biologic being only about 5 percent less than those per approved pharmaceutical.[38] Given the large variation across projects, this implies the average capitalized costs are likely not statistically different from one another.

Finally, where does this leave us in terms of the economics of vaccines, which along with pharmaceuticals have lower success probabilities than biologics? This remains an open question. The only information we could uncover on this issue was in a 2005 presentation to investors and analysts by GlaxoSmithKline vaccine officials, which stated that clinical development of vaccines was increasingly complex, but "still somewhat more economical compared to Pharma" and with a "high success rate post 'proof of concept' [of] 70 percent."[39]

2

Planning for Vaccine Launch

After candidate vaccines have survived various preliminary scientific and potential commercial feasibility screens, but long before actual product launch, vaccine developers engage in an extensive and lengthy process of planning for it. Among preparations that must take place are specification and construction of manufacturing facilities, detailed coordination discussions with government agencies such as the Centers for Disease Control and Prevention, the Advisory Committee on Immunization Practices (ACIP), and other public and private payers. Logistical issues such as when the vaccines would be administered within existing pediatric, adolescent, or adult vaccination schedules also need to be addressed and resolved. In this chapter we focus on issues faced by vaccine manufacturers as they continue development and plan for vaccine product launch, and compare them with those faced by developers of pharmaceuticals and other biologics.

Manufacturing Facility Complexity, Scale Economies, and Costs

One characteristic of vaccine manufacturing that distinguishes it from pharmaceutical manufacturing (but somewhat less so from the manufacturing of other biologics) is the timeframe within which key decisions must be made. A number of interviewees stressed, as does the existing literature, that the critical decision to build manufacturing capacity to substantial scale must typically be made relatively early in the vaccine development process, years before final licensure approval by regulatory authorities. More specifically, manufacturing scale-up from pilot batches into vats for vaccines typically occurs in late phase II of clinical development, considerably sooner than the more common phase III timing for pharmaceuticals.[1]

It is useful to distinguish the building of a manufacturing facility for a new vaccine from the adaptation of an existing facility to manufacture an annually updated flu vaccine, and from the construction of a new or expanded plant for an already marketed vaccine.[2] Building a new vaccine facility typically takes three to five years. First is the design phase, with iterations between actual construction and revised or refined designs. This is followed by intense process and product facility validation for the various stages of raw material inventory, incubation in between processing, refrigeration, and final finish processing.[3] Manufacturing requires a great deal of capital, with the equipment usually highly specialized and customized and having no other economically viable uses.

Thus, the at-risk investment involves substantial sunk costs. While manufacturing facilities for small-molecule pharmaceuticals are often relatively interchangeable, vaccine facilities are typically uniquely dedicated. Furthermore, interviewees agreed that equipment operators in vaccine manufacturing are more highly educated than those in pharmaceutical (though not necessarily other biologic) manufacturing, with most having bachelors' degrees in science or engineering, as opposed to high school diplomas or equivalents, and a substantial portion holding doctorates. As a result, labor costs for vaccine manufacturing are relatively high, and, as discussed below, a substantial portion is fixed.

In part because most vaccines are injected into the body[4] and reach the bloodstream without encountering the natural defenses of the gastrointestinal tract, and in part because they typically originate from living organisms that exhibit substantial random and unpredictable variability, standards for production sterility and consistency are much stricter for them than for pharmaceutical tablets and capsules that are administered orally and are chemically based. Thus, quality assurance is extremely important for vaccines. Environmental controls are comprehensive, with rooms and vents monitored continuously for particulate levels and microbial contamination.[5] Consistency across batches is paramount, and batch analyses must be repeated frequently. This focus on tracking processing and ensuring that vaccine process characteristics are all robust within preset parameter ranges is typically greater than with pharmaceuticals, since with chemically synthesized molecules the analytical characterization of the final product is less random and more definitive. Since the end products of vaccine production cannot be inspected with chemical precision, the processes by which they are made are instead required to meet stringent verifiable standards.[6] For vaccines (and for other biologics), product and process are inextricably linked, with control of process affecting control of product.

After verifying that pilot and larger-scale batches are sufficiently similar, companies typically do a number of "practice runs" with new facilities before carrying out the phase II and phase III studies. Later on, in the course of filing for product license approval, vaccine developers must also submit extensive historical process and product documentation to the FDA to gain final manufacturing establishment licensure approval (ELA). Once having granted these approvals, the FDA continues to inspect, monitor, and audit individual batch releases, ensuring that manufacturing process and product operations are consistent within preset ranges. Samples of each manufactured lot must be submitted to the FDA for approval before the lot can be sold.[7] Notably, and in contrast, pharmaceutical developers need not file ELAs, only product license applications (PLAs, also called new drug applications); beginning in 1996, developers of some nonvaccine biologics were exempted from filing ELAs as well, and required only to file PLAs.

Another useful distinction regarding manufacturing capabilities concerns the duration of the process. For a manufacturer with licensed facilities and products, it takes between six and eighteen months to produce a batch of a vaccine, depending on the complexity of the final product.[8] A firm with a vaccine PLA but not an ELA would need two to five years to produce a different vaccine at the same manufacturing site, and four to six years if it were entering with a completely new plant.[9]

One consequence of this substantial research and development and regulatory oversight of manufacturing facilities for entirely new vaccines is that scale economies are substantial, with marginal or incremental costs of producing additional liters of vaccine much smaller than average costs, where average costs also include earlier R&D and subsequent regulatory compliance costs. Such scale economies reflect the sunk R&D and regulatory compliance costs, but also costs specific to each batch. Batch costs have both fixed and variable components. Fixed batch costs include the amortized depreciation costs of the physical plant and equipment testing, setup costs, and, especially, batch-testing costs involving highly skilled labor. The variable costs of batch runs include costs of raw materials, nutrients, process labor, and packing materials, and, for childhood vaccines, the excise taxes from which no-fault liability claims are paid.[10] Regarding the variable cost component for each batch, while savings can, in principle, be achieved by producing larger batches in larger vats, opportunities for doing so with biologic organisms may be limited by technical and quality-control variables. Specifically, while larger vat capacity could yield larger lot sizes, a single consistency failure in vaccine from a large vat could reduce final product inventory levels unacceptably. Hence, vaccine manufacturers undertake risk analyses to determine the benefits and costs of larger vat and batch sizes, based on how likely they are to result in greater volumes of discarded production or, in some cases, even delayed production of final product.

According to the Institute of Medicine, citing contract work performed by the Mercer Management Consulting Company, about 60 percent of total vaccine production costs are "semi-fixed," defined as excluding R&D sunk costs but including the fixed batch-testing costs. Costs that are essentially fixed per batch constitute about 25 percent of total non-R&D production costs, while fully variable costs comprise the remaining 15 percent.[11]

As emphasized by Scherer, scale economies are therefore likely to be greatest for entirely new vaccines.[12] They are also present but not as large for annual flu vaccines whose yearly incremental R&D and qualification costs are much smaller, and are likely present but still smaller for plants expanding production of existing facilities. Even in this last case, however, scale economies continue to be present at the level of the individual plant; as a result, vaccine manufacturers typically tend to concentrate production at single plants rather than at different sites, thereby exploiting the cost advantages of spreading fixed costs over a larger number of vats and batch lots at a single site.

In a 2005 study, Arnould and DeBrock argued that, while early in the life of a new (unpatented) vaccine there may be a substantial number of manufacturers, firms compete for volume as the product ages by bidding low prices. Smaller-volume firms experience higher costs and gradually exit, and only the lowest-cost manufacturers remain, leaving production for a given vaccine highly concentrated in one or two firms.[13] We return to the consequences of this market dynamic later on when we examine industry structure and recent instances of vaccine shortages in the United States.

Coordination with Public Health Officials and Payers

Earlier we noted that during the vaccine development process, manufacturers interact extensively with public health agencies and payers, ensuring that the final product will fill unmet needs and fit within recommended vaccination schedules and guidelines. Developers also communicate and work with the Centers for Disease Control and Prevention and other payers in undertaking cost-effectiveness analyses, preparing the market for the new vaccine.[14] Although such communication is technically not required by law, it is, de facto, absolutely critical.

An important way in which vaccines differ from other biologics and pharmaceuticals is that, following approval by the FDA, the manufacturer effectively needs a favorable recommendation from the Advisory Committee on Immunization Practices, an advisory committee to the CDC, to sell the vaccine in the United States. The ACIP advises the two large government payers—the U.S. Department of Health and Human Services (DHHS) and the CDC—on whether the vaccine should be included on recommended immunization schedules.[15] Among the criteria considered by the ACIP and its subcommittees are cost-effectiveness and cost-benefit issues, the impact of the new vaccine on pediatric, adolescent, and adult immunization schedules, and whether adequate systems are in place for delivery of the vaccine. The ACIP typically forms a working group to evaluate different aspects of the vaccine, including its intended population, dosing, and scheduling, several years in advance of the developer's FDA submission. This evaluation process takes place over several years, with the full working group typically meeting three times annually. While the FDA and ACIP evaluations run in parallel, FDA approval is a necessary step before the ACIP finalizes any recommendations.

Following FDA approval, the ACIP reviews the final clinical data dossier and then decides whether to recommend that the CDC and the DHHS include the vaccine on the national immunization schedules. The ACIP can make one of three recommendations: to endorse universal vaccination to the indicated population; to defer the decision to individual states; or to decline to endorse or choose to delay a decision while the advisory committee continues to work with the CDC, possibly considering recommending vaccination for only a subset of the population.

For the developer, universal recommendation is, obviously, the most desired outcome. If a vaccine is accepted by the CDC and DHHS, a number of events typically follow, including adoption of the vaccine on state immunization schedules, inclusion in the Vaccines for Children program, which purchases vaccines (see below), and inclusion in the American Academy of Pediatrics Report of the Committee on Infectious Diseases (known as the "Red Book"), which, among other actions, issues guidelines for immunization practices to pediatricians. Only rarely do states deviate from CDC national recommendations.[16] In essence, an ACIP universal recommendation sets a medical practice standard for physicians.[17]

If, on the other hand, the ACIP and CDC were to decline to recommend a vaccine, the manufacturer would need to make its case individually to each state, a much more onerous and complicated process. Finally, the ACIP and CDC can advise that the vaccine be administered based on an assessment of an individual's risk profile (not universally), based on considerations such as likelihood of exposure to the target disease or certain behavioral characteristics. With no mandate for immunization at either the federal or state level, the decision to vaccinate rests with the individual and/or parent and physician. In this case, the burden of educating parents and physicians would be entirely borne by the vaccine manufacturer, who would not benefit from CDC and DHHS educational and outreach efforts.[18]

One important feature of the ACIP review process is that if a vaccine is recommended by the CDC for routine use and added to the national immunization schedules, the CDC will also allocate funds to help states pay for the cost of administering the vaccines and to help patients pay for the vaccine itself. According to Morgan Stanley,

> In the case of pediatric vaccines, about 55 percent–60 percent are purchased directly or indirectly by the federal government through the Vaccines for Children program. This program is a federal entitlement that provides free vaccines to *uninsured* children 18 or under. Under this program, the CDC negotiates the prices of vaccines but the purchases are actually made by the states at the federal contract price.[19]

Federal recommendations also play a very important role for the approximately 45 percent of pediatric vaccine purchases that fall outside the public sector. While private insurers are not required to follow CDC national recommendations (as the benefits they offer depend on the competitive situations they face), these insurers are unlikely to pay for vaccinations that are not recommended for routine use by the CDC.

Distribution and Delivery Channels and Payers

The paths traversed by a vaccine, beginning at the manufacturer's plant and ending with the patient (consumer), are very different from those traveled by pharmaceuticals and, to some extent, from those for other biologics. Here we distinguish between vaccine *distribution*, which refers to the transport of vaccines from the manufacturer to the health-care provider, and vaccine *delivery*, which refers to the provision and administration of vaccine immunization services by the health-care provider to the patient.[20]

Distribution. Only a small proportion of pharmaceuticals are sold directly to health-care providers or pharmacies.[21] Pharmaceutical manufacturers usually sell their products directly to chain warehouses and national or regional wholesalers who, in turn, then sell to providers (physicians or hospitals), to pharmacies, and, to a limited extent, to group purchasing organizations. Finally, retail and mail-order pharmacies, as well as hospitals, dispense the pharmaceuticals to patients. Tablets and capsules of pharmaceuticals are typically shipped in various sizes—bottles of 30, 100, 500, and 1,000 units, for example—which mail-order firms often repackage into bottles of ninety days' supply. In most cases, physicians do not purchase pharmaceuticals, and therefore do not bear inventory costs.

In contrast, vaccines have tended to be distributed in at least three ways.[22] First, they may be distributed in bulk to public buyers, shipped directly by the manufacturer in single or multidose vials[23] to a limited number of state government depot sites (one or two per state). From there they are distributed to clinics, hospitals, and physicians' offices, in some cases after repackaging into smaller multidose vials, separate needle-syringe doses, or filled syringes without needles. Second, vaccines may be distributed in considerably smaller volumes directly from manufacturers to private clinics and physicians' offices, which purchase and bear the inventory costs of storing them. Finally, vaccines in varying shipment sizes may be distributed from manufacturers to wholesalers, who may undertake secondary packaging before reselling to private physician practices and clinics, the latter again bearing the purchase and inventory costs of acquiring and storing the vaccines. Some vaccines are shipped as lyophilized (freeze-dried) powders that must be mixed with a liquid (called a diluent) in a process known as reconstitution before they can be administered.

One way in which vaccines differ from pharmaceuticals is that to retain its efficacy, a vaccine often must be transported and then stored under "cold-chain" refrigeration and minimal-light conditions.[24] This requirement raises at least two issues. First, while vaccine manufacturers can monitor and control the transport and storage conditions for large bulk shipments to a limited number of state collection centers, doing so for smaller-volume shipments to geographically dispersed clinics and physicians' offices is more challenging, particularly when third-party shippers are involved. This challenge in turn introduces other issues, such as liability for variations in temperature or light control and return policies for spoiled products. Second, the provider typically pays refrigeration and other storage costs. The unique requirements for temperature and light ranges for different vaccines can impose considerable equipment costs on providers, in addition to the product acquisition costs they already bear.[25]

A major change involving distribution channels has recently occurred. In years past, physicians' offices, health centers, and rural health clinics had to order vaccines through third-party distributors or wholesalers, imposing significant administrative costs on medical offices. In September 2006, the Centers for Disease Control and Prevention announced that the distribution of vaccines for the Vaccines for Children program[26] would be centralized under a contract with McKesson Specialty, a business unit of McKesson Corporation. Previously, McKesson had been one of the few companies providing influenza, pneumonia, and hepatitis B vaccines to the long-term care market. The CDC believes this centralization of distribution with McKesson will facilitate efficient ordering and shipping.[27]

Another recent change is that pharmaceutical wholesalers are now entering the vaccine distribution chain, reflecting a similar evolution that has taken place for other biologics, with firms known as specialty pharmacies emerging in the last decade to serve as intermediaries between manufacturers and providers. In recent years, a number of these specialty pharmacies have merged with or been acquired by pharmaceutical wholesalers, including McKesson.[28] Both wholesalers and specialty pharmacies typically sell to physicians' offices and clinics, which then bear the financial and storage risks.

Delivery Channels and Payers. According to a 2003 national survey, about 61 percent of vaccines administered to young children were delivered exclusively by private-sector providers, 16 percent via the public sector, and 23 percent by a combination of the two or another type of provider, such as the military. Another survey indicated that 32–58 percent of adults were vaccinated in their doctors' offices, 2–35 percent in the workplace, and 5–14 percent in alternative locations, such as stores or pharmacies.[29] The large ranges reflect in part uncertainty regarding the role of non-physician-office clinics.

In several important ways, the delivery issues for vaccines are similar to those for other biologics. For example, biologics and other therapies administered by physicians or health-care providers, such as chemotherapies, entail the purchase and storage of the product by physicians' offices, requiring them to bear both acquisition and storage costs (including the cost of appropriate equipment). Administration may involve injection, infusion, or intravenous procedures, as well as the associated transport and storage. One major difference, however, is that for many biologics, the acquisition cost per unit of administration, which can be as much as thousands of dollars for a single treatment, is much higher than for vaccines. Hence, while issues of spoilage, return policies, and inventory holding costs are important for vaccines, they likely are less significant than they are for many other "high-touch, high-cost" biologics.[30]

In the United States, payers and purchasers differ considerably for child and adult vaccines.[31] A provision of the Omnibus Budget Reconciliation Act of 1993 was the establishment of the Vaccines for Children (VFC) program to remove cost as a barrier to the immunization of children.[32] As an entitlement under Medicaid (and therefore not subject to periodic appropriations from Congress), the VFC program provides vaccines free to children under nineteen years of age who seek immunizations at federally qualified health centers or rural health clinics and meet at least one of the following criteria: Medicaid-eligible; uninsured; American Indian or Alaska Native; or under-insured. While the provider may charge a fee to administer the vaccine, the immunization cannot be denied if the fee cannot be paid. Private providers enrolled in the VFC program determine eligibility for free vaccines by ask-ing a parent or guardian if the child meets the above criteria, with no further verification required.[33]

Whereas prior to 1993 roughly 50 percent of pediatric vaccine pur-chases came from the private sector, under the VFC program this fell to approximately 10–20 percent. The federal government committed to pur-chasing enough vaccine to immunize 60 percent of preschool children, with the remaining 20–30 percent of public-sector purchases made by state gov-ernments at the federally negotiated prices.[34] The purchases were to cover all existing ACIP-recommended pediatric vaccines, as well as any new vac-cines added to the recommended schedule. States could purchase additional quantities of the vaccines at federal contract prices for any other categories of children. States with universal purchase programs (providing vaccines free for all children) could distribute childhood vaccines to any health-care providers licensed to administer them, subject to minimal constraints.[35]

Although we discuss pricing issues separately below, two points are worth noting here briefly. First, by expanding the number of children eligible to receive free vaccines, the VFC program prompted an increase in the number of vaccine doses sold. At the same time, the increase in the share of public-sector purchases (typically at lower prices than those paid by the private sec-tor), reduced, on average, the price received by the manufacturer per vaccine administered. We have not found literature on the net impact of the VFC program on manufacturers' sales revenues, but according to interviewees, manufacturers and payers both recognized these potential tradeoffs.

Second, prior to the VFC program, the federal government procure-ment contract was awarded to the single lowest-priced bidder, resulting in low prices and uncertainty regarding who would win the bid, and thereby creating uncertainty among potential suppliers as to what demand they would face for their product. In contrast, under the VFC program, all manufacturers of a vaccine are allowed to list their prices, regardless of whether they provide the lowest bid or not. This system enables states to consider issues other than price, such as security of supply (due to manu-facturing problems) and contractual quantity purchase commitment provi-sions, in making their vaccine purchase decisions. Manufacturers are permitted to change their prices several times a year.[36]

In 2002 about 57 percent of vaccines recommended for children were purchased through federal contracts, with most of that (about 84 percent) coming through the VFC program. Of the 43 percent that went to the pri-vate sector, most was purchased by individual providers who were then reimbursed by third-party payers (such as Medicare, Medicaid, or a private insurance plan). Other public funds used to purchase vaccines have come from federal discretionary funds in the section 317 grant program (11 per-cent of 2002 public purchases) and from state and local funds (5 percent of public purchases). The section 317 program is

> a discretionary federal grant program to all states, six cities, territories and protectorates which provides vaccines to under-insured children and adolescents not served by the [VFC] pro-gram, and as funding permits to uninsured and underinsured adults.[37]

In contrast to the VFC program, section 317 requires an annual appro-priation by Congress. Hence, while VFC-eligible children can automatically receive ACIP-recommended vaccines, access is not guaranteed for those relying on section 317 discretionary funds. For example, when the seven-valent pneumococcal vaccine Prevnar (for the prevention of some types of pneumonia) was licensed by the FDA and recommended by ACIP in 2000, VFC-eligible children received it, but many ineligible children did not, in part because there was no contemporaneous increase in section 317 appro-priations. The result was no public-program access to vaccines for VFC-ineligible children in nineteen states. The individual states can finance vaccine purchases for VFC-ineligible children (as of 2002, eight had uni-versal coverage, down from eleven in 1996), but these, too, are subject to state legislative discretionary appropriations.[38]

The number of new vaccines recommended by ACIP for children and adolescents has nearly doubled in the past five years, with the important consequence that the cost of fully vaccinating a child has increased sharply. Gaps have appeared in financial coverage of vaccines for children who are "underinsured" (that is, who have private insurance that does not cover all recommended vaccines); many of them are now unable to receive publicly purchased vaccines in either the private or public sectors. A recent study finds that underinsured children were ineligible to receive publicly purchased meningococcal conjugate vaccine (for the prevention of meningitis) in 70 percent of states, and pneumococcal conjugate vaccine in 50 percent.[39] Between 2004 and 2006, ten states changed their policies to restrict access to selected new vaccines for underinsured children, raising controversy over the prioritization of limited financing for this purpose.[40]

With respect to vaccines for adults, no program analogous to the VFC program exists today. Vaccines for adults are largely purchased in the private sector, and only about 24 percent of individuals under age sixty-five have insurance that covers immunization.[41] Typically, the health-care provider purchases vaccines up front and bills the patient or a third-party payer for reimbursement, plus administration fees. The public health sector has played a minimal role in purchasing adult vaccines; one 2005 study reported that only about 5 percent of influenza vaccines for adults were purchased through the CDC federal contract.[42] Medicare currently reimburses providers for acquiring and administering influenza and pneumococcal vaccines to its beneficiaries, however.[43]

Costs of vaccine administration (as opposed to acquisition), are reimbursed to varying extents by third-party payers. A common theme among those we interviewed and in the literature we reviewed is that providers have typically been reimbursed less than it costs them to administer pediatric vaccines. Particularly for the new and more expensive vaccines, this shortfall is becoming increasingly burdensome for many pediatricians and family practitioners. The per-injection burden has been exacerbated by the sharp increase in the number of vaccines recommended by the ACIP over the last ten years. Moreover, while the availability of combination vaccines has meant fewer painful injections for children, with correspondingly greater comfort and convenience for patients and their parents and improved compliance with recommended vaccination schedules, they have also decreased physician office revenues from vaccine administration, which are typically based on the number of separate injections.[44]

Pediatricians, traditionally among the lower-paid physician specialties, have become particularly vocal concerning nonreimbursed cost increases from vaccine administration, especially when their patient population has been capitated.[45] A *New York Times* article quotes one pediatrician as saying that if a child pulls her arm away from the needle at the last second, "a $120 syringe goes flying through the air and you can't reuse it [and] I'm a good guy . . . but I'm not a social worker."[46] A document prepared by the Task Force on Immunization for the American Academy of Pediatrics estimates that the cumulative inventory costs to immunize one child with all recommended vaccines from birth through adolescence in a private practice setting increased from $22.65 in 1980 for seven injections to $1,641.13 in 2006 for twenty-two to thirty-three injections.[47] In 2005, Medicaid state administration fees for children's vaccines ranged from $2 to about $18 per injection, with a median reimbursement of about $8.50.[48] Currently, a number of studies are underway attempting to estimate the various costs associated with pediatric vaccinations. These include the cost of time spent ordering and maintaining inventory records; management of inventory; special refrigerators and freezers, including backup generators; insurance; unavoidable wastage in multidose vials or when a parent declines an immunization after the dose has been drawn up; and the cost of vaccines that are administered but not paid for.[49]

For adult vaccinations, payment was even less than for children during the 1990s. In 2005, however, Medicare increased the payments considerably. In 2007 they were $18.70 for a first injection and $10.70 for each additional injection per office visit—more than any state paid for administering childhood vaccines.[50]

3

Rolling Out the New Vaccine

We now come to a most exciting time in the life cycle of a potential life-saving vaccine: the new product launch. Successful vaccine candidates spend years undergoing preclinical and then clinical development, are initially produced in pilot batches and subsequently manufactured at scaled-up capacity, become the focus of extensive public- and private-sector payer and provider discussions involving the coordination of pediatric, adolescent, and adult immunization schedules, and, finally, gain FDA approval and recommended immunization status from the CDC and the ACIP. As we noted in chapter 1, the duration of time between phase I trials and product launch, comprising both development and approval stages, has historically averaged close to nine years, with approval times for innovative vaccines eighteen months shorter than those for follow-on vaccines. What are the major issues facing manufacturers as they finally launch and market new vaccines, and how do these issues differ from those faced by manufacturers of pharmaceuticals and other biologics? That is the focus of this chapter. We begin with a challenge that has been much larger for vaccines than for pharmaceuticals and biologics: the threat of product liability.[1]

Product Liability Issues

By their very nature, vaccines introduce into the body some component of an organism that causes disease to stimulate the immunized person's own system to produce antibodies against that disease. As a result, mass vaccinations inevitably involve some risk that a number of individuals will experience an adverse event following immunization.

The extent of mass immunization has been increasing over time. In 1984, American children were routinely vaccinated against seven diseases; by 2005, this number had risen to twelve. In addition, children are now also protected against hepatitis A through immunizations in areas that have high rates of incidence.[2] In spite of extensive safety assessments (such as phase III trials involving 70,000 individuals, and intensive post-launch surveillance), a number of extremely rare but serious adverse events can be expected to occur in the United States, given that over one hundred million immunizations are administered each year.

In the 1970s and 1980s, vaccines for the prevention of pertussis (whooping cough) became associated with several cases of serious brain damage, giving rise to scientific controversy, sharp declines in vaccination rates in some countries, and, in the United States, numerous lawsuits. In Great Britain, in response to a widely disseminated document suggesting a connection between the whole-cell pertussis vaccine and neurological damage in children, vaccination rates fell from more than 80 percent in 1974 to 30 percent in 1978, followed almost immediately by a widespread resurgence of whooping cough.[3] In the United States, as the number of lawsuits filed against manufacturers of diphtheria, tetanus, and pertussis (DTP) vaccines increased, DTP prices rose, in part to meet growing liability insurance costs and in part to cover legal costs incurred in defending lawsuits. Between 1980 and 1987, the wholesale price of the DTP vaccine increased by a factor of more than forty—from $3.89 to $159.31, with about 96 percent of the increase attributed to litigation costs.[4] Prices of other vaccines were also affected, though not as dramatically. By the early 1990s, the number of domestic DTP manufacturers had decreased from four (Wyeth, Connaught, Sclavo, and Lederle) to one.[5] Testifying before a congressional hearing, Lederle, the only remaining commercial supplier at that time, stated that its potential liability was over two hundred times greater than its annual sales.[6]

The U.S. Congress, concerned that liability issues would reduce further the numbers of manufacturers and vaccines in development and, ultimately, decrease rates of vaccination among the public, also recognized society's obligation to compensate those injured by vaccines. In 1986 it passed the National Childhood Vaccine Injury Act, which set up the National Vaccine Injury Compensation Program (VICP).[7] According to Orenstein and others,

The VICP is a no-fault system funded by a seventy-five cent excise tax on each dose of vaccine. People alleging vaccine injury must first file with the program. A vaccine injury table specifies conditions that are automatically eligible for compensation, with no need to prove causation. People alleging injuries that are not in the table must prove that vaccines actually were the cause. After going through the VICP, plaintiffs may accept the decisions and awards or reject them and enter the tort system. If an award is accepted, the plaintiff cannot sue the manufacturer or the vaccine provider.[8]

Provisions of the act specify that a vaccine that prevents only one disease (for example, trivalent influenza vaccine), is subject to the $0.75-per-dose tax, but for one that prevents more than one disease (for example, the measles, mumps, and rubella vaccine), the tax per dose per disease is increased proportionally (in the measles, mumps, and rubella case, to $2.25 per dose).[9] The VICP pays attorneys' fees and costs related to the claim, regardless of whether it is determined to be compensable.

Nearly two-thirds of the petitions filed between fiscal years 1989 and 2007 (5,146 of 7,866) involved claims of death or injury from vaccines causing autism. Between 1990 and 2007, all of the 298 adjudicated claims involving autism were dismissed without compensation; almost 5,000 of the autism-related claims had not been adjudicated. Of the 1995 nonautism claims adjudicated, 871 (44 percent) were compensable, while 1,124 (56 percent) were dismissed. Between 1990 and 2007, nonautism petitioners received a total of about $725 million in compensation, averaging about $850,000 per award; attorneys' fees and cost payments at $29 million were about 4 percent of that amount, or about $34,000 per award. The total amount of attorneys' fees and cost payments for dismissed claims over this same time period was about half as large, at $14 million.[10]

While most observers view the VICP as having been beneficial, critics point to a number of loopholes.[11] First, if dissatisfied with the outcome of its adjudication process, claimants can opt out of the VICP and take their case to a jury. Currently, about three hundred separate lawsuits are pending in U.S. courts from parents claiming their children were harmed by thimerosal, a mercury-containing preservative that for many years was used in multidose vaccine vials to prevent potentially life-threatening contamination with harmful microbes. Since 1999, efforts have been made to eliminate thimerosal, and today its presence as a preservative is negligible.[12]

Second, the VICP does not cover all vaccines, but only those routinely recommended for all children. Adolescents and adults are not eligible to use the VICP adjudication process, with potentially adverse consequences. For example, after LymeRx, GlaxoSmithKline's vaccine for Lyme disease, was launched following FDA approval on December 21, 1998, a substantial number of people claimed it caused chronic arthritis and other ailments. The CDC and the ACIP did not recommend universal pediatric immunization for LymeRx, and since adults constituted a substantial portion of the potential market, LymeRx was not eligible for adjudication through the VICP. While two large epidemiological studies found no evidence that the vaccine caused chronic disease, the injury claims were widely publicized, GlaxoSmithKline spent considerable funds defending their product, and sales of the vaccine declined. On February 16, 2002, just over three years after it had obtained FDA approval, GlaxoSmithKline voluntarily withdrew the Lyme vaccine from the U.S. market.[13]

While product liability is also an issue for nonvaccine biologics and small molecule pharmaceuticals, nonvaccines are generally utilized by ill and nonpediatric populations. Because vaccines are given to millions of healthy children annually, and because rare but serious side effects can reasonably be expected given the widespread utilization, vaccine manufacturers are particularly vulnerable to product liability issues.

Pricing, Product Differentiation, and Marketing

The pricing in U.S. health care of medical products such as pharmaceuticals and biologics is generally quite complex, and vaccines are no exception.[14] It is useful to distinguish between differentiated (or heterogeneous) and undifferentiated (or homogeneous) medical products. With pharmaceuticals, the FDA can rate approved generic drugs as being bioequivalent to the branded innovator products and thereby essentially minimize any perceived difference between brand and generic pharmaceuticals. In contrast, although some vaccines have been on the U.S. market for decades and lack patent protection, currently no generic vaccines are marketed, and to date the FDA has not rated alternative vaccines as being bioequivalent or biosimilar, although the CDC lists alternative suppliers of various vaccines and their prices.[15] A number of recently introduced vaccines are marketed by only one manufacturer, due in large part to patent protection, and in this way are somewhat comparable to alternative brands of pharmaceuticals within a given therapeutic class; but currently, therapeutic competition among alternatives to recently introduced branded vaccines is minimal.

The absence of follow-on vaccines, in contrast to pharmaceuticals, has implications for pricing differences between them. With FDA-approved generic pharmaceuticals, competition among suppliers generally drives prices down toward marginal costs; since fixed and sunk costs for generics (such as for R&D and regulatory compliance) are relatively minor, their average and marginal costs are typically close to one another. Hence, in the United States many therapeutic classes have multiple generic pharmaceutical manufacturers selling the same molecule, and in cases where market segments are sizable, price competition is intense, with generic price approaching marginal cost.[16]

For vaccines the evolution of prices for old products is quite different, for at least three reasons. First, as discussed earlier,[17] very substantial sunk and fixed costs, as well as a lead time of two to five years, are required for a manufacturer to construct facilities, undertake clinical studies, and gain regulatory approval (product and establishment licensure) to produce a "me-too" vaccine product. For generic pharmaceuticals, the costs of gaining approval are much lower, often less than $5 million.[18] A prospective generic vaccine manufacturer also risks loss of significant market share if a superior branded vaccine (offering greater safety, efficacy, or convenience in administration) is introduced, particularly if the subsequent innovator product is placed on the ACIP-recommended dosing schedule. For these reasons, the threat of generic entry is much smaller for vaccines than for pharmaceuticals, at and after the time of patent expiration or other exclusivity loss.

Second, as was also discussed earlier, the manufacturing, regulatory approval, and monitoring characteristics of vaccines comprise fixed costs that are largely unrelated to production volumes and therefore generate very substantial scale economies for an existing manufacturer, such that the firm having the largest production capabilities is also likely to have the lowest marginal cost. As long as prices are greater than marginal costs, the firm will still have incentive to undercut any smaller, less efficient producer by lowering its prices. These relatively low marginal costs may also make it possible for the vaccine manufacturer to price-discriminate, charging different prices to, for example, the public and private sectors.[19]

Third, before 1993, the CDC had a "winner-take-all" policy in accepting only the lowest price bid for federal purchases of a vaccine, which resulted in low prices but great demand uncertainty for the bidding potential suppliers. Combined with substantial scale economies, this policy resulted during the 1970s and 1980s in the exits of numerous manufacturers, leaving only one or two manufacturers of various old vaccines. In 1993 the CDC changed this policy, publicly posting bid prices for all firms with which it negotiated contracts and allowing states to choose among alternative bidders, taking into account both prices and other considerations (for instance, assuredness of supply, minimum and maximum quantities, return policies, and delivery convenience). States could obtain vaccines not included in the Vaccines for Children program at the federally negotiated prices. Prices for any vaccine with a federal contract in 1993 were "grandfathered," allowed to increase at no more than the rate of growth of the Consumer Price Index.[20] It is worth noting that this policy also created incentives to develop new formulation variants of existing vaccines—such as combination products—not subject to the price cap.

What have been the consequences of these policies? For older vaccines, the remaining manufacturers are few, scale economies are present, limited shelf life decreases the ability to stockpile inventory, and the relatively large public-sector price bids are made public. These economics define a Bertrand price-competition framework, and, therefore, we expect prices to be low and close to marginal cost and to one another.[21] This pricing structure is, in fact, what we observe.

In November 2008, for example, CDC prices for the hepatitis A vaccines Vaqta (produced by Merck) and Havrix (GlaxoSmithKline) for pediatric administration were nearly identical at $12.25 per dose (Havrix) and $12.75 per dose (Vaqta) and at $18.99 and $19.75 per dose in ten-pack vials, respectively, for adults; for the hepatitis B vaccines Engerix-B (GlaxoSmithKline) and Recombivax HB (Merck), the prices per pediatric and adolescent dose were nearly identical at $9.50 and $9.75, and ranged between

$23.37 and $24.90 per dose for adults.[22] Similarly, the CDC prices of the two manufacturers still producing the *Haemophilus influenzae* type B (Hib) conjugate vaccine (to prevent bacterial meningitis and related invasive diseases caused by this bacterium) were low but not quite identical, at $8.64 for ActHIB (Sanofi Pasteur) and $11.26 for PedvaxHIB (Merck). For the venerable measles, mumps, and rubella vaccine, MMRII, Merck was the only remaining manufacturer, and its price was $18.26 per dose, while Sanofi Pasteur was the only remaining supplier of the four-dose inactivated polio vaccine, with a price of $11.48 per dose. In each of these examples involving old vaccines, public-sector CDC prices ranged between about 30 percent and 50 percent of those charged in the less centralized private sector, where vaccines are purchased directly by providers—physicians, hospitals, and their group purchasing organizations.[23]

A slightly different case is the five-dose combination pediatric vaccine for diphtheria, tetanus, and pertussis. Here the major change over time, discussed in more detail later in the DTP case study,[24] is that acellular pertussis production has replaced and rendered obsolete whole-cell pertussis production, with no manufacturer currently marketing the older variant in the United States (though it is still marketed in developing countries). Instead, acellular pertussis is combined with old diphtheria and tetanus vaccines in a DTaP combination, ranging in CDC price from $12.65 to $13.75 per dose for brands Tripedia and Daptacel (Sanofi Pasteur) and Infanrix (GlaxoSmithKline); these CDC prices are about 60 percent of the private-sector price.[25]

Interestingly, two manufacturers currently market a Tdap combination variant for those special populations requiring a reduced diphtheria toxoid dose; these formulations are CDC-priced considerably higher and similarly, at $30.75 (Boostrix, GlaxoSmithKline) and $31.75 per dose (Adacel, Sanofi Pasteur), and carry only about an 18 percent discount to the public sector. Also of interest is the fact that the two older influenza vaccines containing the thimerosal preservative, Fluzone (Sanofi Pasteur) and Fluvirin (Novartis), are CDC-priced at $9.97 and $9.25 per dose, respectively—about 25 percent less than the preservative-free Fluzone (Sanofi Pasteur), priced at $13.09 (for children six to thirty-five months old) to $14.25 (children thirty-six months and over). These CDC prices are 18–25 percent less than the private-sector catalog prices, and thus, for influenza vaccines (administered primarily by the private sector), the CDC discounts are comparable to those on vaccines predominantly administered by the public sector.

In contrast to these old vaccines, a number of newer, patent-protected pediatric and adolescent vaccines target diseases for which there previously had been no preventive therapy; these are generally priced much higher. Additionally, since each is exclusively provided by a single manufacturer, their discounts to the public sector are generally smaller. Among these vaccines are Prevnar (Wyeth), a four-dose-recommended pediatric vaccination for prevention of seven strains of pneumococcal infections, whose CDC price at $66.44 per dose is about 20 percent less than the $83.88 private-sector catalog price; Menactra (Sanofi Pasteur), a single-dose vaccine for prevention of invasive meningococcal disease caused by certain serotypes, which is recommended by the ACIP for adolescents between eleven and fifteen years of age and has a CDC price of $76.35 per dose, about 18 percent less than the $93.87 private-sector price; Varivax (Merck), a two-dose pediatric vaccine for prevention of varicella (chickenpox), with a CDC price of $61.50 per dose, about 20 percent less than the $77.51 private-sector price; RotaTeq (Merck), a three-dose pediatric vaccine to protect against five strains of rotavirus, with a CDC price of $57.20 per dose, about 18 percent less than the $69.59 private-sector price; a second three-dose rotavirus recent entrant, Rotarix (GlaxoSmithKline), whose CDC price at $82.25 per dose is 20 percent less than the $102.50 private-sector price; and the most recent entrant, Gardasil (Merck), a three-dose human papillomavirus vaccine for prevention of cervical cancer, currently ACIP-recommended for administration to eleven- to twelve-year-old females and CDC-priced at $100.59 per dose, a 20 percent discount off the $125.29 private-sector price. Hence, the newer, patent-protected brands generally offer higher prices but similar percentage discounts to the public-sector CDC purchaser.

Recall that while combination vaccines offer the advantages of fewer injections (making them more practical and desirable for patients as well as providers), the fewer injections translate into reduced administration-fee revenues for providers (making them less profitable for providers). Whether combination or bundled vaccines can carry prices lower or higher than the sum of the prices of their component vaccines is theoretically ambiguous, and is therefore an empirical issue. Of interest is Merck's Pro-Quad vaccine, a bundled combination of its MMRII measles, mumps, and rubella vaccine, and Varivax for chickenpox. When bundled, the two-dose ProQuad is CDC-priced at $80.75 per dose, only $0.99 more than the sum of the CDC prices for standalone MMRII ($18.26) and standalone Varivax ($61.50); for the private-sector catalog price, however, the ProQuad bundle commands an even smaller premium over the sum of the standalone components ($124.37 versus $124.05 per dose).

Economic theory teaches us that when free entry and exit occur in a market, when competition is extensive, and when consumers and producers are similarly informed, prices will approach marginal cost. As we have seen, for older vaccines, improvements in vaccine safety and convenience, the forces of incumbent firms fighting each other to exploit available scale economies, and the important role of government recommendations concerning preferred vaccines have led to prices that are low and likely close to marginal cost—at least with regard to the CDC prices. In such cases, consumers, not producers, are reaping most of the benefits, as producers are limited in their ability to take advantage of consumers' willingness to pay.

By contrast, since entry is highly restricted for quite some time in new vaccine markets by regulatory and intellectual-property institutions and proprietary manufacturing knowledge, firms can exercise sustained market power and charge premium prices. In such cases, economic theory teaches us, consumers' valuations (not just marginal costs) will have an important impact on prices. As discussed earlier, all currently marketed vaccines are preventive and prophylactic.[26] It is very difficult to identify in advance which unvaccinated individuals would likely contract the disease. In contrast, the specific beneficiaries of many therapeutic pharmaceuticals and biologics are more easily identified, based on diagnoses and laboratory tests. The limited capability to identify and segment likely subpopulation beneficiaries limits, in turn, vaccine manufacturers' ability to charge prices considerably higher than marginal costs.[27]

How profitable are vaccines relative to pharmaceuticals? Although they are imperfect measures of economic profitability, price–cost margins have been estimated separately and then compared for vaccines, other biologics, and pharmaceuticals.[28] In particular, using data from the U.S. Census of Manufacturing for 2002, Scherer estimates price–cost margins that are lowest for vaccines at 56.3 percent, highest for other biologics at 71.4 percent, and in-between for pharmaceuticals (including both branded and generics) at 62.3 percent.[29]

Particularly for new vaccines, producers would prefer to price at levels reflecting the value to consumers and payers, rather than at the marginal costs of production. To quantify the value of benefits consumers realize from being vaccinated, we can turn to the market research conducted by manufacturers to assist them in setting their prices for patent-protected new vaccines; such research is also undertaken by major purchasers, such as the CDC. How are the values (rather than costs) of vaccines to consumers assessed?

Although beyond the scope of this book, a vast literature in health economics looks at the cost-effectiveness and cost–benefit aspects of medical therapies.[30] The two kinds of studies typically differ, depending on the range of costs and benefits taken into consideration. Costs can include both direct and indirect costs, while benefits encompass both reduced mortality and morbidity and, in some cases, improvements in quality of life.[31] Cost-offset studies examine the extent to which the incremental costs of purchasing and administering a new therapy are offset by lower costs elsewhere in the health-care system, such as in reduced office, inpatient, or emergency-room visits. Even if cost-offset analyses reveal a negative impact (when acquisition and administration costs are greater than any reductions in health-care costs elsewhere), utilizing the new therapy may well still be economically optimal, depending on the extent and valuation of such benefits as declines in morbidity and mortality and improvements in quality of life.[32]

In the current vaccine context, researchers have sought to quantify the direct costs prevented by using the vaccines (those associated with the treatment, complications, and *sequelae* of diseases that are avoided by vaccination, including outpatient and inpatient costs) as well as the societal costs (direct costs plus indirect costs, such as productivity losses due to premature mortality or permanent disability, or opportunity costs associated with caregivers who missed work to care for their sick children, or with patients themselves for missed work).

Recently, researchers at the CDC published an economic evaluation of the routine childhood immunization schedule of seven vaccines that was recommended by the CDC in 2001. Their findings, qualitatively similar to numerous others in the vaccine economics literature, were as follows:

Routine childhood immunization with the 7 vaccines was cost saving from the direct cost and societal perspectives, with net savings of $9.9 billion and $43.3 billion, respectively. Without routine vaccination, direct and societal costs of diphtheria, tetanus, pertussis, *H influenzae type b*, poliomyelitis, measles, mumps, rubella, congenital rubella syndrome, hepatitis B, and varicella would be $12.3 billion and $46.6 billion, respectively. Direct and societal costs for the vaccination program were an estimated $2.3 billion and $2.8 billion, respectively. Direct and societal benefit–cost ratios for routine childhood vaccination were 5.3 and 16.5, respectively.[33]

These findings led the authors to conclude that, from both the direct- and societal-cost perspectives, the 2001 routine childhood immunization schedule resulted in substantial cost savings. Note that this study did not incorporate valuations of changes in morbidity and quality of life, and thus likely understated benefits relative to costs. Hence, while prices of vaccines may be increasingly high (particularly for newer vaccines), the benefits appear to be even more valuable.[34]

Although international issues are generally beyond the scope of this book, it is worth noting briefly that, unlike for prescription pharmaceuticals, little public discussion has occurred regarding the possibility of importing, without FDA approval, lower-priced vaccines from countries abroad, such as Canada or Mexico. It is common practice among pharmaceutical manufacturers to import the active pharmaceutical ingredient and/or the finished pharmaceutical tablet or capsule into the United States, after having successfully complied with regulatory provisions and obtained the required approval from the FDA. Currently, Novartis/Chiron and GlaxoSmithKline already import their FDA-approved vaccines into the United States. Most of the vaccines sold in the United States, however, are also manufactured here.

There are at least two key reasons underlying the absence of public discussion on importation of less expensive, but not FDA-approved, vaccines into the United States. First, pharmaceutical tablets and capsules are very small and easy to transport across borders. In contrast, vaccines (like many other biologics) can only be transported under special thermal (cold-chain) and light conditions and often take up more space than pharmaceuticals, particularly when packaged in single-dose vials with syringes, making them cumbersome to transport across borders. Second, the FDA maintains very tight regulatory controls over the manufacturing and distribution of vaccines, both domestically produced and imported, and unlike the case with pharmaceuticals, it has not been asked by congressional representatives to allow the importation of less expensive vaccines. Simply stated, relative to pharmaceuticals, no comparable political pressure exists to arbitrage against lower prices abroad by permitting importation of vaccines.[35]

Finally, we turn from pricing to marketing efforts. Although data are not readily available, interviews we conducted indicated that, as a proportion of sales revenues, expenditures on visits to physicians' offices by vaccine sales representatives ("detailing expenditures") are much less on average than those for pharmaceuticals. Moreover, while dropping off free samples to physicians' offices is common for pharmaceuticals, virtually no such sampling occurs for vaccines. Several reasons factor into this reduced marketing intensity.

First, other than for annual influenza vaccines, which we discuss in detail in chapter 5, many segments of the market have only one vaccine approved for prevention of the specified disease, with no other vaccine serving as a suitable substitute. Among these are Merck's Gardasil for human papillomavirus, MMRII for measles, mumps, and rubella, RotaTeq for rotavirus, Varivax for varicella, Pneumovax 23 for pneumococcal polysaccharide, and Zostavax for zoster, as well as Sanofi Pasteur's Menactra for meningococcal conjugate and Wyeth's Prevnar for pneumococcal seven-valent. While physicians typically may choose among several available pharmaceuticals to prescribe for a particular condition (for instance, which statin to prescribe for high cholesterol, which proton pump inhibitor to treat acid reflux, which antihypertensive drug to lower blood pressure), for many vaccines the choice is not which to administer, but whether to administer any at all. In such cases, detailers are not needed to convince physicians which vaccine is preferable.

From interviews we learned that while detailing efforts for new vaccines often focus on influencing take-up rates by physicians, relatively little effort is devoted to affecting long-term saturation levels—that is, to increasing the proportion of a physician's eligible patients who are administered the vaccine. More important are attempts to influence the speed of new vaccine diffusion—that is, the willingness of a physician to purchase and then administer a new vaccine. Moreover, in cases where some choice does exist, such as among the five flu vaccines, the value to the manufacturer of gaining an additional patient's utilization is much less for a single annual flu shot (between $10 and $18 annually) than is the value to a pharmaceutical manufacturer of getting a new patient to take a daily branded medicine for a chronic condition (say, $5 daily, or $1,825 annually).

Second, the choice of whether to administer any vaccine at all is, as discussed earlier, decisively affected by the ACIP, whose favorable recommendation essentially sets a minimally acceptable medical practice standard.[36] A theme repeatedly sounded in both our interviews and the literature is that ACIP recommendations are absolutely critical to a vaccine's commercial success. Often cited is the example of GlaxoSmithKline's LymeRx, a vaccine for prevention of Lyme disease, which was withdrawn from the market four years following its approval by the FDA after having received only a tepid recommendation from the ACIP.[37]

Instead of aggressive detailing or advertising in medical journals, vaccine promotion takes the form of substantial interactions with the CDC, the ACIP, various state and national medical associations, public health authorities, and employers' associations. These promotions are typically educational and informational, rather than persuasive. Materials are developed to provide public health and medical officials with data on disease prevalence and severity, vaccine effectiveness, side effects, dosing convenience, and so forth. For physicians who need to advance funds to acquire vaccines for administration in their offices (for vaccines not provided through the VFC and section 317 programs), promotional efforts focus on helping them gain reimbursement and provide information on return policies.

Finally, direct-to-consumer advertising for vaccines has, to date, been confined primarily to magazines targeted at parents and is likely, on average, much less than the amount that is done for other biologics and pharmaceuticals. To the extent, however, that direct-to-consumer advertising informs potential consumers about the availability of new vaccines to treat unmet needs (such as Gardasil for the prevention of cervical cancer caused by the human papillomavirus), particularly for adolescents and adults, this form of marketing could become more prominent in the future as an increasing number of vaccines targeted at these populations are FDA-approved, ACIP-recommended, and launched.[38]

Post-Launch Surveillance

Vaccine utilization and impacts are monitored in a variety of ways following a product launch. A CDC biologics surveillance system collects voluntary reports from manufacturers on the number of doses they distribute. Since some vaccine may be wasted or discarded, this information may overstate how much is actually administered.[39]

An important source of pediatric vaccine utilization data is the annual National Immunization Survey (NIS), which is

> a telephone survey that estimates the vaccination rates of children ages 19–35 months. The NIS comprises seventy-eight independent surveys covering all fifty states and twenty-eight major urban areas. More than one million telephone calls are made annually to yield responses from approximately 30,000 households with children in the appropriate age group. Responsible adults in the households are asked to identify health caregivers, who are then queried about each child's record. Responses are weighted on a number of factors, and attempts are made to correct for households without telephones. The NIS also collects information on sources of vaccination, vaccine safety beliefs, and other important topics.[40]

Additional information is collected by states on immunization coverage at licensed day care centers and at initial and returning school-entry registrations.

Substantial but still incomplete efforts have been underway over the past decade to develop national population registries that will eventually record every childhood immunization administered by any provider, determine immunization needs of individuals, remind parents and providers when immunizations are due, and measure immunization coverage. In 2002, based on self-reported state data, registries contained immunization records on 43 percent of children. The goal of the initiative, "A Healthy People 2010," is the enrollment of 95 percent of children ages six years and under in a population-based registry.[41]

In terms of adult immunization, the National Health Interview Survey, based on a national probability sample of households, contains valuable information, but its sample size is too small to provide useful state-specific data. The Behavioral Risk Factor Surveillance System is a telephone survey conducted by the states which provides national and state-specific estimates of influenza and pneumococcal vaccine coverage.

The effectiveness of vaccines is monitored by the CDC, which is responsible for disease surveillance in the United States. Health-care providers are required to report most vaccine-preventable diseases to their states, and to the CDC and FDA through the Vaccine Adverse Event Reporting System (VAERS). State health departments and the CDC also measure vaccine effectiveness when investigating outbreaks of vaccine-preventable diseases; in some cases, studies are designed prospectively, so that data are collected following study design, whereas in other, retrospective studies, analyses are initiated with data collected previously, often for other purposes. Since the annual influenza vaccines are updated each year, and because of the variability of influenza from year to year, short-term studies examining the effectiveness of flu vaccines in adults tend to be incomplete or nonrepresentative, depending on the flu season.

Recently, the effectiveness of influenza vaccination among numerous cohorts (1990–91 through 1999–2000) of community-dwelling (not institutionalized) elderly members of three health maintenance organizations was studied. Based on claims data from 713,872 person-season observations[42] spanning ten seasons, the study compared hospitalization and death rates among vaccinated and nonvaccinated elderly subjects, adjusting for various potentially confounding factors.[43] The authors found that vaccination "was associated with significant reductions in the risk of hospitalization for pneumonia or influenza and in the risk of death" for this group, and recommended that vaccine delivery to these individuals be improved.[44]

We discuss this study in further detail in our influenza case study, where we also note that during the 2007–8 flu season, the marketed vaccines did not accurately target the predominant flu strains in circulation. This discrepancy resulted in a significant lack of protection, whereby the strains that were not covered by the vaccine accounted for approximately 44 percent of observed flu cases.[45]

Another recent study has reported that observed cases of vaccine-preventable diseases have reached an all-time low in the United States.[46]

For nine of fourteen diseases studied (diphtheria, measles, poliomyelitis, rubella, congenital rubella syndrome, smallpox, mumps, tetanus, and Hib disease), hospitalizations and deaths fell over 90 percent in 2004–6, relative to a pre-1980 baseline. For the remaining four diseases (hepatitis A and B, pneumococcal disease, and varicella), hospitalizations and deaths decreased less than 90 percent; however, vaccines for these diseases were relatively new.

Post-launch vaccine safety is evaluated in a number of ways. As a condition of licensure, the FDA frequently requires the manufacturer to conduct various phase IV studies. In addition to working with the FDA in collecting safety data via VAERS, the CDC supports the Vaccine Safety Data link, which contains the complete medical records of members of seven large health maintenance organizations in the United States. These data can be used to assess, for example, whether the incidence rate of a given adverse event is greater among vaccinated than among nonvaccinated individuals. These various data sources, along with other observational studies, can provide signals associating a vaccine with adverse events, but additional controlled clinical studies are typically required to determine whether the vaccine is the cause.[47]

As noted in the introduction to part I, above, data on the utilization and pricing of vaccines are not considered as reliable as those for other biologics or pharmaceuticals; and while the FDA collects safety data through its Adverse Events Reporting System, the extent to which providers report adverse events to the manufacturer and the FDA is widely believed to be considerably less than complete.[48] We are unaware of any studies comparing underreporting of vaccine adverse events with those for other biologics or pharmaceuticals. Similarly, whether vaccine manufacturers differ in any systematic way from manufacturers of biologics and pharmaceuticals in carrying out phase IV commitments has not, to the best of our knowledge, been addressed.[49]

Industry Structure, Concentration, and Shortages

As discussed earlier, the combined impact of substantial scale economies, regulatory policies, price-bidding procedures, concentrated purchasing power, market acceptance of ACIP recommendations, and obsolescence from improved vaccines has reduced the number of competitors producing vaccines in the United States. This impact is in contrast to many pharmaceutical therapeutic classes, where a number of differentiated branded products often coexist and FDA-approved generics play an important role.

The list of manufacturers licensed for immunization and for distribution of vaccines in the United States provided by the Center for Biologics Evaluation and Research at the FDA website overstates to some extent the actual number currently active, reflecting the exit of some licensed manufacturers from the market.[50] For example, while the FDA lists the Massachusetts Public Health Biologic Lab as licensed to produce tetanus and diphtheria toxoids adsorbed for adult use, and for tetanus toxoid adsorbed,[51] the Commonwealth of Massachusetts has, in fact, closed down those production facilities. Discussions with personnel at the laboratory there revealed that continued production of these vaccines was deemed economically unsustainable. Instead, the lab has recently built new manufacturing facilities for the small-scale production of monoclonal antibodies, under contract to various biotechnology developers.[52] About fifteen years earlier, two state laboratories—those of Massachusetts and Michigan—produced components of DTP for domestic use, but both have now exited this market.[53]

The number of companies manufacturing vaccines within the United States decreased from twenty-six in 1967 to seventeen in 1980, and to three in 2004—Sanofi Pasteur, Merck, and Wyeth.[54] A fourth manufacturer, MedImmune (recently acquired by AstraZeneca) now markets FluMist, a live intranasal influenza vaccine for individuals ages five to forty-nine years, with stock seeds (the microorganisms used to produce the vaccine) developed in California and shipped to the United Kingdom for bulk production, which is then shipped to Pennsylvania for filling and finishing. Vaccines marketed in the United States by GlaxoSmithKline and Novartis/ Chiron are currently manufactured outside the country at FDA-approved facilities.[55] Reasons for the reduction in the number of U.S. manufacturers, as mentioned above, include the relatively small market for vaccines compared to other biologics and pharmaceuticals, numerous mergers, scale economies in regulatory compliance and manufacturing, and the legacies of both the pre-1986 liability policies and the pre-1993 "winner-take-all" price-bidding system of the CDC.[56]

Since the various individual vaccines typically cannot be substituted for one another (either on the demand or supply side), the actual extent of their market concentration in the United States is even greater.[57] As shown in table 3-1, of the eleven vaccines recommended for pediatric use (ages zero to six years), five are produced by only one manufacturer.[58] Five have but two suppliers, and one (for influenza) has three manufacturers. Only one manufacturer of an influenza vaccine, however, has a product that is approved for children under the age of two years.[59]

For young people between the ages of seven and eighteen, the ACIP recommends ten vaccines, six of which have sole suppliers, three of which have two, and one of which (influenza) has four manufacturers. While four of the sole-supplied vaccines are relatively new and patent-protected, two very old vaccines (inactivated poliovirus and measles, mumps, and rubella) are also sole-supplied. Similarly, among the nine ACIP-recommended vaccines for adults ages nineteen and over, six are sole-supplied and two have two suppliers, while only influenza has multiple manufacturers (five, just recently increased from four).[60] Other than for influenza, no ACIP-recommended vaccine has more than two active and FDA-approved manufacturers.

One consequence of this reliance on relatively few suppliers for individual vaccines is the vulnerability of the nation's vaccine supplies to production and/or regulatory shutdowns at manufacturing facilities, which may result in shortages. Indeed, since 2000, vaccines against nine of the twelve vaccine-preventable diseases of childhood have experienced significant supply shortages, requiring adaptations to immunization schedules to reduce the number of doses children receive and prioritization of available vaccines to the groups at highest risk.[61] Similarly, shortages occurred in the United States in 2004 due to contamination in Chiron's United Kingdom influenza vaccine manufacturing facility, resulting in many adults not getting their annual flu vaccinations.

The CDC regularly updates its website announcing current vaccine shortages and delays. During 2007, there were three vaccine shortages, all involving Merck. As discussed in further detail in the varicella zoster case study, production of the varicella zoster virus bulk was temporarily suspended in early 2007 due to low yields from incubation, thereby affecting stocks of finished varicella, MMR-V vaccine, and zoster vaccine, each of which has varicella as a component.[62] Stocks of the finished ProQuad

TABLE 3-1

NUMBER OF MANUFACTURERS OF ACIP-RECOMMENDED VACCINES
POSTED ON CDC VACCINE PRICE LIST, NOVEMBER 5, 2008

Recommended vaccine	Age 0–6 years	Age 7–18 years	Age ≥ 19 years
Hepatitis B	2	2	2
Rotavirus	2	N/A	N/A
Diphtheria, tetanus, Pertussis	2	2	1
Haemophilus influenzae type b	2	N/A	N/A
Pneumococcal	1	1	1
Inactivated poliovirus	1	1	N/A
Influenza	3	4	5
Measles, mumps, Rubella	1	1	1
Varicella/Zoster	1	1	1
Hepatitis A	2	2	2
Meningococcal	1	1	1
Human papillomavirus	N/A	1	1

SOURCE: See tables in appendices C and D.
NOTES: N/A = not applicable (not recommended by the ACIP for that age bracket). Vaccination is considered recommended if the initial administration or booster occurs anywhere within the age bracket. A single manufacturer may have several brands or packaging variants.

(MMR-V) were depleted as of June 15, 2007, although stocks of the finished noncombination varicella and zoster vaccines were deemed adequate to fulfill recommended use.[63]

Merck also experienced production delays for the pediatric and adult hepatitis A vaccines (pediatric and adult VAQTA) in 2007, resulting in back orders. The company temporarily discontinued accepting orders for these vaccines, initially projecting they would become available in mid-2008; the pediatric/adolescent formulation of Vaqta became available for ordering as of December 1, 2008, and Merck anticipates that the adult formulation may be available in the second quarter 2009.[64] GlaxoSmithKline (GSK) also sells pediatric and adult hepatitis A vaccine (pediatric and adult Havrix) and an adult hepatitis A/hepatitis B vaccine (Twinrix). According to the CDC website, GSK has sufficient supply to meet current demands and has initiated plans to increase production of Havrix and Twinrix to help ensure uninterrupted supply for the U.S. market.[65]

A potentially more serious shortage involves Merck's December 2007 recall of ten lots of the *Haemophilus influenzae* type b ("Hib") conjugate vaccine, PedvaxHIB, for protection against bacterial meningitis, pneumonia, and other serious illnesses, and two lots of its combination Hib and hepatitis B vaccine, Comvax, involving between 1 million and 1.2 million doses that were distributed in the United States beginning in April 2007.[66] The voluntary recall was issued as a precautionary measure, for Merck could not ensure the sterility of the equipment used during manufacture of these lots, having discovered during routine equipment testing the presence of the bacteria *Bacillus cereus*. Sterility tests of samples from the recalled vaccine lots themselves did not find any contamination, leading Merck to state that the potential for contamination of any individual dose of Hib vaccine was very low. Children who received Hib conjugate vaccine from the recalled lots did not need revaccination or any special follow-up, as efficacy was unaffected.[67] These vaccine products were still unavailable for direct new purchase order as of November 2008, when the anticipated return availability was projected for mid-2009.[68]

Sanofi Pasteur manufactures and distributes two other Hib conjugate vaccines in the United States, ActHIB (a monovalent Hib vaccine) and TriHIBit (a combination diphtheria, tetanus toxoids, and acellular pertussis/Hib vaccine), which were unaffected by the Merck recall. In the recent past, Merck and Sanofi Pasteur each produced about half of the U.S. Hib vaccine supply. Since Merck does not expect to distribute these vaccines until at least mid-2009, and since short-term production increases from Sanofi Pasteur are limited, the CDC expects that temporary shortages are likely to occur.[69]

Very high coverage rates for Hib vaccine (with about 94 percent of U.S. children ages nineteen to thirty-five months vaccinated in 2006) have resulted in a dramatic decline in the incidence of Hib disease in the United States. The CDC has estimated that in 2006 the incidence in children less than five years old was 99 percent less than before the vaccine was available. The ACIP-recommended schedule for Hib-containing vaccines consists of a primary series (either two or three doses, depending on the formulation) administered beginning at age two months, and a booster dose at twelve to fifteen months. Given the Hib vaccine shortage due to the recall, in December 2007 the CDC, in consultation with the ACIP, the American Academy of Family Physicians (AAFP), and the American Academy of Pediatrics (AAP), issued recommendations stating that providers should temporarily defer the routine Hib vaccine booster administered at twelve to fifteen months, except to certain high-risk children's groups. The CDC announcement noted that the short-term deferral of the booster dose was not likely to result in a significantly increased risk for Hib disease because of herd effects from those already receiving the full series of Hib vaccines and from the continued protection of children with only the primary series. Various other rationing techniques were also recommended, such as providers' ordering only the number of doses likely required to meet immediate needs and not stockpiling inventories.[70] The extended delay in Merck's reentry into the Hib vaccine market, now projected as not occurring before mid-2009, has resulted in various states issuing mandatory guidelines to physicians ordering deferment of the booster for now so that the youngest infants can receive at least the first dose in the primary series, and preferably all three doses.[71]

The causes and consequences of these and other recent vaccine shortages have been discussed extensively elsewhere, and we do not elaborate on them further.[72] As has been discussed by Scherer,[73] among others, however, vulnerability to shortages could be addressed by subsidizing an increase in additional manufacturing capacity.

PART II

Four Case Studies

Introduction to Part II

Having discussed similarities and differences among vaccines, other biologics, and pharmaceuticals through the entire life cycle of medicines, we now illustrate and document some of these distinguishing features of vaccines and their changes over time by examining four case studies. Although we confine our attention to four segments of vaccine markets—diphtheria, tetanus, and pertussis; seasonal influenza vaccines; the multivalent pneumococcal conjugate vaccine (Prevnar); and varicella zoster vaccines—it is worth emphasizing that vaccines are currently marketed to residents in and travelers from the United States (including the military) for many other diseases, such as anthrax, hepatitis types A and B, Japanese encephalitis, human papillomavirus, measles, mumps, rabies, rotavirus, rubella, smallpox, typhoid fever, and yellow fever.[1]

As we shall see, while exhibiting some common themes, the four case studies also demonstrate substantial heterogeneity among vaccine markets, particularly in the ways in which innovation is occurring. For instance, the combination diphtheria, tetanus, and pertussis case documents the nature of competition and product differentiation that has taken place in a mature but still changing product space, where innovation has brought new formulations that have increased convenience, variety, and safety, even as the number of competitors has dwindled.

The influenza case highlights the temporal and logistical challenges facing five competing manufacturers who must coordinate with the FDA, the CDC, and international organizations the development, manufacturing, distribution, and administration of yearly altered flu vaccine formulations. In this market segment product differentiation is limited (although both injectable and intranasal versions are marketed now), and innovation is taking the form of manufacturing methods that make scale-up more feasible—

63

a capability that could be particularly valuable should an avian flu pandemic emerge.

The Prevnar case illustrates the commercial success that has accompanied the first conjugate vaccine indicated for the prevention of about 80 percent of invasive pneumococcal disease in children under age six. The vaccine, whose conjugate process intensifies immunity, is given to infants beginning at only six weeks of age. It is more efficacious in infants than the previous-generation pneumococcal vaccine, which is approved for use only in children over two years of age. The clinical development of Prevnar involved collaboration with a large, closed-staff-model health maintenance organization, using state-of-the-art electronic records. A distinguishing feature of Prevnar is its pricing at a level higher than cost offset, in part because of its nonhealth benefits to children and their parents. Moreover, subsequent post-launch surveillance has revealed that vaccinating infants with Prevnar generates spillover health benefits to older children and adults as well. Prevnar is the first vaccine to reach blockbuster status—that is, having more than $1 billion in annual sales.

Finally, the case of varicella zoster vaccine brings focus to both adult and pediatric vaccines. Zostavax prevents reactivation of childhood chickenpox, or varicella, in adults, for whom the disease is commonly called shingles, herpes zoster, or, simply, zoster. The development of Zostavax involved a long, large, and complex collaboration among the National Institutes of Health (NIH), the industry sponsor (Merck), and the Veterans Administration, with the five-year pivotal trial involving about 38,000 individuals whose medical histories after vaccination were closely monitored by the computerized Veterans Administration medical records system. This case also demonstrates the importance of post-launch surveillance, in that close monitoring of the childhood varicella vaccine has resulted in important changes in the ACIP-recommended number of immunizations, significantly increasing the size of the potential market.

Four themes that the reader will repeatedly discover from these four case studies are: first, that innovation is occurring in all cases but is taking on very different forms in the traditional and novel vaccines; second, that development of vaccines involves extensive collaborations among manufacturers, public health authorities, regulators, and payers; third, that for each of these vaccines, manufacturing is complex and fragile; and fourth, that post-launch surveillance yields very important information concerning the efficacy of immunizations, and evidence regarding how immunity is changing as consumption externalities occur among children and adults.

4

Diphtheria, Tetanus, and Pertussis and Related Combination Vaccines

Scientific advances have greatly expanded the variety not only of the vaccines available to Americans, but also the dosages and formulations of these vaccines. A child who received all the vaccines included on the ACIP's recommended immunization schedule as individual agents would be subjected to nearly fifty injections by six years of age. Manufacturers have devoted substantial efforts, therefore, to combining multiple agents into single injections, without sacrificing efficacy or increasing side effects. Their successes in this regard have clearly been beneficial to children and their parents.

In this case study we review the history and economic drivers of a combination vaccine in the diphtheria, tetanus, and pertussis family of vaccinations. GlaxoSmithKline and Sanofi Pasteur dominate this vaccine family, with multiple products and permutations available in the U.S. market. Their "duopoly" creates unique market dynamics and a delicate balance of supply, pricing, innovation, market share, and competition.

Disease Overviews and Treatments

Diphtheria, which is caused by toxigenic strains of the *Corynebacterium diphtheriae* bacterium, primarily affects the respiratory system. Toxin-producing *Corynebacterium ulcerans*, possibly acquired from dairy animals or unpasteurized dairy products, may also trigger the disease. Since diphtheria is a communicable infectious disease transmitted by inhaling the bacteria, epidemic outbreaks are possible, although very rare. Vaccination efforts have been particularly successful in eliciting immunity and reducing the incidence of diphtheria infection. Inexpensive antibiotic treatments are available to combat the disease in infected individuals; if left untreated, however, it may cause serious complications, and even death.

Pertussis, also known as whooping cough, is another contagious bacterial infection. This respiratory disease, characterized by coughing fits, is sparked by the toxin of *Bordetella pertussis* bacteria and is transmitted through the saliva of infected individuals. Antibiotics, primarily erythromycin, are typically administered both for prophylaxis following exposure and for the treatment of infection.

Vaccines have been moderately effective in reducing the incidence of pertussis. According to the CDC, a significant number of people in the United States, estimated between 5,000 and 7,000, continue to suffer from this infection each year.[1] The World Health Organization (WHO) estimates that in 2000, over 39 million people worldwide were infected with the disease, resulting in 297,000 deaths.[2] People of all ages may be infected, but infants are particularly susceptible to the most severe complications, including death.

Although most cases of severe pertussis and almost all mortality occur in infants, the overall disease burden is increasingly shifting to adolescents and adults. The medical community suggests they are becoming increasingly susceptible due to the waning efficacy of the vaccine, administered decades earlier, as the population ages—which in turn also leaves the susceptible infant population at risk of infection, as their full immunity has yet to be established.[3]

The pertussis vaccine is manufactured in two formulations: whole-organism and acellular.[4] The acellular formulation was developed to elicit an acceptable level of immune response while decreasing the risk of side effects. Initially, the whole-organism version was recommended to establish immunity through a set of three injections for infants, with the acellular formulation utilized only as a booster injection at eighteen months and four years of age. In 2002, however, the acellular replaced the whole-organism formulation to establish initial immunity in children in the United States and some European nations. The whole-organism formulation is still available in other parts of the world, as it remains a highly effective and inexpensive product. While the safety profile of the acellular version represents a significant improvement, the ability of this version to provide long-term protection against the disease is less certain. Some recent studies suggest that an increase in the incidence of pertussis over the past twenty years is due in part to the waning immunity associated with the acellular pertussis agent. Thus, adolescents and adults may be susceptible to this infection even after receiving the recommended childhood vaccinations.[5]

Tetanus is an infectious disease that is not transmitted from person to person, yet it may be prevented with adequate vaccination. The disease is caused by the *Clostridium tetani* bacterium when it infects an open wound. As soil is a reservoir for the bacterium, elimination of the causative agent is infeasible. Initial immunity is established through a series of three early-childhood vaccines and is maintained with booster injections every ten years through adulthood. Following the opening of a wound, anti-tetanus immunoglobulins and/or a tetanus toxoid booster may be administered to provide additional passive protection against infection. In the event of an infection, tetanus is treated with agents that control muscle spasms, anti-biotics, and wound care, as required.

Historical Background and Currently Available Formulations

The earliest standalone versions of diphtheria, tetanus, and pertussis vaccines were developed in the 1920s, and a trivalent combination was available in one injection as early as the 1940s. Next came safer formulations containing less of the active agents, thereby triggering fewer side effects without sacrificing efficacy. Most recently, the traditional DTP combination vaccine has further expanded to include protection against even more diseases in a single injection. The most advanced products are Pediarix, which includes a combination of diphtheria, tetanus, pertussis, polio, and hepatitis B, and Pentacel, which combines diphtheria, tetanus, pertussis, polio, and *Haemophilus influenzae* type b. Pentacel, the first combination vaccine to address these five diseases, received FDA approval in June 2008, whereas Pediarix received approval in December 2002.[6]

In the United States, GlaxoSmithKline and Sanofi Pasteur now battle for shares of the market segment for DTP combination vaccines, following the withdrawal of Wyeth's product from the U.S. market in 2001, for reasons discussed later in the chapter. Table 4-1 lists the dates when the currently

TABLE 4-1

SELECTED VACCINES LICENSED FOR IMMUNIZATION AND DISTRIBUTION
IN THE UNITED STATES, AS OF OCTOBER 2008

Trade name	Company	FDA approval	Dosing
Adacel	Sanofi Pasteur	2005	- Single booster administration - Adolescents and adults, 11–64 years of age
Boostrix	GlaxoSmithKline	2005	- Single booster administration - Adolescents, 10–18 years of age
Daptacel	Sanofi Pasteur	2002	- Use in a four-dose primary series - Infants and toddlers at 2, 4, 6, and 17–20 months of age
Infanrix	GlaxoSmithKline	1997 (doses 1–4) 2003 (dose 5)	- Use in a five-dose primary series - Infants and children 6 weeks through 6 years of age
Kinrix	GlaxoSmithKline	2008	- Use as the fifth dose in the DTaP series and the fourth dose in the inactivated poliovirus vaccine series - Children 4–6 years of age
Pediarix	GlaxoSmithKline	2002	- Use in a three-dose primary series in infants born of HBsAg-negative mothers - Infants and children 6 weeks through 6 years of age
Pentacel	Sanofi Pasteur	2008	- Use in a four-dose primary series - Infants and children 6 weeks– 4 years of age
TriHIBit (Tripedia + ActHIBit)	Sanofi Pasteur	1996	- Use as the fourth dose in the primary series - Children 15–18 months of age
Tripedia	Sanofi Pasteur	1996	- Use in a five-dose primary series - Infants and children 6 weeks through 6 years of age

SOURCE: U.S. Food and Drug Administration 2001, 2002a, 2005, 2006a, 2008b.
NOTE: Additional products containing the diphtheria and tetanus components or the tetanus component only are available through Sanofi Pasteur.

marketed DTaP[7] vaccines received FDA approval, and the various indications for which they are approved.

In the original combination of DTP, each component was inactivated (chemically killed or weakened) while left with the capability of eliciting an adequate immune response. The diphtheria and tetanus components were toxoids, or weakened versions of the harmful toxins that are generated by the bacteria, whereas the pertussis component was the organism itself.

Within the DTP vaccine market, safety concerns have been addressed using two different approaches: key changes to the way the vaccine components are developed, particularly with respect to the whole-cell pertussis component; and a reduction in the amount of antigen present in the booster immunizations, particularly with respect to the amount of diphtheria toxoid.

As the use of the DTP vaccine became more widespread, the incidence of pertussis infection and pertussis-related deaths decreased significantly. However, side effects from the pertussis component of the vaccination, which include fever, inflammation at the injection site, and even more serious conditions, such as seizures, were increasingly recognized. The opportunity to enhance the safety profile of the product sparked an interest in additional research.[8]

To decrease the side effects associated with the whole-cell pertussis antigen, manufacturers developed an acellular pertussis component which utilizes only parts of the pertussis bacterium instead of the whole organism. In the United States, vaccines containing whole-cell pertussis are no longer available, although in other regions of the world, the lower-cost and highly effective whole-cell formulation is still in use. The combination with the acellular pertussis component is abbreviated as DTaP (and sometimes differentiated from the DTwP version, which contains the whole-cell pertussis). Although the acellular formulation has a more acceptable side-effect profile, concerns regarding waning immunity that may be linked to the acellular formulation have recently surfaced (see below).

Currently, a number of DTaP products are available on the U.S. market. Daptacel received FDA approval in May 2002. Aventis Pasteur (which became Sanofi Pasteur when Aventis was acquired by Sanofi in 2005) developed this DTaP vaccine to elicit protection against diphtheria, tetanus, and pertussis in children under seven years of age. It is approved for use in a three-dose series to establish primary immunization against diphtheria and tetanus. A fourth dose, which is typically administered between fifteen and twenty months of age, completes the primary immunization series for pertussis and provides a booster dose against diphtheria and tetanus.[9]

GlaxoSmithKline's contribution to the DTaP supply is its Infanrix vaccine, which received FDA licensure in January 1997. It is indicated for the first five doses of the diphtheria, tetanus, and pertussis immunization series in children less than seven years old.[10]

Sanofi Pasteur's Tripedia vaccine was licensed by the FDA in July 1996. This DTaP vaccine was originally developed by Connaught Laboratories, which underwent multiple acquisitions and is now part of Sanofi Pasteur. Like Infanrix, it is indicated for use as the initial five immunizations to elicit protection against diphtheria, tetanus, and pertussis in children under seven years of age.[11]

The diphtheria component of DTaP has also evolved to provide a better safety profile. Identified by the abbreviation Tdap, vaccines are now available with lower concentrations of diphtheria. This formulation is typically indicated for use as an immunization booster for adolescents who completed the primary immunization series as infants. One Tdap vaccine, Sanofi Pasteur's Adacel, was licensed in the United States in June 2005 as an active booster immunization for people eleven to sixty-four years of age. Adacel contains the same tetanus toxoid, diphtheria toxoid, and acellular pertussis antigens as those in Sanofi Pasteur's Daptacel (the company's pediatric DTaP product). The acellular pertussis and the reduced quantity of the diphtheria toxoid make it suitable for booster administration. Each dose of Adacel is adsorbed (attracted and retained) onto aluminum phosphate as an adjuvant agent to bolster the immunologic effect of the vaccine without triggering unwanted side effects.[12]

GlaxoSmithKline (GSK) manufactures Boostrix, which has been available in the United States since its licensure in May 2005. This version of the Tdap combination vaccine also contains reduced diphtheria toxoid, acellular pertussis, and tetanus toxoid. Activity is bolstered with the use of an aluminum hydroxide adjuvant. Boostrix contains reduced quantities of the same antigens as those contained in GSK's Infanrix (DTaP) vaccine. According to the product label, Boostrix is indicated for use as a booster immunization for adolescents ten to eighteen years of age after initial immunization is established through traditional infant vaccinations.[13]

Evolution of More Convenient Combination Formulations

After the antigens present in the DTaP vaccine were optimized, the manufacturers focused on making vaccine delivery more convenient by increasing the number of diseases that could be prevented with a single injection, with GSK and Sanofi-Aventis (now Sanofi Pasteur) taking different paths. Although the clinical requirements of the next generation of vaccines remained critical (that is, the need to maintain a high level of efficacy and a low level of adverse reactions), additional commercial issues accompanied the development of new products. For example, product differentiation and product confusion, manufacturing and distribution hurdles, physician reimbursement, and ACIP and AAP endorsement all contributed to differing decisions regarding the development of the next generation of products in this market segment.

To differentiate its DTaP product and provide a more convenient delivery formulation for multiple vaccines, GSK developed Pediarix (a DTaP plus recombinant hepatitis B plus inactivated poliovirus vaccine). In parallel, Sanofi Pasteur efforts to extend its product line resulted in the launch of Pentacel (a DTaP plus inactivated poliovirus plus *haemophilus influenzae* type b conjugate vaccine).

GSK received FDA approval for the Pediarix combination vaccine in 2002. According to the prescribing label, Pediarix is "indicated for active immunization against diphtheria, tetanus, pertussis (whooping cough), all known subtypes of hepatitis B virus, and poliomyelitis caused by poliovirus Types 1, 2, and 3 as a three-dose primary series in infants born of HBsAg-negative mothers, beginning as early as 6 weeks of age." The vaccine is not indicated for individuals seven years of age or older.[14]

GSK also received FDA approval for the Kinrix combination vaccine in 2008. This combination agent is similar to Pediarix in that it is indicated for active immunization against diphtheria, tetanus, pertussis, and poliomyelitis caused by poliovirus. Kinrix does not, however, include components to stimulate immunity against the hepatitis B virus. The Kinrix prescribing label outlines the specific indication for use of this product as "the fifth dose in the diphtheria, tetanus, and acellular pertussis (DTaP) vaccine series and the fourth dose in the inactivated poliovirus vaccine (IPV) series in children 4 through 6 years of age whose previous DTaP vaccine doses have been with Infanrix and/or Pediarix for the first three doses and Infanrix for the fourth dose." Although combination vaccines offer increased convenience, the addition of Kinrix to the GSK portfolio highlights physicians' continuing need for the flexibility to dose patients in a manner such that they do not exceed the recommended total number of doses per individual component. Since all agents within a combination do not require the same number of frequency of doses, a broad portfolio of vaccine offerings with various permutations of the possible combinations is made available to meet all possible needs.

Sanofi Pasteur has developed an expanded version of the DTaP vaccine that incorporates additional antigens to elicit an immune response against polio and *Haemophilus influenzae* type b (Hib) in children. Pentacel is the first combination vaccine in the United States to offer protection against these five pathogens in one injection. The diphtheria, tetanus, and pertussis components of Pentacel are similar to those found in Sanofi Pasteur's Daptacel (DTaP) vaccine.

Another component of Sanofi's strategy includes the TriHIBit combination vaccine that was approved by the FDA in September 1996.[15] The TriHIBit product combines two of Sanofi Pasteur's previously licensed vaccines—the ActHIB vaccine for *Haemophilus influenzae* type b and the Tripedia vaccine for DTaP—and enables their administration as one injection. No other DTaP-combination vaccines are approved as separate products and also specifically approved to be administered with another product in the form of a single injection. TriHIBit is indicated only for the fourth (booster) dose of the diphtheria, tetanus, and pertusssis vaccine series and the Hib vaccine series in children between fifteen and eighteen months of age.[16]

Rationalizing the Bundled-Product Landscape

Interestingly, the two key players in the American DTaP market, GSK and Sanofi Pasteur, have both been able to bring multiple products with differentiated benefits into this product space. Since these new bundled combination products were approved after 1994, they enjoy the advantage of not being subject to price caps. The multiplicity of products may, however, cause some confusion among health-care workers in terms of administering the correct vaccine, accurately documenting correct dosage and combination, ordering, and so forth.

The ACIP now recommends that children in the United States receive five immunizations containing diphtheria, tetanus, and pertussis to initiate immunologic protection. The first three injections are typically in the form of the DTaP vaccine (Daptacel, Infanrix, or Tripedia, for example) and are administered at two, four, and six months of age. The fourth dose, also utilizing the DTaP formulation, is recommended between fifteen and eighteen months of age. To complete the series, ACIP recommends children obtain a final dose of DTaP between the ages of four and six years. Booster injections containing a reduced level of diphtheria toxoid (the Tdap formulation) are to be administered between eleven and twelve years of age. Either an Adacel or Boostrix injection fulfills this booster recommendation.

In addition to the expanding combinations that are now available or under development, single- and double-valent vaccines are still produced to minimize unnecessary exposure to multiple components, or to be available for patients who cannot tolerate the full combination. For example, booster doses of diphtheria and tetanus toxoids are recommended every ten years as immunity wanes. Therefore, DT or T vaccines, which do not contain a pertussis component, remain on the market to help maintain the initial immunity throughout life. Furthermore, concerns that the pertussis component could exacerbate an underlying neurological condition have led to an ACIP recommendation to withhold pertussis vaccinations from children with possible neurological disorders, giving the DT or T vaccines further utility in this subset of the population.

Vaccine manufacturers continue to invest in R&D efforts to bring new combination vaccines to the DTP market. According to the National Institutes of Health website, ClinicalTrials.gov, tetanus was the subject of at least ten U.S. clinical trials during 2007. Pertussis was also the subject of at least ten clinical studies, and diphtheria of at least nine. These studies included investigational trials before licensure, as well as phase IV monitoring conducted afterward. Trials were designed with a variety of objectives, including the study of concomitant use of multiple vaccines, the evaluation of safety in the elderly, and the determination of noninferiority of new products.

As the number of available vaccines continues to increase, dosing schedules become ever more complicated, even with the expanded combination products. Physicians, parents, and public health authorities are increasingly focused on developing a clear understanding of the interactions that may occur among vaccines when the combination products are administered during a single visit to the physician's office. For the convenience of the parent and the child, and also to ensure appropriate immunological protection from a public health perspective, minimizing the number of visits to a physician's office remains a goal for vaccine developers.

Manufacturing Issues

In economic terms, the DTP vaccine market is currently a duopoly: two major players (GSK and Sanofi Pasteur) battle for market share, with well-established infrastructures and significant resources throughout the value chain (manufacturing expertise, optimized distribution channels, relationships with purchasers, and so on). Prior to 2001, the market also included Wyeth Lederle, which later became Wyeth Pharmaceuticals. Wyeth's departure triggered a temporary vaccine shortage in 2001–2, which lasted until the other manufacturers could modify their supplies in response to the new market conditions.

Other companies did not enter the DTP market following Wyeth's decision to exit, in part because the vaccine manufacturing process presents a sizable barrier to entry. In fact, manufacturing processes present a significant hurdle even for established players trying to maintain their status in the market. As the FDA updates its current good manufacturing practice (cGMP) regulations, with which manufacturers must comply before products from their facilities may be sold, companies must invest continuously in costly renovations. In a market sector where low price and the potential market share for a given product may not offset the additional investment expenditures necessary to comply with cGMP, companies must decide if continued participation is warranted. Wyeth's DTP vaccine fell victim to this quandary. When, in 2001, Wyeth decided not to upgrade its manufacturing facilities in compliance with an FDA requirement, it determined its best choice was to exit the DTP market entirely.[17]

Pricing and Marketing

Along with all other pediatric vaccines, the DTaP series and its various combinations are included in the Vaccines for Children program.[18] Appendix D presents the 2008 price lists for these vaccines, showing the difference between the CDC's cost per dose and that charged to the private sector. It is worth noting that the private-sector price is a catalog or list price; although private-sector payers in the pharmaceutical market generally obtain chargebacks, rebates, and other discounts depending on their ability to shift market share,[19] the extent to which this occurs for vaccines is unknown. Such discounts off the private-catalog list price are likely to occur only in cases where the vaccines can be substituted for one another, which is infrequent, given the product differentiation that has occurred in the DTaP vaccine segment. As noted earlier, because of concerns about shortages and unanticipated manufacturing problems, it is in the public interest for the number of manufacturers to increase. For a company to enter and/or maintain a presence in the vaccine market, however, long-term profitability must be assured. Interviews with industry and government officials indicated a clear awareness of the fragile balance between lower CDC prices and the long-term sustainability of DTP vaccine development and manufacturing.

Post-Launch Surveillance

Post-launch surveillance studies are sponsored by the manufacturer to assess the impact on human health once the vaccine has reached the market and been administered to the general population. Such surveillance is particularly critical to vaccine manufacturers, given that their products are administered to healthy individuals and have long-lived efficacy. Although investigational trials for vaccines are larger than many standard trials for pharmaceuticals, postmarketing surveillance enables companies, public health agencies, and regulatory authorities to gain access to additional information about the vaccine and further ensure its safety and efficacy. The emergence of electronic medical records has streamlined and reduced the costs of collecting post-launch data.

A manufacturer may also choose to convene a phase IV clinical trial in an effort to extend the range of approved indications, or expand the age group for whom a vaccine is approved. For example, in March 2007, Sanofi Pasteur initiated a phase IV evaluation of the company's Adacel vaccine in individuals sixty-five years of age or older. With estimated enrollment of 1,564 test subjects from various parts of the United States, data collection was not anticipated to be completed until late 2008. If the data from this trial indicate that administration of Adacel decreases the incidence of pertussis among the elderly population, Sanofi Pasteur may be able to secure the first approval for this type of vaccine in that patient segment. This trial is potentially a very useful study, as both the elderly, whose immunity to pertussis may be waning, and some younger individuals, who have yet to establish primary immunity, may benefit.

In addition to the manufacturer-sponsored trials designed to expand the market potential of specific vaccines and other manufacturer-sponsored trials required by the FDA, the U.S. government has also implemented various systems through which adverse events associated with vaccines can be monitored. For example, the CDC and the FDA cosponsor the Vaccine Adverse Event Reporting System. VAERS provides a vehicle for the reporting, monitoring, and review of national data on adverse events and side effects.[20]

Another data collection system of note is the Vaccine Safety Data Link Project (VSD). This tool exemplifies the collaboration that is currently integrating the information, knowledge, and resources of the public and private sectors. The VSD was established in 1990 with the goal of identifying and understanding the serious adverse events that may result from childhood vaccinations and modifying the national immunization recommendations accordingly.[21] It comprises immunization histories for over 5.5 million people each year, with information generated by participating managed-care organizations.

The Long-Term Outlook for the DTP Vaccine Segment

The current environment in the DTP vaccine market segment is clearly characterized as a duopoly market, with Sanofi Pasteur and GSK being the two firms. The very high fixed and sunk regulatory costs and the presence of substantial scale economies make unlikely the entry of new manufacturers to this market segment in the near future. Additionally, as is the case in most traditional vaccine market segments, the DTP combination vaccines offer limited sales potential. Although a large portion of the U.S. population receives the vaccine series, administration is limited to a handful of doses, which leaves manufacturers with limited revenue potential in comparison to the potential market size of a pharmaceutical or other biologic associated with a chronic health condition. As large biopharmaceutical companies consolidate and the vaccine businesses become units within the multifaceted enterprises, R&D investments, economies of scale, profit margins, and potential revenues become increasingly critical factors in the distribution of limited internal resources among vaccines, other biologics, and pharmaceuticals. Although the emergence of additional market entrants is unlikely in the near future, it is critical at a minimum to maintain the duopoly structure to ensure competitive pricing, continued (albeit incremental) innovation, and, most importantly, a reliable supply of these vital vaccines.

Seasonal Influenza Vaccines

The influenza vaccine is unique, in that it must be modified and administered annually to address the specific key strains of a virus that are likely to be responsible for that year's outbreak. This dosing requirement makes it one of the most difficult vaccines to coordinate through development, manufacturing, distribution, and administration. The main issues highlighted in this case study include strategies for product differentiation and market-share competition; manufacturing issues and impending changes to production processes (which may provide a competitive advantage to the first company with a successful cell-culture manufacturing system); vaccine distribution practices and the relationships among the manufacturers, distributors, government and private purchasers, insurers, and physicians; and the investment in an annual vaccine infrastructure that may be particularly valuable when an influenza pandemic threatens.

Influenza Disease and Its Treatments

Influenza, also called flu, is a highly contagious respiratory disease to which the elderly, young children, and individuals with compromised immune systems are particularly susceptible. The Centers for Disease Control and Prevention estimate that 5–20 percent of the U.S. population will contract the flu each year. Over 200,000 people will experience severe complications that result in hospitalization, and approximately 36,000 people will die of the disease.[1] Seasonal influenza manifests as a fever, lethargy, nasal congestion, and muscle aches.

Vaccinations against the flu are currently available in two forms: the flu injection, which typically contains the three strains of the (killed) virus that the CDC expects to be the most common form for that particular year, and the nasal spray vaccine, which contains a live, weakened form of the same viral strains. In this case study, we focus on the economic drivers of these vaccines and unique issues associated with the flu vaccine market in the United States.

Over-the-counter (OTC) remedies may ameliorate symptoms of the flu, and four prescription agents (Symmetrel, Flumadine, Tamiflu, and Relenza) are available to help prevent additional infection or shorten the recovery process in recently infected individuals. These agents may also be effective in reducing the spread of the virus and in minimizing complications of the disease. To best address the public health concern, however, the CDC recommends flu vaccinations each year for people who are at high risk of contracting the disease and for those who care for the high-risk population. While current CDC pediatric recommendations call for vaccinations for children ages six months to about five years, in 2008 the ACIP expanded this population to include those ages six months to eighteen years of age— an increase of about 30 million children, beginning no later than the 2009–10 flu season.[2]

Vaccine Development Timelines

The first influenza vaccines became available in the United States in 1945. Today, the list of annual flu vaccines approved by the FDA for U.S. distribution includes five injectable, trivalent, inactivated vaccines: GSK's FluLaval and Fluarix; Novartis's (formerly Chiron's) Fluvirin; Sanofi Pasteur's Fluzone; and a recent (September 2007) entrant, Afluria, from CSL Biotherapies, a subsidiary of Australian vaccine manufacturer CSL Limited. There is also one live, attenuated intranasal vaccine, FluMist, from AstraZeneca (formerly MedImmune). Both the inactivated and live, attenuated versions of the vaccine are able to trigger the body's production of antibodies and offer protection against subsequent infection.[3]

Because some of the viral strains of influenza that infect people change from one year to the next, manufacturers must update the vaccine annually to replace the previous year's viral strains with those most likely to cause an outbreak of the flu in the following season. The process of selecting which strains to include in the annual vaccine is a highly coordinated, global effort, with the CDC and the World Health Organization designating the strains based on constant global monitoring of influenza, and coordinating efforts with the FDA to provide these strains to vaccine manufacturers. All manufacturers produce vaccines for the United States with the same three viral strains, limiting differentiation among products.[4] Because of the long cycle times associated with vaccine production, the strain selection process must take place between January and March, about nine months before physicians need to have the vaccines on hand (usually October or November). The trivalent influenza vaccine typically contains two influenza type A strains (which are known to infect not only humans and other mammals but also birds) and one influenza type B strain (which evolves relatively slowly compared to influenza type A).[5]

The cross-reactivity of the selected strains—that is, how well they match and immunize against those actually circulating during flu season in the United States—can vary. According to a 2007 CDC analysis, the viruses in the vaccine were well-matched to the predominant circulating viruses in sixteen of the previous nineteen U.S. influenza seasons. Between 1988 and 2006, only the 1997–98 season experienced very low cross-reactivity between the strains in the vaccine and the circulating viruses, although it was also deemed low in 1992–93 and 2003–4.[6] During the more recent 2007–8 flu season, however, the two influenza A strains that were predicted to be the most common types (Wisconsin and Victoria) turned out not to be. Instead, analysis of flu samples from those taken ill attributed 44 percent of cases to two quite different strains (Brisbane/10 and Yamagata), neither of which was included in the vaccine. As a result, the match between the predicted and actual types of infection was rather poor. Nonetheless, as late as mid-February 2008, CDC officials were still recommending that those not having received their annual flu vaccination do so, for even though the vaccine coverage was only partial, it could both prevent infections and lessen their severity, particularly in people at high risk for flu complications because of other illnesses.[7] A record 140 million doses were provided.[8]

This mismatch during the 2007–8 annual flu season potentially created problems for the subsequent 2008–9 season. In most years, only one of the three strains is changed for the coming year, and in some cases two new strains are selected. In anticipation of this carryover, manufacturers frequently begin production activities for at least one of the strains several months in advance of the WHO/FDA strain selection in February or March. Since both A strains were incorrectly predicted for the 2007–8 season, and because this error was not observable until January 2008, the FDA/WHO selection committee recommended at its February 2008 meeting that both A strains be changed for the 2008–9 season. Moreover, they also recommended a change in the single B strain included in the vaccine.[9]

For the first time, therefore, all three strains covered would differ from one year to the next, potentially creating delays for manufacturers in growing and combining them into the vaccine.[10] As discussed below, it typically takes about eight months for the entire influenza vaccine production process to be completed, meaning that for the finished product to begin shipping in late August, production of at least one part of the vaccine must begin in January. This production setback raised the possibility of delays in vaccine shipments in fall 2008, and perhaps even shortages if manufacturers encountered problems in growing any of the three vaccine components. However, in August 2008 the FDA approved all six vaccines for the 2008–9 flu season.[11]

Sanofi Pasteur is currently the U.S. leader in the influenza vaccine market, with the greatest capacity of all influenza vaccine manufacturers. The company's Fluzone product was originally approved by the FDA in the 1970s. Aventis Pasteur, which filed a supplement to its biologics license application in 2005 to gain FDA approval of a preservative-free, single-dose presentation of Fluzone, was subsequently acquired by Sanofi, creating the Sanofi-Aventis Group, in which the Sanofi Pasteur vaccine division was made responsible for Fluzone and other vaccine products. Fluzone is the only influenza vaccine indicated for use both in adults and in children six months of age and older.

GlaxoSmithKline manufactures Fluarix, which initially received FDA approval in 2005. That year, GSK expanded its influenza vaccine capacity with the acquisition of the Canadian-based ID Biomedical Corporation. This acquisition yielded the FDA-approved FluLaval influenza vaccine in 2006. Both FluLaval and Fluarix are indicated for adults eighteen years of age and older.

Novartis's leading product in the U.S. influenza vaccine market, Fluvirin (indicated for individuals ages four years and older), was initially launched by Evans Medical in the 1970s. Through a series of ownership changes, Chiron gained control of the product by 2001, at which time the company received FDA approval for a preservative-free formulation containing only trace amounts of thimerosal.[12] In 2006, Novartis acquired Chiron and subsequently established the world's fifth-largest vaccine business, becoming the second-largest player in the influenza vaccine market.

CSL Biotherapies, a subsidiary of Australian vaccine manufacturer CSL Limited, received FDA approval in September 2007 to market its trivalent, inactivated influenza vaccine in the United States to persons eighteen years of age and older. Manufactured in Melbourne, Australia, and Marburg, Germany, Afluria comes in a preservative-free, single-dose prefilled syringe, as well as in a multidose vial with thimerosal added as a preservative. The CSL influenza vaccine is currently licensed in more than twenty countries worldwide under various trade names; the thimerosal-free version was introduced in 2002.[13]

In 2003, FluMist was launched by MedImmune. Although its intranasal administration represented a significant advancement that was more convenient from a patient perspective than the traditional injectable vaccinations, the freezer-stable formulation of FluMist was inconvenient for physicians from a storage and logistics perspective. Moreover, physicians were not at first reimbursed for nasal administration by most payers, as payment for oral/nasal administration had been eliminated from the Current Procedural Terminology (CPT) physician coding system when the oral polio and oral rotavirus vaccines left the market. With uptake of the vaccine further limited by its restriction to individuals five to forty-nine years of age, the manufacturer was highly motivated to develop a second-generation product that could be stored in a standard refrigerator rather than a freezer, and perhaps be approved for use in younger children, as well. Prospects for the new version became especially promising when payment for administration of oral/nasal vaccine was reactivated, thereby giving physicians incentive to adopt FluMist (as well as Merck's oral RotaTeq vaccine).[14]

In January 2007, the FDA approved the new formulation of FluMist,[15] and in May, an FDA advisory panel unanimously agreed that the vaccine's trivalent benefits outweighed the risks for children between the ages of two and five years; it then voted nine to six in favor of approving the vaccine for children between ages one and five.[16] Later that month, however, the FDA issued MedImmune a warning letter concerning manufacturing problems with FluMist, stating that it would be unable to take action on the pediatric indication supplement for children under age five until the manufacturing issues were resolved.[17] This was a significant setback for the company, as gaining approval for the under-age-five population would have expanded the potential market for FluMist considerably; many children are wary of needles and likely to prefer an intranasal formulation. In addition, other yearly influenza vaccinations were already recommended for children under age five in the United States.[18] In September 2007, the FDA granted MedImmune Vaccines approval to expand the use of FluMist to children ages two to four years.[19]

The case of FluMist illustrates how the traditional demand and supply interaction in the influenza vaccine marketplace is complicated by the role physicians play in the selection of the product. This selection may be based on the direct benefit to the patient (avoiding an injection may be an incentive to adopt the intranasal delivery system, for example), or it may be limited by the physician's available resources (such as adequate storage space for a new product in the freezer, or ability to forgo payment for administration). FluMist is a key example of a seemingly superior product that initially experienced only limited success due to distribution and storage challenges in the supply chain, additional issues regarding appropriate reimbursement for administration, and lack of FDA approval for use by children between ages two and five.

Thimerosal Preservative Issues

In accordance with FDA regulations, manufacturing processes or multi-dose-vial presentations of vaccines may incorporate preservatives to prevent contamination by bacteria or fungi. Currently used preservatives include 2-phenoxyethanol, formaldehyde, Phenol, Phemerol, and thimerosal. Thimerosal, which contains approximately 50 percent ethyl mercury by weight, is used in some but not all of the FDA-approved influenza vaccines; these quantities are documented in table 5-1.

Although no convincing evidence has emerged to suggest that the amount of thimerosal needed to preserve vaccines effectively causes harm

TABLE 5-1

THIMEROSAL CONTENT IN CURRENTLY MANUFACTURED U.S. LICENSED
INFLUENZA VACCINES, UPDATED BY THE FDA MARCH 14, 2008

Vaccine	Trade name	Manufacturer	Thimerosal concentration[b]	Mercury
Influenza, killed	Fluzone[a]	Sanofi Pasteur Inc.	0.01 percent	25 µg/0.5 mL dose
	Fluvirin	Novartis Vaccines and Diagnostics Ltd	0.01 percent	25 µg/0.5 mL dose
	Fluzone (no thimerosal)	Sanofi Pasteur Inc.	0	0
	Fluvirin (preservative-free)	Novartis Vaccines and Diagnostics Ltd	< 0.0004 percent	< 1 µg/0.5 mL dose
	Fluarix	GlaxoSmithKline Biologicals	< 0.0004 percent	< 1 µg/0.5 mL dose
	FluLaval	ID Biomedical Corporation of Quebec	0.01 percent	25 µg/0.5 mL dose
Influenza, live	FluMist	AstraZeneca	0	0

SOURCE: Adapted from U.S. Food and Drug Administration 2008a, table 3, 11–13.
NOTES: a. Children under three years of age receive a half-dose of vaccine—that is, 0.25 mL (12.5 µg mercury/dose). b. Preservative-free vaccines contain only trace amounts of thimerosal. The thimerosal and mercury concentrations for the recently approved Afluria vaccines are zero for the thimerosal-free, single-dose prefilled syringe formulation and 0.01 percent and 24.5 mcg/0.5 mL per dose for the multidose vial formulation. CSL Biotherapies 2007.

to healthy individuals, numerous lawsuits have been filed against manufacturers.[20] To minimize potential liability, manufacturers are working to decrease further the use of thimerosal in their products. Thimerosal-free presentations of the influenza vaccine may become available in prefilled syringes, where the appropriate dose for a single patient is packaged individually by the manufacturer and simply awaits a needle for administration. Single-use vials and intranasal formulations are other thimerosal-free options. In addition to the resources that are needed for the development of such formulations, limited production capacity remains the major impediment to this process because individual presentations utilize more capacity than their multidose counterparts.

Guidelines on thimerosal exposure have been established by WHO, the FDA, the U.S. Environmental Protection Agency, and the Agency for Toxic Substances and Disease Registry in the U.S. Department of Health and Human Services.[21] Since significant reductions have been achieved with respect to the amount of thimerosal in other vaccines, the small amount contained in the multidose vials of the influenza vaccine will not cause a child to exceed the recommended total exposure safety levels when it is added to the standard schedule of pediatric vaccinations.

Clinical Development: Testing for Safety and Efficacy

Unlike clinical trials for therapeutic pharmaceuticals or other biologics, trials for prophylactic vaccines typically require large numbers of test subjects because the vaccine is administered to healthy individuals for whom the safety risks must be exceedingly low. In addition, as the schedule of recommended vaccinations continues to expand, new vaccines must not interact with those that were previously or are concomitantly administered.

Clinical trials for influenza vaccines typically utilize surrogate markers (such as antibody levels) to assess safety and efficacy.[22] Since a number of influenza vaccines are currently available, new vaccines are evaluated against the existing products in these respects. Recently, attention has focused on assessing a cell-based rather than egg-based production technique for the flu vaccine market segment; we distinguish these techniques in the following paragraphs. Interest in a novel manufacturing method has arisen in part because of recent shortages, and in part due to production delays associated with the complex manufacturing processes and the wide and unpredictable random variations in demand. The most recent severe shortage occurred in 2004 when Chiron's manufacturing facility in Liverpool, England, experienced contamination and was unable to produce approximately half the anticipated U.S. supply. Although the individuals we interviewed differed in their views of how quickly and effectively new manufacturing techniques would be adopted, most believed that once the supply was available to meet the demand on a regular basis, the most effective and reliably supplied vaccines would garner the greatest share of the market.

In this context, an influenza clinical trial reported by Novartis in October 2006 is of considerable interest. In this phase III trial, which took place in Poland during the 2004–5 influenza season, the Novartis cell-derived influenza vaccine demonstrated an "effective immune response and good tolerability" compared with a conventional, egg-based influenza vaccine. Test subjects included 1,300 adults of ages eighteen to sixty and 1,354 elderly individuals ages sixty and older. (In the course of all phases of clinical development, the vaccine was tested in over 3,400 people.) The European Union's Committee for Medicinal Products for Human Use (CHMP) developed the criteria for evaluation of the vaccine.[23] In June 2007, Novartis announced that the vaccine had been granted European approval. The company claims that this vaccine, with the trade name Optaflu, is based on a proprietary cell-culture technology that will enhance both the flexibility and reliability of the manufacturing process.[24] The results of the Optaflu trial raise a number of issues involving manufacturing, to which we now turn our attention.

Manufacturing Developments: Egg-Based versus Cell-Based Production

As we have already discussed, manufacturing vaccines is a complicated process with high fixed costs, strict and lengthy regulatory requirements, and complex scientific challenges.[25] These conditions present a substantial barrier to entry for potential market participants, And, as a result both of their limited number and the inflexible and relatively unpredictable manufacturing processes currently available, manufacturers have not been able reliably to supply sufficient flu vaccine to meet demand in the United States in a timely fashion. According to the CDC, delays, limited supplies, and tight timelines in manufacturing and distribution have further contributed to supply disruptions over the past seven years.[26] In part, this vulnerability reflects current manufacturing methods, which are rigid, fragile, and not easily scalable.

Egg-Based Vaccine Production. All influenza vaccine in the United States is currently manufactured through a complex process that utilizes chicken eggs as incubators for the annual viral strains. As described above, each year the CDC and WHO identify what they believe will be the three predominant strains for the forthcoming flu season and coordinate efforts with the FDA to provide samples of them, frequently from flu-stricken individuals in the Southern Hemisphere, to influenza vaccine manufacturers. The viral strains are then grown individually while incubated in chicken eggs. By the end of July, all of the virus-containing fluid from the eggs must be harvested to allow enough time to complete the manufacturing process before flu season commences in the Northern Hemisphere in November. Between June and October, the viral strains are purified, inactivated, fragmented, combined, and tested. Testing is critical to assess the yield of each strain and to confirm that the incubation process yields a consistent and robust viral product. Working within an egg-based system that is subject to considerable random and unpredictable production variations presents challenges to reliably obtaining viral concentrations at the level needed to elicit an adequate immune response.

Once the manufacturers and the FDA are satisfied with the product, individual lots are released and shipped to distributors. Ideally, the vaccine becomes available each August, with additional supply reaching physicians as it is produced through November. At the end of the flu season, all unused vaccine for that year must be discarded, as it will not be specific to the following year's virus strains and will therefore no longer elicit the appropriate immunity.

This coordination among the various global and governmental agencies (WHO, the CDC, and the FDA) and the vaccine manufacturers is key to the success of the complex production process each year. But the process has a number of obvious drawbacks. The egg-based system requires costly and time-consuming testing and regulatory review. The challenges of updating the components of the vaccine annually, and not knowing how each new strain will behave in the egg-based manufacturing system, make it difficult to forecast each year's supply. Additionally, the time period from identification of the three likely dominant strains to when the final product needs to reach physicians or clinics is only eight to ten months. This rapid production cycle leaves little room to correct any errors in the process while working to meet the demands of the market. Even with five large manufacturers of flu vaccine, threats of shortages are ever present.

Gaining access to a large supply of eggs that meet the guidelines for egg-based manufacturing is a challenge in itself. As with all live systems, the risk of contamination is also a factor to be considered, as are wide variations that occur in the yield of viral strain from each egg. To maximize yield, scientists work to modify the genetic characteristics that drive replication rates in the selected annual strains while maintaining the appropriate antigenic attributes that stimulate the immune response in humans. Due to its nature and the limited time that can be dedicated to perfecting this optimization process, it is often more successful for some strains and less successful for others. The entire supply of the annual vaccine may be limited by the strain with the lowest replication rate.

Another key limitation of the egg-based system is its lack of flexibility. A manufacturing plan must be determined early in the year, long before the actual market demand can be fully assessed. As the flu season unfolds and the severity of that year's infection becomes clearer, the lengthy initial incubation period limits the manufacturer's capability to respond and modify the supply.[27] Furthermore, if a significant surge in demand occurs, through a pandemic outbreak, for example, the system cannot be modified to react to the immediate needs, and severe shortages will likely result.

While new technologies are under development for use in influenza vaccine manufacturing, they require significant capital investment and continued resources for research. Expanding the capacity of the egg-based system to meet the current market demand is not, however, a priority for the manufacturers, since the demand is inherently highly random and unpredictable. Thus, until the next generation of cell-based technology becomes available, the limited manufacturing capacity of the egg-based system will remain a potentially binding constraint.[28]

Cell-Based Vaccine Production. The cell-based manufacturing process for influenza vaccine uses mammalian cells instead of chicken eggs to grow the viral strains. As illustrated in figure 5-1, the cells are grown in a flask and then scaled up to vats for additional multiplication and growth, after which they are washed and incubated in new media for the addition of the viral strains. The viral strains incorporate into the cells and harness the cellular machinery for replication. The large quantities of the virus that are harvested from the cells then undergo the standard process of chemical

FIGURE 5-1

THE CELL-BASED INFLUENZA VACCINE MANUFACTURING PROCESS

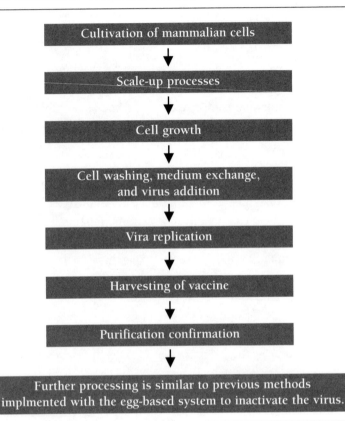

SOURCE: Adapted from Bardiya and Bae 2005.

inactivation and further processing to create a safe and efficacious seasonal influenza vaccine.

Shifting to a cell-based manufacturing process will most likely not offer significant benefits with respect to the per-unit cost of producing the influenza vaccine; indeed, it may increase those costs. This emerging production method offers various other advantages, however, over the traditional egg-based technique, although the extent of such benefits has not yet been fully elucidated and will only be clarified once experience is gained from full-scale production facilities running at capacity. Among the key advantages are the following:

• Flexibility and scalability

• Reliability of supply independent of the number of eggs available and unaffected by the variable characteristics of eggs

• No contraindication for people allergic to eggs

• Viral strains more similar to the actual natural strains because modifications to enhance their replication capabilities in eggs are no longer required, possibly enhancing the immunogenic response

• Potentially greater yield and robust viral proliferation

• Potential applicability during a pandemic outbreak

Despite these advantages, applying these cutting-edge biological techniques and replacing the suboptimal egg-based system will not be the answer to every challenge that influenza manufacturers face. For example, unless a universal vaccine can be developed, annual updates to manufacturing processes will still be required due to the seasonal nature of the disease and the evolution of the virus each year.

Additionally, the tight timeline of development, production, distribution, and administration cannot be eliminated, and intense scale-up in the middle of an unexpectedly severe season is unlikely to occur. Individuals we interviewed believed that, were there to be a pandemic, the projected supply even from egg-based and likely near-term cell-based production combined would be insufficient to meet demand, and that additional supplies from even newer technologies, such as recombinant DNA methods, would be needed.

In April 2007, Novartis secured a positive opinion for its cell-based vaccine, Optaflu, from the Committee for Medicinal Products for Human Use, which supports approval of such products in the European Union, and, in June, Optaflu earned European regulatory approval. Earlier, in July 2006, Novartis had announced plans to build the first manufacturing plant in the United States to utilize the cell-based process for production of the annual influenza vaccine. The Holly Springs, North Carolina–based facility will cost approximately $600 million to establish and will produce fifty million doses of the vaccine each year. The company originally anticipated a submission for regulatory approval of the first cell-based influenza vaccine in the United States in late 2008 or 2009.[29] In January 2009, Novartis announced it will receive an additional $487 million from the U.S. Department of Health and Human Services to develop two new vaccines, for either seasonal or pandemic use, and to fund clinical bridging studies designed to compare the firm's vaccines to existing products in terms of safety and efficacy, potentially expediting FDA approval. Novartis expects the North Carolina plant to be fully operational in 2012.[30]

As the frontrunner in the race to launch the first influenza vaccine in America manufactured using a cell-based process, Novartis currently holds a unique position in the market. Although the final product is not significantly different from those developed through the egg-based process (except for elimination of the contraindication for people allergic to eggs), Novartis will have the opportunity to set itself apart from its competitors with its ability to deliver a more reliable vaccine supply to the market. Moreover, as the company expands its capacity, its market share is likely to grow because Novartis will be able to provide additional supply—a benefit that the currently available egg-based systems cannot offer. Novartis believes that, once the traditional annual demand is met, it will be well positioned to distinguish itself further through novel product enhancements as it speeds down the learning curve of this technology.[31]

The Shift from Egg-Based to Cell-Based Vaccine Production. The transition from traditional egg-based to cell-based vaccine production can be envisaged as involving a number of stages. Figure 5-2 illustrates the advancement in innovation and its impact on the reliability of the vaccine supply over various time intervals. During time interval A of the figure, when the early egg-based manufacturing systems were being established, the reliability of the supply was fragile. Few manufacturers fully understood the process or were able to control the stochastic, random nature of egg production. In time interval B, the reliability of the supply increased significantly, as additional manufacturers entered with egg-based methods and as learning-curve effects and economies of scale became evident. During time interval C, reliability reached a plateau, as the egg-based system was optimized and no new players contributed significant learning to the process.

FIGURE 5-2
TECHNOLOGY SHIFT IN INFLUENZA VACCINE PRODUCTION

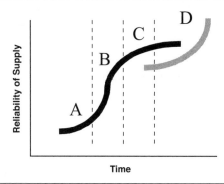

SOURCE: Authors' illustration.

Meanwhile, the gray line represents the development of the cell-based manufacturing systems. As the reliability of the supply from the egg-based method reached its highest point, the cell-based system was just becoming established. Looking to the future in time interval D, a scenario may emerge in which the learning-curve effects and economies of scale become evident, and the innovative cell-based method achieves a high level of reliability, surpassing that of the conventional egg-based tools.

One promising recent development in influenza vaccine technology involves VaxInnate's launch of the first clinical trial to test what some call a "universal" flu vaccine.[32] This product is designed to target the M2 ectodomain (M2e) portion of the flu virus, which is common to all virus strains, and thereby do away with the annual scramble to reformulate the vaccine to protect against the latest strain. Although the M2e portion of the flu virus is limited in its ability to produce an immune response, VaxInnate uses a receptor technology to recognize certain general molecular patterns associated with pathogens and trigger an initial innate immune response. This innate response is rapid because it is the result of the body's recognition of only general molecular patterns, but its lack of specificity may limit its capability to fight off certain infections. The VaxInnate technology addresses this by harnessing the immune system's more specific adaptive response, physically combining the vaccine antigen with bacterial flagellin, and thereby creating a more potent antibody response.[33]

A particularly attractive feature of the VaxInnate technology is the production of the vaccine in bacterial cell systems rather than egg-based ones, cutting manufacturing time and lowering costs, perhaps to levels affordable in poorer countries.[34] Also, because of its universal properties, the vaccine can be manufactured and then stored, inventoried in case of a pandemic.

VaxInnate announced results from its first phase I trial in August 2008, in which the M2e vaccine was given to sixty volunteers in a double-blinded, dose-escalating study of two doses injected twenty-eight days apart;[35] the vaccine candidate was found to be safe and capable of eliciting a potent response that triggered both arms of the body's immune defense at doses below a microgram of vaccine antigen and without the use of conventional adjuvants.[36] A second VaxInnate flu vaccine candidate entered phase I clinical development in late 2008, with preliminary results expected in early 2009.[37]

In the meantime, in February 2009 two independent research teams announced, within days of one another, the discovery of a human antibody dubbed "supermantibody," that latches on to the stems of mushroom-shaped proteins coating flu viruses that contain critical machinery the virus needs to enter and infect cells. To their surprise, the teams discovered the stem portion does not mutate, leaving it vulnerable to antibodies that specifically bind to it, suggesting that such antibodies could provide the basis of a universal vaccine. This research was conducted on mice; further research and testing on humans are in the planning stages.[38]

Influenza Vaccine Distribution Issues

The currently existing distribution networks for small-molecule therapeutics are relatively straightforward. In contrast, the process of transporting influenza vaccine from the manufacturer to the patient is highly complex. While biological therapeutics and most vaccines share a need for cold-chain distribution, for example, this requirement is further complicated in the case of the influenza vaccine by the seasonal nature of the demand. Whereas the systems for other vaccines and biologics run smoothly and evenly throughout the year, for the influenza vaccine they must be reestablished annually. The reliability of this supply—in terms of both availability and assurance that cold-chain stability has been maintained from production to administration—is critical. With the limited window of time during which the vaccine must be administered each year, proper inventory controls, replenishment orders, and return policies must all be in place.

During our interviews with vaccine manufacturing and delivery experts, we confirmed that companies not only closely monitor their distribution partners to ensure compliance with refrigeration requirements; they are also reassessing their partnership agreements. In addition, they are now revisiting the "build or contract" question of whether to integrate forward into the value chain and be directly responsible for the critical distribution component, instead of contracting it out to partners.

Also complicating the process of distributing the influenza vaccine are the locations of the physicians and nurses administering it. Unlike other vaccinations, immunizing against the flu requires the establishment of new clinics each time the disease season approaches, to help medical personnel reach out to the public at, for example, worksites, pharmacies, shopping malls, and senior citizens' centers. The creation of these ad hoc clinics, and the ordering, payment processing, documenting, and cold-chain monitoring that come with them, present another level of logistical complication.

Extensive Role of Government in Flu Vaccine Supply and Demand

The various relationships, dependencies, and financial incentives among governmental agencies and vaccine manufacturers highlight the magnitude of the impact the influenza virus and its prevention may have on public health. The role of government in vaccine supply and demand is unique to influenza in a number of ways. As we have seen, for example, identifying the strains of the virus that will correspond with the most prevalent strains of infection the following year in the United States requires constant monitoring and assessment on a global level by WHO and the CDC, producing the information based on which the vaccine manufacturers develop their seasonal product. Inaccurate information may result in large financial losses and a significant impact on human health for the duration of that season.

Also unusual is the position the FDA has taken on approving new vaccines for use in the United States when these products have already received licensing approval in other countries. Because of the nature of the influenza vaccine market, the agency is willing to consider applications that include surrogate marker data[39] in combination with postmarketing studies from abroad to assess clinical effectiveness. Thus, manufacturers and the public will benefit from more rapid ways of obtaining the safety and effectiveness data required for FDA approval.[40]

Third, in no other vaccine arena is the government interested in directly supporting innovation for seasonal prevention as well as overall pandemic preparedness. This interest is derived in part from the public health benefits and externalities that emerge with infrastructure development. For example, in June 2007 the U.S. Department of Health and Human Services announced an award of over $132 million to Sanofi-Aventis and MedImmune to retrofit their existing American manufacturing facilities for pandemic influenza vaccine production. Sanofi-Aventis and MedImmune are contributing $25 million and $14 million, respectively, of their own resources to this effort.[41]

The seasonal flu vaccine market represents a unique combination of concentration and competition. For most other types of vaccines, economic factors have driven the number of manufacturers to one or two major players per market (Merck, for example, is currently the only manufacturer for the varicella vaccine, and DTP combination vaccines are only provided by GSK and Sanofi Pasteur). The influenza vaccine segment, however, boasts six key players in the United States, including GSK along with its Canadian subsidiary, ID Biomedical Corporation of Quebec, Novartis (formerly Chiron), AstraZeneca (via the acquisition of MedImmune), Sanofi Pasteur, and CSL Biotherapies. All but AstraZeneca market a trivalent inactivated injectable formulation of the flu vaccine, with little differentiation among products since they all address the same three viral strains.

Even with many manufacturers contributing to the annual supply, the threat of a severe shortage or rationing of influenza vaccines still exists. Such a scenario would be possible if one manufacturer encountered difficulties in the inflexible and lengthy egg-based manufacturing process described above, for example. As the DHHS grants to Sanofi-Aventis, MedImmune, and Novartis demonstrate, the U.S. government is investing in infrastructure to help provide the system with surge capacity in the event of compromised supplies from key manufacturers or a larger-than-anticipated need prompted by a pandemic outbreak. Governmental incentives are aimed, first, at stabilizing and driving demand; second, at encouraging existing manufacturers to invest in maintaining good manufacturing processes certification instead of bowing out of vaccine production to invest in other segments of their business (for example, ceasing development of advanced vaccines manufacturing technologies to engage in pharmaceutical R&D instead); and third, at attracting new players with advanced technologies to the market.

Finally, governmental programs such as the Vaccines for Children program also help to stabilize and drive demand, which is critical for flu vaccine manufacturers given that with today's technology, each year's supply must be used in the year in which it is produced. Wide variations in demand make production planning and, eventually, the profits of this industry particularly uncertain. The ACIP recommendation may expand eventually to include universal vaccination, once production capacity and vaccine supplies are at a level to meet the needs of everyone for whom the influenza vaccine may be appropriate.[42] For the 2007–8 flu season, the CDC estimated that a record 132 million total doses of vaccine were produced for U.S. use, considerably more than the 102.5 million produced for the 2006–7 season; for the 2008-09 season, the CDC estimates as many as 146 million doses will be available, with as many as 50 million doses being thimerosal-free or preservative-free. Given then current ACIP and CDC recommendations, in 2007–8 about 75 percent of Americans were recommended to be vaccinated with the influenza vaccine.[43]

Pricing, Marketing, and Nonprice Competition

As noted above, vaccine production has increased over the last several years. According to a CDC September 2006 press release, manufacturers expected to release over 100 million doses of the influenza vaccine during the 2006–7 flu season.[44] In part this market size reflected the fact that, for the first time, the ACIP endorsed, and the Vaccines for Children program funded, pediatric use for children ages six months to fifty-nine months.[45] Moreover, even though a new Medicare Part D prescription-drug benefit was implemented in January 2006 involving a variety of beneficiary copayment provisions, individuals covered by Medicare Part B remained eligible to receive the flu vaccination at no cost, with no deductible or copay charged to the patient.[46] Most private insurance providers also covered the

TABLE 5-2

INFLUENZA VACCINE MANUFACTURERS FOR
THE 2008–9 INFLUENZA SEASON

Manufacturer	Vaccine	Formulation	Thimerosal preservative	Age indication
Sanofi Pasteur Inc.	Fluzone, Inactivated TIV	Multidose vial	Yes	6 months and older
		Single-dose, prefilled 0.25 mL syringe	None	6–35 months
		Single-dose, prefilled 0.5 mL syringe or vial	None	36 months and older
Novartis Vaccine (formerly Chiron Corporation)	Fluvirin Inactivated TIV	Multidose vial	Yes	4 years and older
		Single-dose, prefilled 0.5mL syringe	Preservative-free (1 mcg or less mercury/0.5mL dose)	4 years and older
MedImmune Vaccines Inc.	FluMist LAIV	Single-dose sprayer	None	Healthy persons 2–49 years
CSL Biotherapies	Afluria Inactivated TIV	Single-dose prefilled 0.5mL syringe	None	18 years and older
		Multidose vial	Yes	18 years and older
GlaxoSmithKline Biologicals (subsidiary of GlaxoSmithKline PLC)	Fluarix Inactivated TIV	Single-dose prefilled 0.5 mL syringe	Preservative-free (1 mcg or less mercury/0.5mL dose)	18 years and older
ID Biomedical Corporation (subsidiary of GlaxoSmithKline PLC)	FluLaval Inactivated TIV	Multidose vial	Yes	18 years and older

SOURCE: Centers for Disease Control and Prevention 2008a.

cost of the vaccination. For the 2008–9 season, uptake among children less than five years of age is expected to increase, since one product (FluMist) has been newly licensed for healthy persons two to forty-nine years of age, expanding the market which previously had been restricted to ages five to forty-nine.[47] For uninsured individuals and those who do not receive Medicare benefits, the cost of the seasonal influenza vaccine could range from a low of $10 to a high of approximately $20 per dose. Table 5-2 documents the vaccines available in the United States during the 2008–9 influenza season, along with various characteristics of each product; appendix D provides 2008 prices, with CDC prices ranging from $9.25 (Fluvirin) to $18.50 (FluMist) per dose.

The marketing initiatives associated with the influenza vaccine represent joint efforts by the public and private sectors. For example, the CDC has developed extensive websites, campaigns, and initiatives to assist with community outreach efforts educating people about the benefits of seasonal vaccination. Additionally, manufacturers have initiated programs to help ease the burden on the physicians who administer the vaccines. In 2005, for example, manufacturers implemented a policy enabling providers to return unused vaccines for a credit, thereby paying only for the cost of shipping the returned products.[48]

More generally, market competition has led manufacturers to differentiate themselves through ancillary benefits provided to physicians in addition to the vaccine itself. Such benefits include, in addition to return policies, educational and software services and materials and grace periods on payments due for the vaccine products.

Post-Launch Surveillance

Each flu season the CDC's Influenza Division collects, compiles, and analyzes information on influenza and vaccination activities in the United States, weekly from October through May. The CDC also studies samples of influenza viruses circulating during that season to evaluate how close a match has been achieved between the three virus strains in the vaccine and the circulating viruses, and it regularly conducts effectiveness studies, attempting to quantify any differences in hospitalizations, mortality, and other medical events between those individuals who are vaccinated and those who are not.[49]

Because of the inherent interseasonal variability in circulating flu strains and in the closeness of match between the three strains included in the vaccine with those circulating, the effectiveness of flu vaccinations is likely to vary somewhat by year. To evaluate their effectiveness over a longer time period, the CDC authored research in 2007 examining differences in medical claims between vaccinated and nonvaccinated individuals in cohorts of community-dwelling (that is, noninstitutionalized) elderly members of three health maintenance organizations, over various time periods within the ten annual flu seasons between 1990–91 and 1999–2000. Recall from a discussion earlier in this chapter that during this time period, the vaccine–virus antigenic match was good to excellent in all seasons except 1992–93 and 1997–98, when the match was poor.[50] Using statistical (specifically, multivariate regression) techniques that attempted to control for differences among individuals in addition to whether or not they were vaccinated, the study authors analyzed 713,782 person-year observations.[51] Vaccinated subjects were slightly older than nonvaccinated subjects and had higher prevalence rates of all baseline medical conditions except dementia or stroke.

In terms of effectiveness, the analysis showed that, on average and other things being equal, influenza vaccination was associated with a 27 percent reduction in the probability of being hospitalized for pneumonia and for influenza, and a 48 percent reduction in the probability of death. Estimated effectiveness varied across seasons. In the two seasons prior to 2000 in which there was a poor match between the vaccine and the circulating virus strains, vaccination was associated with only a 37 percent reduction in the probability of death, whereas in seasons with a good match, the reduction in mortality was 52 percent; differences in hospitalization for pneumonia and for influenza between good- and poor-match flu seasons were generally not statistically significant. Additional analysis revealed that the reduction in hospitalizations associated with flu vaccination was particularly large for high-risk individuals who had one or more major coexisting conditions at baseline. According to the authors, vaccination rates of elderly persons at the time of the study remained stagnant and well below the 2010 goal of 90 percent. Clearly, these results convincingly highlight the importance of widespread vaccination, and of accurately predicting which virus strains are likely to predominate during an impending flu season.

Pandemic Issues

Although experts are uncertain when the next pandemic flu will arise, the importance of preparedness is relatively undisputed. Government economists estimate that the impact of a mild to severe flu pandemic would range from 1 to about 4 percent of gross domestic product and result in substantial mortality.[52] In the event of such an outbreak, a strong and flexible infrastructure by which seasonal influenza vaccines can be manufactured and distributed will be necessary to avoid major adverse consequences. From a manufacturer's perspective, capabilities and lessons learned in the development of seasonal influenza vaccine may spill over into those required for the successful development of other pandemic flu vaccines, and vice versa.

In April 2007, for example, Sanofi Pasteur, a critical supplier of the seasonal influenza vaccine in the United States, received FDA approval for the first vaccine for humans protecting against the H5N1 influenza virus (bird flu),[53] as the result of the combined efforts of the company and various U.S. governmental agencies, including the FDA and the National Institutes of Health, and the European Union's European Medicines Agency (EMEA). Sanofi Pasteur's investment in this vaccine has readied the public should the H5N1 virus develop the ability to spread from human to human without an avian host.

Beyond such recent successes, additional research efforts are still necessary to combat the unpredictability of pandemic threats. Uncertainty surrounding the size of the surge in demand in the event of a pandemic, the timing of this surge, the price that the vaccine market will bear, how recipients will be prioritized as shortages emerge, and the role of the government in battling the outbreak will create high-risk opportunities for the manufacturers who decide to become involved in the pandemic arena. Governmental programs have partially mediated the market risk, however, by providing companies with monetary support for the pandemic programs[54] and by sponsoring and making basic scientific and other intellectual contributions to further these efforts. The role of the government and its ability to offer incentives to manufacturers capable of participating in pandemic preparedness are critical to managing and mitigating the public health risks of such an outbreak.

Future Issues and Challenges

Economic drivers of ongoing research efforts affecting the future of the influenza vaccine market include the need to meet demand reliably each year and the desire to address concerns regarding the weakened immune response often seen in the elderly population. In late 2008, for example, GlaxoSmithKline announced it was initiating recruitment for a 43,000-volunteer trial, all adults ages sixty-five and older, in fifteen countries. The phase III trial will compare a single annual dose of a new vaccine utilizing an adjuvant similar to one produced for an EMEA-approved pandemic vaccine to a currently available vaccine.[55] Other vaccine makers are focusing R&D on manufacturing issues. In addition to the promising cell-based manufacturing technology that may yield vaccines for distribution in the U.S. market as early as the 2009–10 influenza season, manufacturers are researching new ways to enhance the immune system's response to such vaccinations, such as VaxInnate's "universal" influenza vaccine and the "supermantibody," discussed earlier.

To date, a limiting factor in influenza vaccine production has been the availability of the inactivated viral strains. By using less inactivated virus per vaccine, more doses may be produced. Adjuvant technology, which is currently implemented in the diphtheria, tetanus, and pertussis combination vaccines, may help alleviate some of the supply constraints and also elicit a greater immune response in adult and elderly populations. Although not present in the currently marketed seasonal influenza vaccines, adjuvant technologies have been implemented in vaccines targeted at an influenza pandemic, should one arise.[56] For example, Novartis's Focetria vaccine, which received European Union approval in May 2007 and will be utilized when a pandemic is imminent, contains the proprietary adjuvant MF59. The MF59 adjuvant is able to extend the vaccine supply by bolstering the effect of a lower concentration of viral antigens.[57]

More recently, in May 2008, GSK received final EMEA approval for a vaccine branded Prepandrix, intended for use in advance of a bird flu pandemic. Prepandrix is designed to raise immunity against several strains of the lethal H5n1 virus, using an adjuvant technology that allows a low level of active ingredient to be used in each administered dose. The concept of a pre-pandemic influenza vaccine is based on using the currently circulating H5n1virus to make a vaccine with the ability to raise immune protection against potential drift strains—that is, alterations in the strains resulting from small, gradual changes in the genetic material that occur through random and unpredictable mutations. Prepandrix can be stockpiled in advance of a pandemic. If a pandemic were to occur, manufacturers would then attempt to isolate the strain causing the outbreak and make a more precise and targeted vaccine.[58]

In this chapter we have documented the extraordinary collaborative efforts among various stakeholders in the development, manufacturing, and coordination among public health authorities, payers, and physicians, as well as the distribution and post-launch surveillance, that result in annually modified seasonal influenza vaccines delivered to the United States market each fall. To meet the threat from global pandemics involving other viral strains, such as that for avian flu, will likely require even greater coordination among nations, regulators, public health officials, and manufacturers. Fortunately, much has been learned from experiences with annual influenza vaccines—knowledge that can help build the foundations of effective antipandemic programs and policies.

6

Prevnar—The Seven-Valent Pneumococcal Conjugate Vaccine

Prevnar is Wyeth's seven-valent conjugate vaccine approved for the active immunization of infants and toddlers against pneumococcal diseases such as pneumonia, bacterial meningitis, and bacteremia (bloodstream infections). Prevnar was launched in the United States in 2000 and in the European Union in 2001. It is the only pneumococcal conjugate vaccine approved for use in the United States.[1]

Disease Background

Streptococcus pneumoniae, or pneumococcus, causes invasive infections, such as bacteremia and meningitis, as well as pneumonia and upper respiratory tract infections, including otitis media (earache) and sinusitis. Pneumonia and otitis media are particularly common; the latter is the leading diagnosis for the administration of antibiotics to children in developed countries. Pneumococcal infection therefore has a significant impact on the quality of life of both children and adults (especially the elderly).[2] Before 2000, pneumococcal infections annually caused 100,000–135,000 hospitalizations for pneumonia, 6,000,000 cases of otitis media, and 60,000 cases of invasive disease, including 3,300 cases of meningitis.[3] There are approximately ninety different pneumococcal serotypes (that is, groups of microorganisms), although the majority of disease is caused by fewer than thirty.[4]

Before the introduction of Prevnar, pneumococcal polysaccharide vaccines had been available for some time.[5] Existing polysaccharide vaccine technologies use the outer coat of the bacterium to trigger an immune response from the body. Pneumovax 23, developed by Merck, contains the polysaccharides of twenty-three different serotypes and has greater than 90 percent serotype coverage.[6] It has a prevention rate of 56–81 percent for pneumococcal infections and contains sixteen more serotypes of *S. pneumoniae* than Prevnar.[7] Because polysaccharide vaccines such as Pneumovax 23 are not effective in very young children, however, they have not been introduced into the ACIP's universal childhood immunization schedules. Pneumovax 23 is indicated in children two years of age or older having chronic illnesses specifically associated with increased risk of pneumococcal disease or its complications.[8] Prevnar, on the other hand, can be administered to infants as young as six weeks.[9]

Preclinical Research and Development

Two teams of researchers, one at the National Institute of Allergy and Infectious Diseases (NIAID) of the National Institutes of Health and the other at the University of Rochester, were among the first to develop and test the concept of a "conjugate" vaccine—one that is made more effective by linking it to a protein that spurs an infant's immune system to fight an infection especially vigorously. The researchers demonstrated that the coupling of a protein to an existing polysaccharide vaccine evoked an immune response in infants that could not be elicited with the polysaccharide vaccine alone.[10]

In the 1970s, the teams first used the technology to target a bacterium known as *Haemophilus influenzae* type b (Hib), the leading cause of bacterial meningitis. After initial tests in the early 1980s were successful, the Rochester team attempted to persuade a pharmaceutical manufacturer to license the technology, but the offer was declined. Instead, the researchers went into business together and created a company, Praxis (now part of Wyeth Pharmaceuticals), to make the Hib vaccine.[11] It was approved by the FDA in 1990—the first vaccine in twenty years to be recommended by the FDA for universal use in children.

S. pneumoniae is the second microbe to be targeted by a "conjugate" vaccine based on the Rochester technology. A third set of conjugate vaccines that targets the microbe meningococcus, based on the same technology, is available in some parts of the world, including the United Kingdom, but not in the United States;[12] for Americans between eleven and fifty-five years of age, the quadrivalent meningococcal conjugate Menactra is indicated.[13] The development of Prevnar began in the 1980s. Prevnar, which includes a mutant form of diphtheria toxin that spurs the immune system to fight the *S. pneumoniae* microbe effectively, targets the seven most common serotypes of *S. pneumoniae*, responsible for approximately 80 percent of invasive pneumococcal disease in American children less than six years of age.[14] The complex development process required creation of a separate preparation of each of the seven included serotypes, which were then separately added to the vial to make the seven-part vaccine.[15]

Clinical Development: Testing for Safety and Efficacy

Following preclinical development of Prevnar, clinical trials were required to demonstrate its safety and efficacy. To conduct a large enough phase III clinical trial both to track confirmation of the disease and demonstrate efficacy, Wyeth went to Kaiser Permanente in Northern California (KPNC). KPNC is a nonprofit, group-model HMO which provides comprehensive health care to over eight million members, primarily on the West Coast and in Colorado, and has an extensive electronic health records network.[16]

KPNC presented a number of strategic advantages for conducting clinical trials. First, the HMO had a heterogeneous, ethnically diverse patient population well representative of the U.S. Census population at large.[17] KPNC had direct access to this population, as well as comprehensive database systems that allowed Wyeth to follow the clinical-trial population and recover *every* case of invasive disease.[18] Investigators could rely completely on the KPNC database because invasive diseases are reportable diseases— that is, diseases considered to be of such importance to public health that physicians and laboratories are required to report every diagnosis of them. This requirement permits surveillance, which in turn allows tracking for study purposes. Also, while patient recruitment for a clinical trial typically can be a limiting factor, it was relatively easy to recruit patients for Prevnar trials because the vaccine targeted an unmet medical need.

The Prevnar phase III clinical trial was designed as a randomized, double-blinded trial that took place over three years. Approximately 38,000 infants were assigned randomly to receive four doses of either Prevnar or an investigational meningococcal C conjugate vaccine control (Meningitec) at two, four, six, and twelve to fifteen months of age. Also administered were routinely recommended vaccines, which changed during the trial to reflect changing recommendations from the American Academy of Pediatrics and the Advisory Committee on Immunization Practices. Trial designers estimated that a cumulation of seventeen cases of invasive disease was needed to meet FDA statistical standards for determining whether the vaccine was effective; a split of fifteen to two or better in favor of Prevnar was required to establish a statistically significant difference between the two study groups. Once the seventeenth case of infection was diagnosed, the blind on the study was broken, and researchers determined that all seventeen cases occurred in the meningococcal control group.[19]

According to an industry representative we interviewed, the cost of the clinical trial was roughly $1,000 per patient, implying that this pivotal trial cost its developer around $38 million. Among the factors driving the cost upward were the large number of patients enrolled and the duration of the trial, which continued into phase IV. Mitigating cost somewhat was, among other things, the lack of invasive testing of subjects (for example, blood samples did not need to be taken).

Manufacturing Issues

The manufacture of vaccines is typically much more complex than that of small-molecule drugs, such as capsules or tablets. This difference is due in part to the use in vaccines of living organisms or their products, as opposed to a more predictable chemical process, and also to the subsequent complexity of the quality control and compliance processes. According to industry representatives we interviewed, it takes approximately five years to build and validate a vaccine manufacturing facility. As a result, it is necessary to commit to building facilities at the same time that pivotal clinical trials are beginning and while their outcome is still uncertain.

Prior to initiating phase III trials, Wyeth built a pilot-scale manufacturing facility for Prevnar. Ensuring its compliance with current good manufacturing practice regulations required developing manufacturing processes that would mimic the full-scale processes. After Wyeth built its full-scale facility, it then needed to demonstrate a link between the vaccine manufactured in the pilot-scale facility (used in the efficacy trial) and that manufactured in the commercial facility. A trial was run in which lots from the commercial facility were compared to lots from the pilot-scale facility. It was especially challenging to prove reliably that the lots were similar, given the seven different serotypes in the vaccine, which generated multiple dimensions of comparison.[20]

Currently, Prevnar is manufactured in two facilities that were licensed in 2000 after inspections by reviewers from the FDA's Center for Biologics Evaluation and Research (CBER). Since then, to improve compliance and increase production capacity, Wyeth has made significant changes in these facilities and in its manufacturing and quality control processes. Over $300 million in capital was invested in Prevnar facilities between 2000 and 2007, and operating expenses nearly doubled between 2004 and 2007. Over two thousand people are presently involved in the manufacture of Prevnar, and an additional five hundred are employed to ensure Wyeth is compliant with all regulatory requirements.[21] Manufacturing Prevnar requires a complex, fifteen-step process that typically takes twelve months from the start of the manufacture of one (out of seven) polysaccharides to final filling of the vials and release.[22]

Several shortages have occurred in the manufacturing of Prevnar since its licensure, beginning in August 2001. An industry representative attributed Wyeth's shortages to a variety of factors. In 1995, when the company built its first full-scale manufacturing facility, it anticipated competition for the FDA's approval of pneumococcal conjugate vaccine from other manufacturers, most likely Merck and GSK. Its prospective competitors encountered a series of problems in their clinical development programs, however, and Wyeth became the sole supplier of the conjugate vaccine (although nonconjugate Pneumovax 23 was available) in 2000. The result was significant unanticipated demand, upon the vaccine's gaining FDA approval. The complexity of manufacturing the vaccine was also much greater than anticipated, as was the flatness of the initial learning curve. To address the manufacturing issues, Wyeth added redundancies to each step of the process, including new conjugation lines, multiple fill/finish facilities, and the development of a new polysaccharide manufacturing site, thus freeing the company from reliance on any one particular step in the manufacturing process or one particular manufacturing facility.[23]

Securing a Listing on the ACIP Recommended Schedule

In addition to obtaining FDA approval, to be commercially successful a vaccine must be recommended by policymakers for its specific use before being marketed in the United States. Recommendations by the ACIP and the American Academy of Family Physicians to add the vaccine to the childhood immunization schedule are critical to boosting sales. Sales also depend on the size of the subpopulation for which the vaccine is recommended. To develop recommendations for Prevnar, the ACIP formed a working group consisting of scientists from the CDC, voting members from the ACIP, liaisons from the AAFP, other physicians, and representatives from Wyeth (at that time, Lederle Laboratories).

The working group needed to decide for which ages and populations Prevnar should be recommended. Since the data clearly showed a high incidence of invasive disease during the first two years of life, with decreasing rates thereafter, unanimity was reached on the importance of vaccinating children less than two years old. The cut-off points for "catch-up" vaccination after two years of age, however, were less clear, because the data showed that, as incidence rates for invasive disease dropped, the morbidity rate also dropped, and serotype distribution changed, which lowered protection against all serotypes. Further complicating the question were other data documenting that blacks, Alaskan natives, and American Indians ages two to five years had higher incidence rates of pneumococcal disease than whites ages two to five, and concerns that these populations would not be able to afford catch-up vaccinations. Therefore, the major ACIP issue became the question, for which populations should the catch-up vaccinations be recommended?

In the end, the ACIP recommended routine vaccination of children up to two years of age and catch-up vaccination for children in high-risk groups, such as those between the ages of two and five years with sickle-cell disease or human immunodeficiency virus (HIV). No ethnic groups were explicitly included at the recommendation level. However, instead of a universal recommendation, the ACIP advised that use of Prevnar be considered for children in specific ethnic groups, including Alaskan natives, American Indians, and blacks. The vaccine was made available to eligible persons in these groups through the Vaccines for Children program. The AAFP maintained its earlier position of catch-up vaccination through five years of age for children at high risk, including certain ethnic groups.[24]

As this controversy illustrates, government regulatory agencies and professional provider bodies face many struggles and challenges in their policy recommendation decision-making processes, as they attempt to take into consideration and balance multiple scientific, financial, socioeconomic, public health, and societal perspectives.

Pricing and Marketing

At the time of Prevnar's launch in 2000, Wyeth made a potentially industry-changing decision by pricing the vaccine at a seemingly high private-sector price of $58 per dose, or $232 for the four-dose regimen. Before Prevnar, vaccines were typically expected to be priced at the break-even cost to society—that is, the price at which vaccination costs would be offset by direct medical costs elsewhere in the health-care system, but not taking into account indirect costs such as increased parental absenteeism and reduced workplace productivity. For Prevnar, however, as one industry representative put it in an anonymous interview, "Cost effectiveness studies weren't conducted, cost benefit studies were conducted." Research sponsored by the CDC found that the vaccine would be cost-effective if the drug were less than $46 per dose,[25] based upon the established direct cost to society. Wyeth industry representatives pointed out, however, that Prevnar also had indirect benefits to society, such as saving parents work time they would otherwise lose caring for children with illnesses that would have been prevented by the vaccine.

An industry representative we interviewed explained the factors at Wyeth that drove this aggressive pricing strategy. Just three years before Prevnar gained FDA approval, Wyeth had licensed RotaShield, a rotavirus vaccine, which it withdrew from the market fifteen months later due to safety concerns. The episode had demonstrated to the company the considerable risks involved in spending ten to twelve years developing a vaccine and building manufacturing capacity, only to end up with an unmarketable product. Also, due to greater costs of being in business and increasing costs of R&D, the vaccine development group at Wyeth believed it needed to prove to corporate headquarters that vaccines could be profitable. "We were competing with colleagues on the drug development side for resources. We reached the decision that we needed to make Prevnar profitable in a competitive way," said an interviewee at Wyeth.

Profitability for Prevnar has, in fact, turned out to be the case. Despite encountering supply shortages and resistance from payers to its high price, Prevnar has become the first vaccine to reach blockbuster status (that is, having more than $1 billion in annual global sales), with 2007 sales reaching nearly $2 billion.[26]

Numerous individuals we interviewed in the vaccine industry stated that Prevnar transformed the vaccine business almost overnight. Dr. Stanley Plotkin, professor emeritus at the University of Pennsylvania and consultant to Aventis Pasteur Ltd., one of the four large vaccine makers, told a journalist, "Wyeth's success has shown other companies that there is a potential for vaccine blockbusters."[27] Recent projections, as well as data presented in table I-1 in the introduction to this book, indicate the vaccine market is growing at double digits annually, outpacing other infectious-disease biologics and small-molecule pharmaceutical sectors.[28]

Post-Launch Surveillance

In addition to tracking patients prior to licensure, monitoring them after licensure is especially important to developers and payers to ensure vaccines provide continued immunity. The Active Bacterial Core surveillance (ABCs), a component of the CDC Emerging Infections Program, has conducted a number of surveillance studies to compare the burden of invasive pneumococcal disease before and after the introduction of Prevnar. In one study, using data from seven geographic areas (total population, 16 million) with continuous participation from 1998 to 2001, the researchers concluded, "The use of the pneumococcal conjugate vaccine is preventing disease in young children, for whom the vaccine is indicated, and may be reducing the rate of disease in adults. The vaccine provides an effective new tool for reducing disease caused by drug-resistant strains."[29] The suggestive finding that consumption externalities from pediatric vaccinations of Prevnar were spilling over into the adult population was exciting and, to some extent, unexpected.[30]

To evaluate the possible adult spillover phenomenon in greater detail, another CDC study examined invasive pneumococcal disease continuously from 1998 to 2003 in defined populations in eight states (total population, 18 million). Using ABCs data from the two years before Prevnar licensure (1998–99) and the four subsequent years, the study evaluated the incidence of all invasive disease, of disease caused by specific pneumococcal serotypes, and of common disease syndromes. The CDC's objective was to determine whether incidence of invasive pneumococcal disease, disease characteristics, or the spectrum of patients acquiring these illnesses had changed among adults ages fifty years or older in the time since licensure.

Consistent with Prevnar's ability to interrupt transmission, a decline in invasive pneumococcal disease incidence among older adults was observed as early as 2001, the year after Prevnar's introduction to infants, and even more so by 2003. These CDC findings indicated that for every direct case prevented by vaccination of children with Prevnar, two cases were indirectly prevented.[31] The trend led the study authors to conclude that "use of conjugate vaccine in children has substantially benefited older adults."[32]

The Evolving Competitive Landscape

The critical patent for Prevnar expired on January 7, 2007.[33] Unlike small-molecule pharmaceuticals, vaccines hardly ever face competition from generics, but instead are challenged by follow-on and next-generation vaccines.[34] The success of effective pneumococcal vaccination has created incentives for competing therapies in clinical development. One potential competitor for Prevnar is GlaxoSmithKline's Synflorix, a ten-valent conjugate pneumococcal vaccine. Synflorix may be more efficacious than Prevnar because it contains antigens to three more serotypes. Since GSK is targeting only the pediatric population for Synflorix, however, while Wyeth is seeking to have approval of Prevnar extended to adults over age fifty (see below),

Synflorix is unlikely to present a serious challenge to Prevnar's position based on better efficacy unless GSK extends its target population to adults as well. Nonetheless, to fend off the threat of competition, Wyeth is developing a thirteen-valent version of Prevnar, which was recently granted FDA Fast Track designation.[35] The company expects to complete its United States filing for pediatric use of the vaccine in the first quarter of 2009.[36]

Even if the thirteen-valent version is successful, Synflorix may still pose a serious challenge to Prevnar for the specific indication of acute otitis media (AOM, or earache). At a presentation to investors and analysts in 2005, a GSK official cited promising preliminary data from a clinical trial involving about 4,900 children in the Czech Republic that showed this vaccine effective in preventing AOM; currently, Prevnar has no AOM indication approval.[37] AOM remains a significant childhood disorder and is the most frequent reason for pediatric office visits in the United States, accounting for approximately 20 million visits annually. By three years of age, 83 percent of children will have had at least one episode of AOM. The most common pathogen for AOM is *S. pneumoniae*, although it is responsible for only about 40 percent of all cases. The seven types of pneumococci targeted by Prevnar account for about 70 percent of all pneumococcal AOM in young children and are somewhat more likely than other types to be resistant to antibiotics. Whether GSK is able to produce positive efficacy data for AOM and obtain FDA approval for that indication may be a critical factor in the eventual U.S. success of Synflorix. Notably, in late January 2008, the EMEA accepted for review a dossier submitted by the company, in which GSK sought approval not only for invasive pneumococcal disease, but AOM infections as well.[38]

Meanwhile, as noted above, Wyeth is seeking to expand the approved use of the Prevnar vaccine to protect adults over age fifty from pneumonia, making it the first pneumococcal conjugate vaccine for that age group. Wyeth notes that pneumonia represents a significant disease burden in adults, with over 500,000 cases caused by *S. pneumoniae* occurring annually in the United States, and believes that Prevnar could prevent 40–60 percent of these cases. The additional indication for adults could also increase sales of the vaccine by more than $1 billion a year.[39]

Currently, a twenty-three-valent polysaccharide vaccine (Merck's Pneumovax 23) is available for adults as a single dose at age sixty-five, although it has significant limitations. Protection from polysaccharide vaccines decreases over time for several reasons. First, they do not stimulate development of memory B-cells and therefore prevent the body from responding to reinfection. Second, immune response does not increase and may decrease with repeated doses. These vaccines also have limited coverage. Wyeth has proposed that a primary dose of Prevnar be given at age fifty, followed by an injection at age sixty-five of the twenty-three-valent polysaccharide and then a booster dose of Prevnar at age seventy, giving expanded coverage and protection against invasive pneumococcal disease. The company already reports promising preliminary data with Prevnar in those over the age of seventy, showing a very acceptable safety profile, no serious vaccine-related systemic reactions, and a superior antibody response compared to the polysaccharide vaccine. The clinical trials to establish Prevnar's long-term efficacy and safety, necessary to gaining FDA approval for use with adults, could be difficult to carry out, however. The proposed schedule of injections administered twenty years apart to older adults will present significant challenges in terms of maintaining contact with elderly subjects and minimizing attrition. An additional challenge for Wyeth will be demonstrating that the addition of Prevnar to adult vaccination schedules provides a genuine cost–benefit improvement.[40]

Emerging Challenges: Replacement Phenomena

According to a study published in the *New England Journal of Medicine*, serious diseases such as meningitis and bloodstream infections due to strains of *S. pneumoniae* not covered by Prevnar have risen by about 50 percent since the vaccine's introduction, though the amount of disease caused by these strains is still low. For reasons that are not entirely clear, a corresponding increase in less serious diseases, such as ear infections and pneumonia, has been more substantial. Recent studies have indicated that strains of *S. pneumoniae* not covered by Prevnar multiply in the noses and throats of children after they are given the vaccine. Although Prevnar reduces the amount of the seven strains it covers, the other strains completely fill the gap—so the total amount of *S. pneumoniae* found in children's noses and throats is not reduced by vaccination. This "replacement" phenomenon is something that occurs commonly throughout nature. When physicians give antibiotics to treat an infection, new bacteria that are resistant to the antibiotic quickly fill in the space left by the susceptible bacteria.[41]

Recent evidence demonstrates that ear infections due to other species of bacteria are also on the rise, now that those caused by *S. pneumoniae* have decreased. This shift may make it necessary in the future to treat ear infections with different antibiotics, since the bacteria filling in the gaps are not always susceptible to the drugs currently utilized. The rise in nonvaccine strains of *S. pneumoniae* has been especially concerning in high-risk patients—those with HIV or sickle-cell disease, for instance—whose immune systems are weaker. A pediatric infectious disease physician at Boston Medical Center explained to us that the strains not covered by Prevnar are weaker than the covered strains, and high-risk patients are more susceptible to these less virulent strains that healthy people usually can resist.

The rise in nonvaccine strains of pneumococcus is likely to continue and is being closely monitored by epidemiologists. Experts suggest the best way to curb it would be to develop new vaccines to cover more strains. A more inclusive vaccine would be particularly important for the developing world, where pneumococcal strains not included in Prevnar have always been a more important cause of disease than in the United States.[42]

Implications for the Developing World

Acute lower respiratory infections are responsible for close to two million deaths per year; a large proportion of these are caused by *S. pneumoniae*. Most victims are children in developing countries. A study in The Gambia (a small country in western Africa) has indicated that more than one-third of these deaths might be caused by *S. pneumoniae*.[43] The bacterium also causes other serious illnesses, such as meningitis and septicaemia. Although pneumonia deaths far outnumber those from meningitis, in nonepidemic situations *S. pneumoniae* is a major cause of meningitis fatalities in sub-Saharan Africa; of those who develop pneumococcal meningitis, 40–75 percent either die or are permanently disabled. Children infected with HIV/AIDS are twenty to forty times more likely than others to contract pneumococcal disease.

Currently, Prevnar does not include two serotypes (types 1 and 5) that cause a high percentage of pneumococcal illness in developing countries.[44] Wyeth has completed evaluation of a nine-valent conjugate vaccine, however, that does include them. One phase III trial involving 40,000 people was completed in South Africa in 2002, and another with 17,437 subjects was concluded in The Gambia in 2004. In the South African trial, the vaccine reduced invasive disease caused by the relevant serotypes by 83 percent in children not infected with HIV and by 65 percent in HIV-infected children. Results from the Gambia trial showed the vaccine was 77 percent effective in preventing infections caused by the relevant serotypes; that it resulted in 37 percent fewer cases of pneumonia (as confirmed by chest X-ray) compared with a control group; and that recipients experienced a 16 percent reduction in overall mortality. Despite these positive results, Wyeth abandoned its nine-valent experimental vaccine to focus its development efforts on a single, thirteen-valent conjugate pneumococcal vaccine for global distribution. Developing-country vaccine manufacturers, such as the Serum Institute in India, have initiated development of conjugate vaccines as well, and vaccines based on common protein antigens of pneumococcus are also in the pipeline.[45]

Determining reliably the extent of pneumococcal disease in developing countries is challenging, since many lack the laboratory facilities, expertise, and resources to do so. As a result, public health decision-makers there are often unaware of the prevalence of a disease and of the toll it exacts in death and disability. Furthermore, because data are scarce, the appropriate serotype valency targeted to these countries has not yet been conclusively established. Although trial results to date are encouraging, concerns remain that prevention of pneumococcal disease from some serotypes may be offset by an increase in incidence from others.[46]

Another issue is the price of the pneumococcal vaccine. Not yet set for developing countries, it may be too high for them to afford without special financing arrangements. A solution may be an innovative financial initiative, Advanced Market Commitment (AMC), which promises manufacturers that if they develop a vaccine meeting certain technical specifications, donors will commit to purchasing it on behalf of developing countries at a price much higher than these countries traditionally pay.[47] In February 2007, the Global Alliance for Vaccines and Immunization (GAVI) announced that five nations, together with the Bill and Melinda Gates Foundation, had committed $1.5 billion to launching the first AMC to help speed the development and availability of a new vaccine targeted to pneumococcal disease.[48] A press release from GlaxoSmithKline commended the donors and said the company looked forward to working with the World Bank and the donor governments on details of the plan. GSK has a ten-valent pneumococcal vaccine in late stages of development which appears to be effective against the pneumococcal diseases with greatest incidence in the developing world.[49]

Conclusion

The Prevnar case study highlights the significant and ongoing challenges encountered by manufacturers when developing a vaccine against multiple serotypes whose incidence differs considerably across the globe, and whose prevalence can be replaced in response to the vaccine's success. It also attests to the advantages of conducting clinical trials in large pediatric populations whose close monitoring is facilitated by extensive electronic medical records, such as those kept by Kaiser HMO—conditions not found in the developing world.

Finally, the Prevnar case is important because Wyeth pioneered in pricing Prevnar aggressively in the United States, arguing successfully that the benefits of a pediatric vaccine are not confined to the reduction in direct medical costs attributable to vaccination, but must also take into account the reduced workplace absenteeism and greater productivity of children's parents. Moreover, post-launch surveillance has uncovered consumption externalities from pediatric vaccination with Prevnar, in which older children and adults have subsequently experienced reductions in the occurrence of diseases such as pneumonia.

7

Varicella Zoster Vaccines

The varicella zoster virus (VZV) is one of eight herpes viruses known to affect humans. During the initial infection, the disease caused by the virus is called chickenpox, or varicella disease. The symptoms characteristic of varicella are itchy rashes, consisting of clusters of small raised or flat spots, fluid-filled blisters, and crusting. A reactivation of the infection that occurs later in life is commonly called shingles, herpes zoster, or simply zoster.

Varicella is an acute, highly contagious viral disease with worldwide incidence. While mostly a mild disorder in childhood, the disease tends to be more severe in adults. It may be fatal, especially in newborns and in immunocompromised persons (that is, those whose immune systems have been impaired by disease or treatment).[1] Prior to the introduction of the vaccine, about four million cases occurred per year in the United States, with typically a hundred or fewer deaths. Although those who became infected with the disease were mostly children, the majority of deaths (as many as 80 percent) were among adults. Additionally, chickenpox led to the hospitalization of about ten thousand people each year.[2] Complications included bacterial infection of lesions, pneumonia, Reye syndrome, and other central nervous system manifestations.

Following infection, viruses remaining dormant in the nerves can reactivate and cause zoster (shingles), a disease mainly affecting the elderly and immunocompromised persons. Individuals with shingles can pass the virus to individuals who have never had chickenpox. While individual cases may be prevented or modified by varicella zoster–immune globulin or treated with antiviral drugs, the disease can only be controlled by widespread vaccination.

In temperate climates of the Northern Hemisphere, varicella occurs mainly in the period from late winter to early spring. Secondary attack rates

118

TABLE 7-1

TIMELINE OF VARICELLA VACCINE DEVELOPMENT

Year	Event
1953	Varicella pathogen is isolated.
1974	Varicella vaccine is developed at Osaka University in Japan.
1995	Varivax varicella vaccine, developed by Merck, is licensed in the United States.
2000	Varivax II, second-generation (refrigerator-stable) version of Varivax, is launched.
2005	ProQuad, MMR-varicella vaccine, developed by Merck, is licensed in the United States.
2006	Zostavax, shingles vaccine developed by Merck, is licensed in the United States.

SOURCE: Authors' research.

reach close to 90 percent in household members who are not immune. The varicella zoster virus is transmitted by droplets, aerosol, or direct contact; patients are usually contagious from a few days before rash onset until the rash is covered by a crust or scab. Once a case has occurred in a susceptible population, it is very difficult to prevent an outbreak. High rates of vaccination are therefore needed to induce herd immunity.

The history of the development and marketing of the varicella zoster vaccines is summarized in table 7-1. In 1974, more than twenty years after the varicella pathogen was first isolated in 1953, a vaccine preventing varicella was developed at Osaka University in Japan. Initially working independently but later on collaborating, scientists from Osaka and Merck developed a superior vaccine that was introduced in the United States in 1995. Since then there have been significant improvements in the varicella vaccine, as well as in the prevention of varicella zoster in adults. As we shall see in this chapter, the history of varicella and varicella zoster vaccines highlights the critical roles played by collaborations between the public and private sectors, and the importance of cost-effectiveness studies and public information campaigns in facilitating widespread adoption of vaccines. The varicella history also reminds us of the vulnerability of supplies to manufacturing problems and the value of post-launch surveillance in monitoring the effectiveness of vaccinations, which in this case resulted in significantly altering the ACIP recommendations to include a second dose for all children.

Preclinical Research and Development

For centuries, varicella was considered a benign, inevitable disease of childhood. Complications were generally mild and rarely severe, and virtually every individual was infected by adulthood. In certain groups such as children with leukemia, however, infection was associated with a high risk of serious complications. Concerns about the severity of varicella in this immunocompromised population led to the initial development and testing of a live, attenuated vaccine,[3] with studies first conducted in the 1970s. Both Merck and researchers at Osaka University in Japan developed their own vaccines. In the late 1970s, Merck and Osaka University formed a collaboration, in which Merck eventually obtained United States license rights to the Oka strain of the varicella virus from Osaka's Biken Institute.

The varicella virus vaccine was first licensed for use among high-risk children in several European countries in 1984, in Japan in 1986, and in Korea in 1988. In Japan and Korea, licensure was extended to healthy children in 1989; after the administration of more than two million doses in these countries, no concerns about vaccine safety had been identified.[4] In the United States, Merck's Varivax was approved for prevention of chickenpox by the FDA in 1995.

Even as the development of its Varivax vaccine for immunization against the varicella virus was taking place, Merck also began developing ProQuad, a vaccine combining Varivax with MMR II for measles, mumps, and rubella. Merck's objectives were to reduce the number of injections, improve timely vaccination coverage, reduce the costs to health-care providers of stocking and administering separate vaccines, and decrease the health-care costs for extra visits to physicians' offices.[5]

Clinical Development: Testing for Safety and Efficacy

Since its development in 1974 at the Biken Institute, the original Oka-strain live, attenuated varicella vaccine, which was first tested in leukemic children, has been studied in a large number of clinical trials. The largest study was carried out by the Varicella Vaccine Collaborative Study Group. Over the course of a decade, this group immunized approximately six hundred children with leukemia in remission, most of whom were still receiving maintenance chemotherapy. Following the apparent success of the vaccine in these children, trials were begun in healthy children in the mid-1980s, and development shifted away from immunocompromised patients, who were at risk for side effects in the clinical studies. Scientists hoped that vaccination of healthy children would provide indirect benefits to immunocompromised children who could not risk being vaccinated themselves.[6]

During the 1980s and 1990s, clinical trials for the varicella vaccine were carried out by Merck in approximately 9,000 healthy children and 2,000 healthy adults.[7] The vaccine was shown to be highly immunogenic, with almost all children developing antibodies and cellular immunity after a single dose. About 85–90 percent of vaccinated children were completely protected from developing varicella. In the remaining 10–15 percent who caught the disease, the infection was usually extremely mild and without complications.[8]

As a result of these numerous and large clinical studies, Varivax was approved by the FDA in 1995 for the prevention of chickenpox. The ACIP recommended one dose of Varivax for children twelve months to twelve years of age and two doses for adolescents and adults thirteen years of age and older; as discussed below, this recommendation was later changed to two doses for children, as well.[9]

In 1984, as the clinical development of Varivax was ongoing, that of the combination vaccine ProQuad began. The pivotal trial was designed as a noninferiority trial, a protocol which is sometimes necessary when the availability of existing effective treatments makes it unethical to include a placebo—that is, nontreatment—group. The goal of a noninferiority trial is to establish that the test group receiving a combination vaccine fares no worse than the group receiving only the separate component vaccines. The clinical trials for ProQuad, which included over 5,800 subjects, evaluated the immunogenicity, antibody persistence, and safety of ProQuad compared to its component vaccines, Varivax and MMR II. Immune responses were the key endpoint measures in the trials, which were quantified by the percentage of subjects responding to the vaccines. Evaluation of potential interactions involving immune responses and safety among the component vaccines was also included in the trial design.

A major challenge in developing a combination vaccine is that it is often difficult to predict interactions among components. In early ProQuad clinical studies, suboptimal varicella responses were observed as the result of such interactions. A new dose-response study involving different component doses was conducted to establish the optimal potency range for varicella. Following successful noninferiority trials, ProQuad was approved for use by the FDA in September 2005.[10]

The third vaccine in Merck's varicella vaccine franchise, Zostavax, was approved by the FDA in 2006 for prevention of shingles in adults ages sixty and older.[11] The clinical study of Zostavax was one of the largest adult vaccine trials in medical history. The trial, involving roughly 39,000 adults ages sixty and older, was conducted by the Department of Veterans Affairs (VA), in collaboration with the National Institute of Allergy and Infectious Diseases of the National Institutes of Health and Merck, at twenty-two U.S. research sites over a period of five years.[12] The primary endpoint measure was the burden of illness due to herpes zoster, based upon the incidence of the disease in test subjects with and without vaccination, as well as the severity and duration of the associated pain and discomfort in those who contracted the illness. The secondary endpoint was the incidence of postherpetic neuralgia (a form of neuralgia with intractable pain that develops at the site of a previous eruption of herpes zoster).[13] The study was made possible in large part because of the closed network characteristic of the VA hospitals and clinics and their thorough medical records, which kept track of all visits within the network.

As an aside, we note here that this large, long, and complex trial demonstrated the benefits of a collaboration among academics, governments, and industry in clinical trial design and implementation—a mode of collaboration with a long history in vaccine development.[14] The Cooperative Studies Program (CSP) of the Veterans Administration, for instance, which conducts large clinical trials focused on veterans' health problems, has been cited by the National Institutes of Health for its role in improving clinical practice. As noted by the VA, CSP is unique among research networks because it is part of the Veterans Health Administration, the nation's largest health-care system. The program has access to a large pool of veteran patients who volunteer for studies. It is well-equipped to conduct trials "in-house," with pharmaceutical support and study subjects, research teams, and clinicians who can employ study findings in their practices, and effective electronic health records all on hand.[15]

Manufacturing Issues

The varicella vaccine presented Merck with challenges not only in development and clinical testing but in production as well, owing to the complexity of the required manufacturing process. As with other live, attenuated virus vaccines, regulatory oversight is much more stringent than that governing the manufacture of either therapeutic proteins or small-molecule pharmaceuticals. In part, this is because vaccines are much more difficult to characterize analytically than can be done by chemical synthesis formulae for many pharmaceuticals. Because analyzing such a large molecule is so challenging, historically there has been a tendency in development for the manufacturing process of producing the vaccine itself to define the product, rather than to characterize the final product analytically. Any changes in either scale or process must leave the product unchanged in terms of its efficacy and safety, with satisfactory proof of this demanded by the FDA for each manufactured lot. Any change in manufacturing process or scale is typically accompanied by very sophisticated and extensive analytical characterization and, in some cases, a requirement for additional clinical testing, simply to prove equivalence between the modified and old versions of the vaccine.

For licensure of ProQuad, consistency of the manufacturing process was supported by clinical trials, the objective of which was to show equivalence of clinical response among the manufactured vaccine lots. In each study, 4,000 subjects were enrolled, involving three lots of a four-component vaccine, MMRV, and, for comparison purposes, an active control consisting of the three-component MMR vaccine plus the singleton varicella vaccine, with the treatment group receiving two injections, designated as MMR + V. The first step showed consistency of the three MMRV lots by evaluating antibody response rates, whose differences from one another were found to be statistically insignificant. The second step established that the combined responses of MMRV were not inferior to those of MMR + V.

This level of strict regulatory oversight affects every step in the manufacturing cycle of a vaccine, from the testing of the cell line used to produce it to the testing of the final product. All processes are described and characterized in great detail, including the nature and performance of the specific equipment used for each step. These requirements create an essential rigidity in approach which is unforgiving of an error in judgment, so that any misstep along the way can result in a very time-consuming (sometimes years-long) and expensive correction in the manufacturing process.[16] A varicella shortage that occurred in late 2001, for example, was caused by voluntary manufacturing modifications made by Merck in response to an inspection carried out under current good manufacturing practice regulations.[17]

An added complication is the difficulty of growing high concentrations of varicella virus. Manufacturing sufficient quantities of Zostavax and Pro-Quad (both of which require higher concentrations than needed for Varivax) has proved very difficult for Merck. In 2007, the company warned of a shortage in ProQuad for this reason and shifted its available supply of weakened virus to the manufacture of Varivax and Zostavax, since they require less of it.[18]

Pricing and Marketing

When Varivax was approved by the FDA and ACIP for distribution in 1995, it was initially priced at $55 per dose for the private sector, with a single-dose regimen recommended for pediatric use. According to Merck, this relatively high price was justified by the complexity of manufacturing and handling the vaccine and the fact that it served a significant unmet need.

The claims concerning the value of Varivax were over and above savings found by a cost-effectiveness study conducted in 1994 to evaluate the economic consequences of a routine varicella vaccination program for healthy children. The study documented that such a program would prevent 94 percent of all potential cases of chickenpox, providing that the vaccination coverage rate was 97 percent or more at school entry. It reported that if one dose of vaccine per child were recommended at a cost of $35 per dose, the total annual direct cost would be $162 million. From the societal perspective, which includes parental work-loss (reduced absenteeism from work) as well as medical costs, the program would save more than $5 for every dollar invested in vaccination. From the narrower perspective of the health-care payer, however (which takes into account only medical costs and ignores work-loss consequences), the program would cost approximately $2 per chickenpox case prevented, or $2,500 per life-year saved. From both a societal and the narrower payer's perspective, the program was deemed to be cost-effective at $35 per dose or less.[19] With the private-catalog launch list price at $55 per dose in 1995—$20 in excess of the narrow cost-effectiveness threshold of $35—Varivax was one of the first vaccines to be value-priced—that is, priced valuing reduced parental work absence, and thereby significantly above the estimated cost-effectiveness level.

The initial adoption of Varivax was slowed by its relatively high price, as well as by the public perception that chickenpox was a "harmless" disease. Merck sought to counter this perception by focusing its marketing efforts on educating the public about the severity and burden of the disease. The company compiled and publicized data such as the number of deaths and hospitalizations caused by chickenpox and used its sales force to inform nurses and physicians of these statistics. Partnerships were created with the CDC and various immunization groups, such as the Immunization Action Coalition, to educate the public. Merck also had to overcome parents' hesitation to vaccinate their children, based on their uncertainty regarding the duration of immunity granted by the vaccine and the fear that their children would become susceptible to the zoster form of the virus; we discuss this issue below.

Post-Launch Surveillance

In addition to the clinical trials that evaluated the effectiveness of the varicella vaccine prior to licensure, post-launch surveillance has been conducted, resulting in important changes to the ACIP recommendations that have significantly enlarged the potential market and enhanced Varivax sales. Before the introduction of the vaccine in 1995, varicella was a universal childhood disease in the United States. Since it was not a nationally notifiable infectious disease,[20] data were not available through the National Notifiable Disease Surveillance System to monitor the impact of the vaccination program. Accordingly, in 1995, the year in which Varivax was launched, the CDC, in collaboration with state and local health departments, instituted an active surveillance project in three communities. Its objectives were to establish baseline data and monitor trends in varicella disease following introduction of the vaccine.[21] Analyses of this population and other studies conducted after licensure indicated that one dose of varicella was only 80–85 percent effective against the disease. Therefore, 15–20 percent of children were still at risk because they had no immune response, or because the vaccination was only partially effective.[22]

In 2007, a *New England Journal of Medicine* article reported that the disease pattern for varicella was changing. Before 1995, 73 percent of cases occurred in children ages six years or younger; by 2007, however, the peak incidence of the disease among vaccinated children was occurring at ages six to nine and among unvaccinated children at ages nine to twelve. The study also found that the greater the elapsed time since receiving the vaccine, the more likely children were to have moderate to severe cases of the disease.[23]

Based on having access to earlier studies reporting similar results, in June 2006 the ACIP provisionally recommended adding a second dose to the varicella vaccine regimen.[24] The CDC subsequently published a final recommendation in 2007 supporting the two-dose regimen, thereby substantially increasing potential sales of the vaccine.[25]

Emerging Challenges and Issues

Merck is the sole manufacturer and supplier of varicella vaccine in the United States. Sanofi Pasteur's Varicelle Merieux and GSK's Varilrix are marketed only outside the United States, primarily in European markets, where concerns regarding childhood immunization with varicella vaccine have so far prevented their widespread use.[26] Intellectual property regulations have also kept competitors out of the U.S. market. Merck's status as the sole supplier of varicella vaccine in the United States, the ACIP recommendations increasing the number of doses required for immunization from one to two, and low yields of the varicella zoster virus have all contributed to shortages of the vaccine.[27] Merck dealt with this in 2007 by temporarily suspending production of ProQuad, whose stocks at the company were entirely depleted as of June 15. In June 2008, Merck announced that while manufacturing of the bulk varicella had resumed, the company's process improvements still needed to be cleared before wider use of the ingredients in finished vaccines could resume. In the meantime, Merck was not accepting orders for ProQuad, and while it was accepting orders for Zostavax, the company warned that customers could face shipping delays of as many as six weeks. Instead, Merck was giving priority to Varivax (for pediatric uses, to prevent varicella) over Zostavax (for adult use, to prevent shingles). When production of ProQuad would resume was unclear.[28]

Also in question was whether waning immunity to varicella could lead to higher rates of shingles, which tends to strike people ages fifty and older. Prior to the introduction of the vaccine, the spread of chickenpox provided a natural boost to the immune system of adults who came into contact with younger persons infected by the varicella zoster virus. Some experts now believe natural periodic exposure to persons with varicella may provide immunity against shingles. As more children have become immunized, however, the natural virus is no longer in widespread circulation. The result may be an increase in the incidence of zoster among persons who have had chickenpox, as well as a decrease in the average age at which zoster occurs.[29] This complex interaction illustrates nature's ability to adapt to changing environments in surprising ways, and highlights the importance of monitoring closely the prevalence and incidence of infectious diseases, as well as having in place a reliable and accurate post-launch surveillance system for vaccines.

PART III

Ongoing and Future Issues
in Vaccine Policies and R&D

Introduction to Part III

In the preceding chapters we have considered a number of important issues by presenting case studies of the product life cycles of four vaccine market segments, from intellectual property protection and clinical development through pricing and marketing to post-launch surveillance, comparing them along the way with small-molecule pharmaceuticals and other biologics. These case studies have illustrated some of the changing dynamics among these diverse vaccine markets: innovation in the form of more convenient formulations among mature DTP vaccines, coordination issues with annual influenza campaigns, the world's first "blockbuster" vaccine, and challenges in developing and then tracking the impacts of a novel vaccine to prevent the reemergence of chickenpox as shingles in the adult population. In each case, we have seen that consumption externalities play an important role, in some cases even spilling over from vaccination of children to reduced incidence of illness in adults.

In this final part of the book we will examine issues that were only briefly touched upon in the four case studies, but are extremely important to the future of the U.S. vaccine industry. Combination vaccines to prevent measles, mumps, and rubella, one of the largest vaccine market segments in which consumption externalities play a prominent role, have been the focus of a lengthy and intensely passionate controversy pitting the scientific integrity of vaccine manufacturers and public policymakers against the claims of well-organized and media-savvy patient advocacy groups and personal-injury lawyers that allege these vaccines cause autism. In the next chapter, we review the histories of this enduring dispute, and trace events leading up to critical quasi-judicial decisions occurring, beginning in 2009, in both the United States and the United Kingdom. This is followed by the conclusion to the book, in which we describe the expanding focus of vaccine R&D, and the policy issues these efforts may raise in the future.

8

Challenges in Maintaining
Public Trust in Vaccine Safety

That's the problem with vaccines. When they work, absolutely nothing happens. Nothing.

—Paul A. Offit[1]

Tolerance for risk is a particularly volatile issue for vaccines, since most are administered to healthy children, and inflicting harm on them through vaccinations seems especially devastating and regrettable. Completely risk-free vaccines do not exist, however, and with millions of children receiving vaccinations each year, manufacturers, researchers, providers, and public health authorities must confront the challenge of responsibly communicating, in a balanced manner, both the benefits and risks of vaccinations. Events of the past decade suggest that overreactions by the public to claims of potential harm from vaccination are not only possible, but may well lead to unintended harm of a different sort, and a decline in public trust in the vaccine delivery system.

We now examine two recent and ongoing examples of apparent overreaction to claims of harm from vaccine immunization, one in the United Kingdom and the other in the United States, involving the combination measles, mumps, and rubella (MMR) vaccine. Both hinge on a pervasive—though ultimately unfounded—belief that children who receive these vaccines are placed at risk for developing autism.

The Autism "Epidemic"

The term "autistic" was first coined in the late 1940s by psychoanalyst Leo Kanner, who reported eleven cases of children exhibiting an "extreme autistic aloneness." According to the medical historian Jeffrey Baker, Kanner identified children with this condition who eliminated all social contact, displayed little emotion, and expressed what he called an "obsessive desire for the maintenance of sameness."[2] Over the next several decades, researchers noted that a relatively large proportion of such children were born to highly educated parents. One Freudian hypothesis held that autism in infancy emerged in response to rejection of the child by an emotionally distant (albeit well-educated) parent—the so-called "refrigerator mother." An alternative theory attributed autism to biological origins. Over the years these different schools of thought have been embraced by different groups of parents and professionals.[3]

In recent history, the "mainline" community of autism researchers has envisaged autism as a neurodevelopmental condition. This view typically has four tenets:

- The causes of autism are fundamentally biological and likely genetic, and specifically not associated with parental behavior; in this sense, they are similar to the causes of cerebral palsy or Down syndrome.

- Autism is best characterized and conceptualized as a wide spectrum or continuum of disorders, rather than a single condition having narrow and specific manifestations.

- Treatment for autism must be rehabilitative rather than curative.

- Early referral and intervention offer the greatest hope for positive outcomes.[4]

In the past two decades researchers, providers, and parents from the mainline community have devoted enormous and intense efforts to promoting the use of screening tools and special education programs in schools for autistic children. Among their accomplishments in the United States was helping Congress to pass the Individuals with Disabilities Education Act in 1991, which officially added autism to the list of covered disabilities, thereby encouraging acceleration of diagnoses and early treatment. The rise in autism diagnoses since then has been precisely what the mainline community strove for and expected: It has emulated the rising diagnostic rates for other mental disorders, such as depression and anxiety, that occurred as awareness of these conditions increased. It has also raised the issue of whether the underlying incidence of autism is increasing, or if instead it is only the diagnosis of autism that is on the rise, reflecting increasing awareness and/or a broadening of the definition of what constitutes autism. What has been frustrating to the mainline community, however, is the gap that all too frequently has opened up between rising demand for and limited supply of autistic therapeutic services, which has resulted in long queues and office visits with physicians unfamiliar with the condition and its treatment. Lacking the institutional resources to solve this quandary, those in the mainline community have turned to each other and to the Internet.[5]

Meanwhile, an "alternative" community of researchers, providers, and patient advocates has also viewed autism in biomedical terms. Instead of envisaging it as a spectrum or continuum of disabilities, however, this community has characterized the condition as a heterogeneous collection of discrete disorders sharing a common manifestation, yet having different causes and etiologies. Notably, this alternative view offers hope that at least some forms of autism are not only treatable but might, in fact, be curable.

One branch of the alternative community focuses on special diets, linking a hypothesized intestinal abnormality to toxins or opioids traveling to the brains and nervous systems of children. This viewpoint, known as the "leaky gut" theory, has been promoted by the Autism Research Institute in San Diego, California, which provides parents and providers with educational materials and tools as they interact with autistic children. It has gained some credibility because its founder was one of the original debunkers of the "refrigerator mother" hypothesis.[6]

Other groups have advocated a procedure called chelating, in which children are injected with ethylenediaminetetraacetic acid (EDTA), a chemical that binds to mercury and helps remove it from the body. EDTA chelating therapy has never been shown to mitigate symptoms of autism, nor is it approved by the FDA for this purpose; furthermore, it may have adverse consequences.[7] In August 2005, a five-year-old boy in suburban Pittsburgh died from an arrhythmia (abnormal heartbeat) caused by the injection of the chelating agent EDTA.[8] Nonetheless, it is estimated that currently about ten thousand autistic American children are given mercury-chelating agents annually.[9] Although the National Institute of Mental Health (NIMH) in 2006 gave preliminary approval to fund a clinical trial evaluating mercury chelation as a therapy for autism, a subsequent animal study found that the drug to be used in the trial caused cognitive impairments in rats that did not have exposure to heavy metals. This led an NIMH institutional review board to conclude that there was no clear evidence for direct benefit to the 120 autistic children who would participate in the chelation trial and that the study presented more than a minimal risk. As a result, the NIMH called off the trial, stating that the agency would use the funds earmarked for the chelation trial for other research on the causes of autism. Autism support and advocacy groups expressed disappointment with cancellation of this trial.[10]

The medical historian Jeffrey P. Baker has argued that it was among these various alternative-community parental advocacy groups, not the medical or educational professions or personal-injury lawyers in the United States, that the notion of an "autism epidemic" was originally spawned and promulgated.[11] In 1998, in the midst of the alternative community's speculations as to what might be causing such an epidemic, the *Lancet*, a mainstream and prestigious British medical journal, published a study of autistic children. In the massive press coverage that accompanied the article's release, author Andrew Wakefield and some of his coauthors causally linked the increasing rates of autism diagnoses with widespread immunization via the combination measles, mumps, and rubella vaccine. This claim would have an enduring impact on vaccine development and policy in both the United Kingdom and the United States.

The MMR Three-in-One-Jab Panic in the United Kingdom

Combination vaccines are popular among children, their parents, and health providers because they reduce the number of painful injections children need to have, as well as save parents' time by cutting down on doctors' appointments. Maurice Hilleman at Merck's vaccine division developed the first combination MMR vaccine, which was launched by Merck in 1971 in the United States and in 1988 in the United Kingdom, where it was dubbed the "three-in-one jab."[12]

On February 28, 1998, ten years after the vaccine's introduction in Britain, Dr. Andrew Wakefield, a gastroenterologist surgeon, together with twelve other researchers affiliated with London's distinguished Royal Free Hospital and School of Medicine, published an article in the *Lancet*, reporting results from an investigation of "a consecutive series" of twelve children with chronic enterocolitis (inflammation of the large and small intestines) and regressive development disorder (later called autism).[13] Among their findings, the authors stated that "onset of behavioural symptoms was associated by the parents with measles, mumps, and rubella vaccination in eight of the 12 children" and occurred remarkably rapidly following immunization: "In these eight children, the average interval from exposure to first behavioural symptoms was 6.3 days (range 1–14)."[14]

The article's conclusions were cautious and qualified. "We have identified a chronic enterocolitis in children," the authors wrote,

> that may be related to neuropsychiatric dysfunction. In most cases, onset of symptoms was after measles, mumps, and rubella immunization. Further investigations are needed to examine this syndrome and its possible relation to the vaccine.[15]

But at a crowded prepublication press conference at the Royal Free Hospital on February 26, 1998, five of the coauthors were much less cautious, and instead linked autism causally to the MMR vaccine. The physicians' theory was that in some of the children the combination vaccine damaged the immune system, which could not cope with simultaneously receiving tiny doses of three separate diseases.[16] Because the immunocompromised intestinal surface was unable to provide an adequate barrier, they speculated, harmful proteins were allowed to enter the bloodstream and travel to the brain, where they might have caused autism.[17] Dr. Wakefield was particularly concerned about the measles virus component within the MMR vaccine, purported to persist in the gut, which, he claimed, caused the damage.[18]

When the five doctors were asked if, given their findings, parents should continue having their children vaccinated with the MMR three-in-one jab, Dr. Wakefield replied that the possibility of a link among intestinal disorders, autism, and MMR vaccination could no longer be ignored. "It's a moral issue," he said, "and I can't support the continued use of these three vaccines given in combination until this issue has been resolved."[19]

These oral comments were much more provocative than the nuanced text in the *Lancet* article. Moreover, credibility for the study's independence had been enhanced in the acknowledgments section of the article, which stated that the study was "supported by the Special Trustees of Royal Free Hampstead NHS [National Health Service] Trust and the Children's Medical Charity."[20] The study also appeared to conform to professional standards with regard to ethical approval and informed consent, with the authors claiming that "investigations were approved by the Ethical Practices Committee of the Royal Free Hospital NHS, and parents gave informed consent."[21]

Wakefield's study clearly did not provide scientific evidence supporting a causal link between MMR vaccinations and autism. The suspicious proteins were not identified. Furthermore, since at that time about 90 percent of British children had received their MMR vaccinations soon after their first birthdays, and because symptoms of autism usually appear when a child is between one and two years of age, it wasn't really surprising that Wakefield and coauthors had found twelve children who had become autistic within two weeks of receiving the MMR vaccine. Nor had Wakefield and coauthors compared the incidence of autism in children who had received the MMR vaccine with those who had not. Even if they had done so and found a higher incidence in those receiving the vaccine, additional scientific research would have been necessary to establish that the vaccination, rather than some other factor more common among vaccinated children than among nonvaccinated children, caused the greater incidence of autism. Finally, Wakefield and his supporting cast had not carefully considered the public health consequences of their recommendation—the possibility that fewer children would be immunized with the combination MMR vaccine and be at risk of catching measles, mumps, or rubella.

Several of Wakefield's coauthors disagreed with his interpretation of their findings, and the Department of Health also vigorously dissented.[22] However, with his charisma, humor, cultured British accent, good looks, and apparent warmth toward autistic children and their parents ("Everything I know about autism, I know from listening to parents"), Wakefield became an instant media darling.[23] The British public listened when Wakefield expressed contempt for the "villainous" public health officials and vaccine companies:

> We are in the midst of an international epidemic (of autism). . . .
> Those responsible for investigating and dealing with this epi-
> demic have failed. Among the reasons for this failure is the fact
> that they are faced with the prospect that they themselves may
> be responsible for the epidemic. Therefore, in their attempts to
> exonerate themselves, they are an impediment to progress. I
> believe that public health officials know that there is a problem;
> they are, however, willing to deny the problem and accept the
> loss of an unknown number of children on the basis that the
> success of public health policy—mandatory vaccination—by
> necessity involves sacrifice.[24]

To make matters worse, British public health officials were already on the
defensive. A few months earlier, during an epidemic of mad cow disease,
they had declared British beef to be safe, only to ban it from the marketplace just a short time later.[25] Could Britons trust these same authorities to
tell the truth about the MMR vaccine, or were they covering something up?
Were Wakefield and coauthors revealing a massive scandal?

The day after the press conference, London tabloids responded with
headlines such as "Ban Three-in-One Jab, Urge Doctors." Tony Blair, then
Britain's prime minister, added fuel to the controversy by refusing to disclose whether his son Leo had received the MMR vaccine, stating it was a
private matter. Rumors circulated that the Blairs had traveled to France to
have the separate single jabs from a private (that is, not of the British
National Health Service) provider.[26]

Public health authorities urged parents to continue having their children vaccinated with the three-in-one jab, emphasizing the lack of scientific
evidence supporting Wakefield's provocative recommendations. In March
1998, a Medical Research Council expert panel found "no evidence to
indicate any link" between the MMR vaccine and autism in children, and
an April 1998 Finnish report concluded that, based on the findings of a
fourteen-year study, the MMR vaccine was not dangerous.[27] Nevertheless,
MMR vaccination rates in Britain for children under age two subsequently
fell from 91.5 percent immediately before Wakefield's warning to 79.9 percent in 2003—considerably less than the World Health Organization's estimated critical herd immunity rate of 95 percent;[28] and within months of

the Wakefield press conference, one children's hospital near Dublin, Ireland, admitted a hundred children with measles, three of whom died.[29]

In the immediate aftermath of the *Lancet* article and the publicity surrounding the press conference following its publication, Wakefield's supporters and detracters engaged in heated debate. Press coverage was extensive, with much public attention focused on parents of autistic children, who organized themselves into potent, media-savvy advocacy groups. Dr. Richard Horton, a colleague of Wakefield's at the Royal Free Hospital and the *Lancet* editor who had handled the manuscript, strongly supported the article. "Progress in medicine depends on the free expression of new ideas," Horton declared. " . . . In science, it was only this commitment to free expression that shook free the tight grip of religion on the way human beings understood their world."[30]

Meanwhile, epidemiologists, medical researchers, and public health officials in various countries carefully examined medical records in an effort to assess whether children who had received the MMR vaccine were at greater risk of autism than those who had not. Fourteen groups of investigators, examining the records of more than 600,000 children, all concluded that the incidence of autism was the same in the two groups. Their clear and consistent conclusions were that no credible evidence supported the claim that MMR vaccines caused autism, and that parents who chose not to have their children vaccinated were not reducing the risk of autism. Instead, they were increasing the risk of their children's experiencing potentially serious cases of measles and other infections.[31]

Then came the bombshell. Suspicious of the claimed extent and speed of onset of autistic behavioral symptoms following MMR vaccination, the *Sunday Times* of London initiated an investigation in December 2003, headed up by a reporter named Brian Deer.[32] Deer soon learned that instead of having been identified through routine physician referrals, most of the twelve children in the Wakefield study had, with their parents' consent, been recruited by a British solicitor, Richard Barr, who for some time had been attempting to raise a speculative lawsuit against the MMR vaccine manufacturers.[33] Deer discovered that at the time Wakefield's article was published in the *Lancet*, the parents of ten of the twelve children already had received legal aid from Barr to sue the manufacturers; those of the eleventh were American and not eligible to sue; and the twelfth child's parents joined the lawsuit four years later, after being visited by a lawyer.[34] Moreover, two years before the publication, Wakefield had launched a research collaboration with Barr, aided by a contract with Barr's team paying Wakefield £150 per hour on top of his Royal Free Hospital salary. Barr obtained additional funding from the Legal Aid Board, which authorized up to £55,000 from public funds for Wakefield to do "clinical and scientific" tests on ten of Barr's child clients.[35]

Although the *Lancet* had strict requirements for authors to report possible conflicts of interest, Wakefield did not disclose this funding or his collaboration with Barr in the published article, nor did he notify his article coauthors. Moreover, the authors' claim that "investigations were approved by the Ethical Practices Committee" of the Royal Free Hospital was later denied by both the chair of the committee and the dean of the Royal Free and University College Medical School.[36] Deer uncovered additional information suggesting that Wakefield had altered the medical records of study subjects, that test results from cerebrospinal fluids of the twelve children taken earlier via lumbar puncture had revealed no measles virus in any of them, and that, almost nine months before publication, Wakefield and the medical school had filed the first in a series of patents relating to the MMR vaccine, including one for a single vaccine against measles which, if successful, would likely have competed with the MMR three-in-one jab.[37]

Within a month of the appearance in the *Times* of Deer's investigation exposing Wakefield, the editors of the *Lancet* responded to six serious allegations of research misconduct that had been raised. They stated that three of the allegations had been answered appropriately through clarifications provided by Wakefield (a conclusion later challenged by Deer),[38] but that with respect to the other three,

> We regret that aspects of funding for parallel and related work and the existence of ongoing litigation that had been known during clinical evaluation of the children reported in the 1998 *Lancet* paper were not disclosed to the editors. We also regret that the overlap between children in the *Lancet* paper and in the Legal Aid Board funded pilot project was not revealed to us. We judge that all this information would have been material to our decision-making about the paper's suitability, credibility and validity for publication.[39]

In the same issue of the *Lancet*, ten of the twelve coauthors retracted Wakefield's interpretation of findings in the February 1998 article, stating:

> While much uncertainty remains about the nature of these changes, we believe it important that such work continues, as autistic children can potentially be helped by recognition and treatment of gastrointestinal problems.
>
> We wish to make it clear that in this paper no causal link was established between MMR vaccine and autism as the data were insufficient. However, the possibility of such a link was raised and consequent events have had major implications for public health. In view of this, we consider now is the appropriate time that we should together formally retract the interpretation placed upon these findings, in the paper, according to precedent.[40]

Late in 2001, after Wakefield had failed to honor an agreement with the Royal Free Hospital to undertake "properly organized research to verify his claims," the doctor's employment at the medical school was terminated, "albeit with substantial compensation."[41] Subsequently, he moved to the United States, where he is now executive director of the Thoughtful House Center for Children, in Austin, Texas, a nonprofit school and clinic that treats children with autism from all over the world.[42]

To many, including numerous parents of children with autism who were Barr clients and formed advocacy groups such as Justice Awareness and Basic Support (JABS) and Allergy-Induced Autism,[43] Wakefield remains a hero, "a tragic figure bravely standing up against a medical establishment determined to crush him."[44] In a November 2000 *60 Minutes* interview with Ed Bradley, Wakefield described his beliefs and commitments:

> Should we stop, should we go away, should we stop publishing because it is inconvenient? I've lost my job. I will never practice medicine in (England) again. There is no upside to this. But if you come to me and say, "This has happened to my child," what's my job? What did I sign up to do when I went into medicine? I'm here to address the concerns of the patient. There's a high price to pay for that. But I'm prepared to pay it.[45]

In June 2007, after undertaking a preliminary investigation, the British General Medical Council announced that its Fitness to Practise Panel would be holding hearings to consider whether to remove the physician license registrations of Wakefield and two of his coauthors, professors John Walker-Smith and Simon Murch. Among the allegations to be considered by the panel were those mentioned above concerning research misconduct and failure to disclose conflict of interest, as well as newer ones: the exploitation of autistic children with high-risk medical procedures, such as colonoscopies and lumbar punctures, that were not clinically necessary; and the alleged purchase by Wakefield of blood samples from children for £5 at a birthday party attended by his son.[46]

The General Medical Council disciplinary hearing began on July 17, 2007. At an interview given just prior to his appearance at the hearing, Wakefield continued to link autism with the MMR vaccine. "My concern," he said,

> is that it's biologically plausible that the MMR vaccine causes or contributes to the disease in many children, and that nothing in the science so far dissuades me from the continued need to pursue that question. The trend in autism has gone up sharply in many countries. It's interesting that the increase coincides in many places with the introduction of the MMR vaccine. That doesn't make it the cause. But it's an observation that needs to be explained, because there was clearly some environmental change at that time that led to growing numbers of children becoming autistic. It's a legitimate question if MMR is one of those factors. I fear that it may be.[47]

The public hearings focused on professional conduct issues and were not to arbitrate "between competing scientific theories generated in the course of medical research."[48] After a recess, they resumed on March 27, 2008. As parents of autistic children supporting him held signs reading "Stop the Witch Hunt" and "We're With Wakefield," Wakefield testified before the General Medical Council panel. Asked by his attorney whether he had acted improperly, Wakefield told the panel, "Absolutely not."[49] Meanwhile, the National Autistic Society issued a statement pleading that the case not be allowed "to increase the lack of sympathy that some parents of children with autism have encountered from health professionals." Some parents, said the statement, had "reported to the NAS that in some cases their concerns [had] been dismissed as hysteria following previous publicity around the MMR vaccine."[50] Further details of the proceedings have been withheld until their scheduled completion in late 2008 or early 2009.[51] A conclusion is now expected in April 2009.[52]

Additional research by the investigative reporter Brian Deer, based on hospital and other records and published in 2009, appears to indicate that virtually all of the twelve children had begun developing symptoms of autism well before their MMR injection. Moreover, at least one parent of a child in whose intestines the measles virus was said to have been found took samples to three other laboratories, each of which was unable to find the virus. Deer also reported that with considerably less than the 95 percent of the pediatric population vaccinated, Britain has lost its herd immunity; while in 1998 when Wakefield's initial research was published, 56 cases of measles were reported, in 2008 1,348 measles cases were reported, up 36 percent from 2007.[53]

Mercury, Vaccines, and Autism

The allegation that the MMR vaccine might be a cause of autism migrated quickly from Britain to the United States, where it attracted attention from parents, environmentalists, the media, politicians, and personal-injury lawyers. The origins of American MMR and thimerosal litigation go back, however, to events that preceded publication of the provocative Wakefield article in February 1998.[54] The passionate disputes regarding thimerosal are remarkably enduring and seemingly endless, with U.S. public health authorities unintentionally providing ammunition to all combatants. We begin with some history.

Among environmental scientists, a long and infamous history links methylmercury environmental pollution to serious mental-development disorders of the human fetus and infant. Methylmercury was once widely used in developing countries as a fungicide, where it played an important role in the "Green Revolution" following World War II. It is also synthesized by bacteria residing in mercury-polluted soil and waters, from which it is passed up through the food chain and eventually concentrated in fish consumed by humans.[55]

In an environmental disaster that began in Japan in the 1950s, a chemical company discharged mercury effluent into Minamata Bay. This practice was eventually implicated by the Japanese government in 1968 as the cause of deaths among fish, birds, and cats, and profound neurological impairments in humans; bacteria in waters had converted the inorganic mercury into methylmercury, resulting in several thousand diseased individuals. Distressing photographs of mercury-poisoned children taken by W. Eugene Smith for *Life* magazine during the 1960s revealed children with spasticity, seizures, deafness, and severe mental retardation. The substantial proportion of these children who were born to asymptomatic mothers led to the realization among environmental scientists that fetuses might be more vulnerable to mercury poisoning than adults.

Another environmental disaster occurred in Iraq in 1971–72, when more than 6,000 farmers and their family members were hospitalized for methylmercury poisoning; of them, 459 died. The source of the poisoning was homemade bread that had been derived from a wheat seed contaminated by fungicide. Extensive analysis of Iraqi victims provided the basis upon which the U.S. Food and Drug Administration constructed, in the late 1970s, the first set of standards defining safe methylmercury exposure for adults.

Determining safe exposure standards for fetuses and newborns was more challenging, for several important studies in the 1980s produced inconsistent findings, eventually resulting in differing recommendations from various U.S. agencies as to safe exposure levels to methylmercury. Although the different studies generally agreed that fetuses were more sensitive to methylmercury than adults, the neurological, cognitive, and linguistic developmental delays detectable in those with greater exposure were rather subtle and required sensitive and sophisticated testing. Notably, any link between methylmercury and the much more obvious autism spectrum disorders was never even considered or discussed.[56]

In September 1997, the U.S. Congress considered renewal of 1992 legislation called the Prescription Drug User Fee Act, which provided for commitments from the FDA to review product license applications for drugs more quickly, in return for user fees submitted by industry sponsors.[57] Congressman Frank Pallon from New Jersey attached a simple, 133-word amendment to the reauthorization bill, known as the FDA Modernization Act of 1997, giving the FDA two years to "compile a list of drugs and foods that contain intentionally introduced mercury compounds and (to) provide a quantitative and qualitative analysis of the mercury compounds in the list."[58] Among these compounds was thimerosal, a preservative that had long been used to prevent bacterial contamination in multidose vials of pediatric vaccines. The concern was that, cumulated over a series of vaccinations, the total amount of thimerosal exposure for a child could be substantial.

It is essential at this point to note that the pertinent substance in thimerosal is ethylmercury. While methylmercury and ethylmercury are chemically quite similar, the difference between them is substantial, and comparable to the distinction between ethanol (the form of alcohol in wine) and methanol, its highly toxic and lethal counterpart (a poisonous and flammable liquid synthesized into fuel, solvents, and antifreeze, and used in the manufacture of formaldehyde).[59]

In May 1999, the FDA reported that by six months of age, infants might receive a total of up to 187.5 µg of ethylmercury—75 µg from three doses of the DTP vaccine, 75 µg from three doses of the Hib vaccine, and 37.5 µg from three doses of the hepatitis B vaccine—although this maximum was unlikely to be experienced by a majority of children, since thimerosal concentrations historically had varied by manufacturer.[60] Since no safety guidelines were available for ethylmercury, the FDA examined its own safety guidelines for methylmercury (environmental mercury), as well as those of the Environmental Protection Agency and the Agency for Toxic Substances and Disease Registry, to determine whether these amounts were safe.

As we have noted above, however, although the two molecules differ by only one carbon atom, they are quite different. Inorganic mercury from volcanic eruptions, burning coal, and water erosion from rocks is converted to organic methylmercury by bacteria in the soil. Methylmercury then enters the water supply and eventually the food chain; it is omnipresent in the environment and unavoidable.[61] Because methylmercury is excreted from the body much more slowly than the ethylmercury in vaccines (and is therefore more likely to cumulate), its safety guidelines were not very informative for evaluating the safety of ethylmercury-containing thimerosal.[62]

In late June 1999, FDA officials convened a meeting with representatives from the Centers for Disease Control and the American Academy of Pediatrics, who, along with the ACIP, make and publish national vaccine recommenda-tions.[63] Participants realized that no studies were available comparing neuro-logical outcomes in children who had received thimerosal-containing vaccines with those who had not, although studies of children who had consumed large amounts of mercury from fish in their diets and were apparently unaffected provided some assurance of safety.[64]

On July 9, after considerable debate, the CDC and AAP decided to exer-cise caution, albeit in an ambiguous manner. Specifically, they asked manu-facturers to remove thimerosal from their vaccines as soon as possible, and in the interim they recommended that physicians suspend the birth dose of the hepatitis B immunization—which at the time contained thimerosal—in children who were not at risk for hepatitis B. The accompanying AAP press release seemed contradictory, however. It stated,

> Parents should not worry about the safety of vaccines. The cur-
> rent levels of thimerosal will not hurt children, but reducing
> those levels will make safe vaccines even safer. While our cur-
> rent immunization schedules are safe, we have an opportunity
> to increase the margin of safety.[65]

Not wanting to risk their longstanding collaboration with the ACIP and AAP, manufacturers complied with the CDC/AAP request. With the excep-tion of some flu vaccines that still contained trace amounts,[66] thimerosal was removed from all pediatric vaccines by packaging them in single-dose vials that did not need a preservative; manufacturers' actions were swift and com-prehensive, resulting in almost complete removal by the summer of 2001.[67]

But physicians and other observers were confused by the CDC/AAP precautionary move and by the rapid response of vaccine manufacturers in removing thimerosal. How could the removal of something that had not been found to be harmful make something safer? Did vaccine manufac-turers remove it because they knew there was a safety problem? Meanwhile, less than a year and a half before, Andrew Wakefield's article purporting to show a link between autism and the MMR vaccine had made its appearance in the *Lancet*. Many parents, frightened by the sudden change in policy and perhaps generally aware of news concerning the vaccine scares in the United Kingdom, reasoned that thimerosal was being removed because it was harmful. Fueled by additional support from parent groups and religious organizations opposing compulsory immunization in general, the Wakefield phenomenon began to erode public trust in the U.S. vaccine delivery system.

The fallout from the July 1999 CDC/AAP precautionary announcement was considerable, causing substantial collateral damage and harm. About 10 percent of U.S. hospitals suspended use of the hepatitis B vaccine for all newborns, regardless of their risk level,[68] and the proportion of hospitals failing to vaccinate infants born to high-risk seropositive mothers rose more than sixfold, from 1 percent to 7 percent in the months during which the birth dose of the hepatitis B vaccine was suspended.[69] A three-month-old Michigan child who became infected with hepatitis B virus died of a massive infection shortly thereafter.[70]

The CDC/AAP announcement also galvanized the emerging parent and provider advocacy groups, who claimed that thimerosal-containing vaccines were linked to the "autism epidemic." One self-designated group of "mercury moms" created an advocacy organization, SafeMinds, which commissioned journalist David Kirby to write about the thimerosal–autism controversy.[71] The resulting book, *Evidence of Harm*, reported on alleged secret meetings by the CDC, intrigue among public officials and manufacturers, and the failure of public health officials to fulfill their professional obligations.[72] *Evidence of Harm* became a sensational hit, resulting in interviews of the author by radio personality Don Imus and *Meet the Press* host Tim Russert. Soon it became one of the best-selling health books in the United States, and, even months after its publication, the thimerosal–autism story continued to play a prominent role in news coverage.[73]

Politicians quickly joined the chorus of those casting vaccine manufacturers and public health officials in the role of villains. Representative Dan Burton, a Republican congressman from Indiana and chairman of the House Committee on Government Reform, opened hearings on April 6, 2000, focusing on the possible link between thimerosal and autism, after having been convinced by members of SafeMinds that he should shift his focus away from the MMR vaccine.[74] Burton began by pointing to a picture of his granddaughter, stating that she had "almost died after receiving the hepatitis B shot."[75] In the same picture, with his head on her shoulder, was his grandson. Burton said that according to doctors, after the boy received "nine shots on one day, the MMR and the DTaP and the hepatitis B, within a very short period of time he quit speaking, ran around banging his head against the wall, screaming and hollering and waving his hands, and became totally a different child. And we found out that he was autistic."[76] One of the hearing speakers was Dr. Andrew Wakefield.[77] Notably, in the United Kingdom, the MMR three-in-one jab formulation did not contain any thimerosal, so it was not an issue there. Nevertheless, the MMR vaccine scare (minus the thimerosal element) began to flourish in the United States. In his November 2000 appearance on *60 Minutes* with Ed Bradley, Wakefield was asked if he would give his own children the MMR vaccine, to which he responded, "No, I wouldn't. . . . I would most certainly vaccinate them. I would give them (separate shots of) measles, mumps and rubella vaccines."[78]

Between 2001 and 2007, no less than eight safety review panels conducted by the Institute of Medicine (IOM) reassured the public on the safety of vaccines.[79] Two detailed reviews by the IOM concluded that the available evidence failed to support any causal link between mercury in vaccines and the increasing prevalence of autism.[80] Nevertheless, the final report of Congressman Burton's House Committee on Government Reform, issued in 2003, stated that "thimerosal as a preservative used in vaccines is directly related to the autism epidemic,"[81] and concluded, "Our public health agencies' failure to act is indicative of institutional malfeasance for self-protection and misplaced protectionism of the pharmaceutical industry."[82]

The 1998 CDC/AAP request for vaccine manufacturers to remove thimerosal from their vaccines and the manufacturers' rapid and relatively complete response to do so created conditions for the confluence of a number of forces, bringing together parents of children with autism seeking an explanation and wanting to spare others of their devastating experience, families dealing with guilt from having been accused of accommodating "refrigerator mothers," environmental groups sensitive to the damage wrought by the discharge of mercury into waters, personal-injury, class-action lawyers perceiving the potential for lucrative and massive damage claims against the well-funded vaccine manufacturers, the media seeing a sensational story of vaccines that were supposed to be lifesaving and instead were causing harm, and politicians sensing an opportunity both to demonstrate empathy for devastated parents and to achieve publicity and visibility.[83] Political strife did not split across party lines, but exposed intraparty feuds. Even as Representative Burton chastised vaccine manufacturers and public health officials, in November 2002, other congressional Republicans inserted language into a massive, 475-page homeland security bill, prohibiting parents from suing vaccine manufacturers. In January 2003, after a public outcry, the proposed language was scrapped.[84]

Although manufacturers moved rapidly to eliminate thimerosal from their vaccines, various states began enacting laws completely banning the vaccines or, in some cases, only allowing trace amounts of thimerosal in certain flu vaccines. On May 14, 2004, Iowa governor Thomas J. Vilsack signed into law a bill banning thimerosal, becoming the country's first state to do so.[85] Soon thereafter, on August 26, 2004, Governor Arnold Schwarzenegger banned vaccines containing thimerosal from California.[86] Since at that time the supply of thimerosal-free flu vaccine was very limited, Schwarzenegger's prohibition essentially prevented many California children from being vaccinated for influenza.[87] In a number of other states, legislation banning thimerosal was signed into law or introduced but not enacted.[88]

Not long after California banned vaccines containing thimerosal, in June 2005, Schwarzenegger relative Robert F. Kennedy Jr., describing himself as "an attorney and environmentalist who has spent years working on issues of mercury toxicity," authored an exposé of the mercury/autism controversy that was published in *Rolling Stone*.[89] Kennedy cited some of the same secret meetings as had journalist David Kirby, and referred to several studies suggesting that "ethylmercury is actually *more* toxic to developing brains and stays in the brain *longer* than methylmercury."[90] Suggesting the alleged mercury poisoning surpassed even the harm caused by asbestos and tobacco, Kennedy concluded, "I devoted time to study this issue because I believe that this is a moral crisis that must be addressed. If, as the evidence suggests, our public health authorities knowingly allowed the pharmaceutical industry to poison an entire generation of American children, their actions arguably constitute one of the biggest scandals in the annals of American medicine."[91]

Kennedy's reference to asbestos and tobacco harm again raised concerns over liability from injury due to vaccine immunization, concerns that have long played an important role in Congress. Recall that the federal Vaccine Injury Compensation Program was adopted by Congress in 1988 in response to a panic over the pertussis portion of the DTP vaccine.[92] Although most U.S. public health officials believed that the claims of adverse side effects from the DTP immunization were unfounded, some families who sued manufacturers won very substantial awards from sympathetic juries who were otherwise convinced. Several vaccine manufacturers began exiting the DTP market, others threatened to do so, and public health officials feared a loss of herd immunity. The result was the creation of the VICP.

To win an award from the VICP, a claimant must show that a child had one or more of several listed adverse reactions within a short timeframe following vaccination, in which case the VICP usually presumes the adverse reaction was caused by the vaccine. An advisory committee provides counsel regarding changes to the list of adverse events as consensus views evolve with the publication of new studies and findings. If families claim that a vaccine caused an adverse reaction that is not on the list, the burden of proof rests with them. Proof of causation does not need to be at the level of so-called scientific certainty or "proof beyond a reasonable doubt," but must only meet the lower standard of "the preponderance of the evidence" demonstrating that causation is "more likely than not."[93]

Currently, autism is not on the list as an adverse reaction from any vaccine; the VICP program has rejected about three hundred such autism claims outright.[94] In early March 2008, however, news emerged that in the previous year the VICP had agreed to award damages to the family of Hannah Poling, conceding that a connection existed between her autistic symptoms and the vaccines she received, though the connection was by no means simple.[95] In 2000, because of a series of ear infections, nineteen-month-old Hannah had fallen behind in the vaccination schedule, so in a single day she received five inoculations covering nine diseases (measles, mumps, rubella, polio, varicella, diphtheria, pertussis, tetanus, and *Haemophilus influenzae*).

A confounding factor is that Hannah was also diagnosed with a mutation in a gene linked to mitochondrial dysfunction in basic cell metabolism. Mitochondria serve as power generators for each cell in the body, converting food and oxygen into energy. When mitochondria fail, they cause such wide-ranging symptoms as muscle weakness, diabetes, developmental delays, and susceptibility to infection.[96] The VICP panel concluded that the vaccines had "significantly aggravated an underlying mitochondrial disorder, which predisposed [Hannah] to deficits in energy metabolism," causing brain damage with "features of autism spectrum disorder."[97] Notably, the decision did not address the issue of whether it was thimerosal—or something else in the vaccines—that was at fault. (Recall, too, that in response to a July 1999 request by the CDC/AAP, manufacturers began removing thimerosal from all vaccines except influenza vaccines, completing the process in 2001, a year after Hannah's inoculations.)

Indeed, following the decision, CDC director Dr. Julie Gerberding was quoted as saying, "The government has made absolutely no statement about indicating [sic] that vaccines are the cause of autism, as this would be a complete mischaracterization of any of the science that we have at our disposal today."[98]

While personal-injury lawyers were delighted with the decision (one attorney representing more than 1,200 families with vaccine injury claims was quoted as saying, "It's a beginning"),[99] others, such as Dr. Paul Offit, author and division chief of infectious diseases at the Children's Hospital of Philadelphia, chastised the VICP panel decision, rebuking them for having abandoned the "preponderance of scientific evidence" standard, and instead exhibiting a willingness to adopt a much weaker "biological plausibility" hypothesis. According to Offit, "The system worked fine until a few years ago, when vaccine court judges turned their back on science by dropping preponderance of evidence as a standard. Now, petitioners need merely propose a biologically plausible mechanism by which a vaccine might cause harm—even if their explanation contradicts published studies."[100]

In June 2008 the New York Times reported a second case of a child who became autistic shortly after receiving FluMist, an intranasal influenza immunization. The individual was a six-year-old girl from Colorado, suffering from a mitochondrial disorder, who received the flu vaccine FluMist on January 11, 2008, developed autism-like symptoms within a week, and died on April 5, 2008.[101] Since FluMist protects against influenza (unlike the MMR vaccine), and since it does not contain the preservative thimerosal, this incident raises issues distinct from the various controversies discussed above. Instead, it has induced researchers to examine a different hypothesis, namely, that vaccination contributes to the activation of an underlying mitochondrial genetic disorder which, in turn, produces the autism.[102]

While scientists pursue intriguing new hypotheses, progress will likely be elusive, since both autism and mitochondrial disorders are poorly understood. Moreover, screening children prior to vaccination is infeasible, since currently no reliable test is available to screen for mitochondrial disorders.[103] Meanwhile, public officials continue to link vaccinations with autism. Asked about the link between vaccines and autism as he campaigned in summer 2008, for example, Republican presidential candidate Senator John McCain was quoted as saying, "It's indisputable that autism is on the rise among children. The question is, what's causing it? And we go back and forth, and there's strong evidence that indicates that it's got to do with a preservative in vaccines."[104]

Several weeks after the VICP panel decision on Hannah Poling's case, the CDC announced the formation of a working group tasked with choosing the most important safety questions for the centers to research over the coming five years. As part of this process, the group was explicitly requested to obtain significant public input in setting priorities, including hearing from vaccine critics, apparently to ease skepticism that public health authorities were hiding or discounting information concerning vaccine safety.

With the exception of the single decision involving Hannah Poling, by 2008 the almost five thousand autism-related claims at the VICP had not been adjudicated.[105] In an effort to resolve such claims more expeditiously, the VICP had announced as early as 2002 that it would have a small number of test cases (initially, nine were expected) examining general causation issues but not dealing with specific issues of harm to any particular child.[106] Although the test-case study originally was envisaged to be completed in two years, the first case was not brought before Special Master George L. Hastings Jr. until June 11, 2007.[107] The legal procedure is called the Omnibus Autism Proceeding at the U.S. Court of Federal Claims in Washington, D.C.[108] The approximately 4,900 petitioners are represented by the Petitioners' Steering Council (PSC), which initially requested that three different theories of general causation be considered: the theory that MMR vaccines and thimerosal-containing vaccines can combine to cause autism; the theory that thimerosal-containing vaccines alone can cause autism; and the theory that MMR vaccines alone can cause autism. The presiding special masters instructed the PSC to designate three test cases for each of the three theories.

Between June 11, 2007, and November 9, 2007, three different special masters each presided over a test-case hearing in a different location in the United States involving the first theory. After the conclusion of those hearings, the parties engaged in a lengthy process of filing written briefs analyzing the evidence in each of the three cases. According to a September 29, 2008, autism update statement, the special masters would issue written rulings on the three test cases involving the first general theory "as soon as possible."[108] Evidentiary hearings on the second general theory took place between May 12 and July 22, 2008. In late 2008, the parties were still exchanging written briefs. The special masters will analyze these briefs and the evidentiary record before issuing written rulings.[109] Regarding the third general theory (that MMR vaccine alone can cause autism), the parties have filed documents indicating no need for a third round of test cases, arguing that the theory has already been presented, in effect, as part of the first theory. Therefore, no further test case proceedings have been scheduled.[111]

On February 12, 2009, three special masters, ruling separately on petitions brought forward by three families on behalf of their children, issued decisions stating that the evidence presented did not prove a link between autism and the MMR vaccines. Special Master George L. Hastings, Jr. wrote as follows:

> I concluded that the evidence was overwhelmingly contrary to the petitioners' contentions. The expert witnesses presented by the respondent were far better qualified, far more experienced, and far more persuasive than the petitioners' experts, concerning most of the key points. The numerous medical studies concerning these issues, performed by medical students worldwide, have come down strongly against the petitioners' contentions. Considering all of the evidence, I found that the petitioners have failed to demonstrate that thimerosal-containing vaccines can contribute to causing immune dysfunction, or that the MMR vaccine can contribute to causing either autism or gastrointestinal dysfunction. I further conclude that while Michelle Cedillo has tragically suffered from autism and other severe conditions, the petitioners have also failed to demonstrate that her vaccinations played any role at all in causing those problems.[112]

In past decisions involving claims unrelated to autism, some families have complained bitterly about the VICP process. Any petitioner dissatisfied with a decision can file a regular lawsuit alleging that a product is defective, and the named defendant can be found liable. To win such a case, a petitioner needs to persuade a jury not only that the vaccine harmed an individual child, but also that it had a defective design or failed to carry adequate warnings. In nonautism cases to date, relatively few who have been denied compensation have subsequently sued a vaccine manufacturer.[113]

Although decisions by the special masters of the U.S. Court of Federal Claims may bring closure to some petitioners, most observers agree that controversy regarding vaccines causing autism will not suddenly vanish. Parents have already cited "fatal flaws" in the VICP proceedings, such as differences in discovery rules between civil courts and the vaccine court, and have declared that "families are forced to sue the government, which has no incentive to settle and can drag out cases for years while children go untreated."[114] Some claimants are attempting to bypass the VICP process, saying their claims should be exempt from the process because thimerosal is not included in the legal definition of a "vaccine," or arguing that it is an "adulteration." Others are suing companies that make or have made thimerosal (such as Eli Lilly), arguing that preservative suppliers are not vaccine manufacturers.[115]

Meanwhile, the evidence against any link between thimerosal and mental ability and behavioral problems in children continues to cumulate. For example, in a CDC-sponsored study of 1,047 children between the ages of seven and ten whose exposure years earlier to mercury from thimerosal could be determined from computerized immunization records, medical records, personal immunization records, and parent interviews, a series of standardized tests assessing forty-two neuropsychological outcomes were conducted. Results from the study, published in the *New England Journal of Medicine* in September 2007, showed that only a few statistically significant associations with exposure to mercury from thimerosal could be detected, all of them small and almost equally divided between positive and negative effects. The authors concluded, "Our study does not support a causal association between early exposure to mercury from thimerosal-containing vaccines and immune globulins and deficits in neuropsychological functioning at the age of 7 to 10 years."[116] A spokesperson for the parents' advocacy group SafeMinds criticized the study, citing its small sample size and 30 percent participation rate, and stating instead that the results were "inconclusive and the interpretation of the data . . . too sweeping."[117] Since the data underlying the study will be made available to other researchers by the CDC, the spokesperson encouraged other scientists to apply alternative methodologies to the dataset. Notably, while the *New England Journal of Medicine* study explicitly excluded examination of the autism-spectrum disorders and instead focused on forty-two other neuropsychological outcomes, results from another CDC-sponsored study focusing on the causal link to autism are expected to be made public sometime in 2008 or 2009.[118]

Within the next year or so, therefore, the passionate and enduring controversies linking the MMR vaccines, thimerosal, and autism will reach critical decision points, with perhaps very significant impacts on vaccine manufacturers, public health authorities, the scientific community, and families. The journey to this point has been a rough one for many, but from it much can be learned concerning responsible communication of risks and benefits from vaccinations. As one observer has recently commented:

> During the next few years, thimerosal will probably be removed from influenza vaccines, and the court cases will probably settle down. But the thimerosal controversy should stand as a cautionary tale of how not to communicate theoretical risks to the public; otherwise, the lesson inherent in the collateral damage caused by its precipitous removal will remain unlearned.[119]

Conclusion:
Beyond The Turning Point—
The Expanding Focus of Vaccine R&D

Vaccine manufacturers have long been a cost-effective but commercially dormant component of the health care industry; in recent years, however, they have experienced spectacular growth in revenues. Between 2005 and 2007, for example, manufacturers' revenues from sales of vaccines in the United States more than doubled, from $2.8 to $6.1 billion, an average compounded annual growth rate of about 48 percent. With an average growth rate of only about 6 percent between 2001 and 2005, it appears that in terms of their commercial prospects, vaccines have reached and soared beyond the turning point.[1] There are now two blockbuster vaccines, with annual sales exceeding $1 billion—Wyeth's Prevnar for pneumococcal disease and Merck's Gardasil for prevention of cervical cancer in females. Were it not for manufacturing problems resulting in supply constraints in 2007, Merck's Varivax for prevention of chickenpox would likely have become the third vaccine in three years to attain blockbuster status.[2]

Preliminary estimates suggest very strong continued growth in revenues for vaccine manufacturers in coming years. Estimates from a national survey undertaken by the Centers for Disease Control and Prevention indicate that in 2007, the first full year following launch of Gardasil, about 25 percent of teenage girls had already received at least one dose of Gardasil, which is administered in a three-dose series. This was a very rapid initial uptake.[3] The same survey also showed big increases in usage rates of TDap vaccines Boostrix (GlaxoSmithKline) and Adacel (Sanofi Pasteur), which in 2005 were added to adolescent vaccine recommendations after health officials noticed an uptick in whooping cough cases among teenagers. The proportion of teens receiving Menactra for prevention of meningococcal disease also increased sharply between 2006 and 2007, from 11.7 to 32.4 percent.[4] Even though growth in the share of those eligible to receive Menactra was already substantial between 2006 and 2007, with two-thirds not yet receiving the vaccine, there is much potential for future growth in its usage. According to one report, Merck's expected 2008 revenues from its various vaccines are about $5 billion, consisting of about $2 billion for Gardasil and $3 billion for its other vaccines.[5]

Ongoing research and development by vaccine manufacturers may result in very substantial revenue growth, not just for new vaccines but also for new uses of vaccines already on the market. For example, Merck's Gardasil is currently approved by the FDA for girls and women ages nine to twenty-six, and the CDC recommends Gardasil for all girls ages eleven and twelve. Merck has reported that boys can directly benefit from the Gardasil vaccine, as well. The vaccine has been shown to protect against four types of the human papilloma virus. Two of these strains account for 70 percent of cervical cancer cases, while the other two account for 90 percent of genital warts, the latter of which affects both men and women.[6]

In men, the human papilloma virus can lead not only to genital warts, but also to anal and penile cancer. Gardasil is currently estimated to provide protection for five years.[7] Results of a study including 4,065 men ages sixteen to twenty-six who received three injections of Gardasil or a placebo over a six-month period revealed that participants who received Gardasil were 90 percent less likely to develop genital warts related to the four human papilloma viruses targeted by the vaccine.[8] While the study indicates that boys and men would directly benefit from vaccination with Gardasil, to the extent that males are carriers of the four strains of human papilloma virus that are transmitted sexually, vaccinating males could provide very significant indirect benefits to females in reducing their vulnerability to cervical cancer. This is yet another example of consumption externalities and the herd effect of vaccines, which could provide a very favorable marketing opportunity for Merck's Gardasil. According to one report, Merck plans to file an application soon asking the FDA to approve Gardasil for boys and men ages nine to twenty-six to prevent genital warts.[9]

GlaxoSmithKline, developer of a potentially competing vaccine to Gardasil that targets only two of the four human papilloma virus strains, is currently seeking FDA approval of Cervarix for the prevention of cervical cancer in women. Cervarix does not protect against genital warts in males. In an intriguing test of the herd immunity hypothesis, however, Glaxo-SmithKline is administering Cervarix to both boys and girls in a trial in Finland. Boys are being included in the trial to determine whether vaccinating them will help eradicate cervical cancer in girls and women.[10] If results of these and other trials document a statistically significant and clinically meaningful herd effect from vaccinating boys and men, the potential market for both Gardasil and Cervarix could be very large, indeed.

For growth in vaccine utilization to continue on a sustained basis, it will be critical that the public views vaccines as being safe, effective, and consistent with public health. As we noted in the previous chapter, much passionate controversy has occurred in the last decade concerning alleged causal links between vaccinations and the onset of autism in the pediatric population. Additional rulings by the various special masters in the U.S. Federal Court of Appeals are expected within the coming year, conceivably having important consequences for public confidence in and support of the Vaccines for Children program, as well as for the vaccine industry more generally. The panel of medical officials in the United Kingdom overseeing the hearings in which improper behavior by Dr. Andrew Wakefield is alleged will also be issuing important decisions in 2009, rulings that are likely to be widely discussed.

Turning to the impact of recent market and scientific developments on the incentives for vaccine manufacturers to invest in research and development, we believe a number of recent developments suggest that the future direction of the vaccine markets may differ considerably from the trends of the past. Among those we interviewed, a prominent theme was the very significant increase in research and development, not just to meet current needs for prophylactic vaccines targeted at preventing contagious diseases, but also for therapeutics for diseases such as cancer and cardiovascular, gastrointestinal, and immune system illnesses.[11] This expansion is in addition to the considerable recent R&D focus on bioterrorism agents and pandemics.

From the standpoint of public funding, issues of contagion, externalities, and herd effects for therapeutic vaccines and, perhaps, for some of the bioterrorism agents are quite different from those for existing vaccines that currently prevent infectious diseases. Specifically, if some of the future therapeutics do not involve any consumption externalities, then the rationale for public-sector support in the form of providing them free or heavily subsidizing them may no longer be present. Such considerations have led some vaccine policy analysts to recommend that, in the future, vaccine utilization be subsidized by public funds only to the extent that consumption externalities and herd effects generated by the vaccines can be documented.[12] As with other early-stage biological and basic medical research, however, public-sector support of early-stage vaccine R&D may still be warranted when it generates knowledge spillovers and beneficial scientific externalities that can be appropriated and developed further by other researchers. In such cases a market failure may exist, since the inability to prevent basic R&D knowledge spillovers implies that the private sector cannot fully appropriate them from their R&D, and therefore it faces insufficient incentive to invest in the basic R&D. Such a rationale has long provided the basis for public-sector support of basic research conducted through a competitive program managed by the National Institutes of Health.[13]

Externalities other than herd immunity and increases in basic knowledge may raise issues about the proper mix of public and private funding of vaccine R&D, though. For example, in the influenza case study we noted that recent research is focusing on a "universal" influenza vaccine that is effective for all strains of the flu virus and thus does not require annual updates and modifications. Also attractive is the cell-based manufacturing process that permits more rapid scale-up and the universality that warrants consideration of maintaining stocks of inventory in the event of pandemics.

Meanwhile, several other research teams are attempting to develop a "mega-shot" that provides protection against numerous diseases in a single injection. In this case, questions remain regarding the potential adverse interactions from such a combination product, which will also be subject to development and marketing controversies owing to diffused ownership of the underlying intellectual property.

Manufacturing procedures are also receiving considerable attention, particularly for technologies that would permit more rapid scale-up of production than available from current egg-based procedures. As was discussed in the influenza case study, consensus has not yet been achieved regarding the extent and speed with which mammalian cell-based technologies will, in fact, replace traditional egg-based technologies because of favorable scale-up properties. Further, it is possible that both of these will be leapfrogged by other technologies, such as recombinant DNA manufacturing methods.[14] Other recent research has focused on improved delivery systems, such as edible vaccines, needle-less approaches, and vaccines whose transport and storage does not require cold stability and/or lighting restrictions.

Although the current number of actual vaccine manufacturers in the United States is small, the recent acceleration of R&D efforts for new vaccines suggests that in the coming decade we may witness the launch not only of new companies, but of many new vaccines. Whether these new products will succumb to the same market, regulatory, and public-sector forces that heretofore have contributed to the pattern of dominance in many fragile vaccine markets, eventually resulting in only one or two suppliers, or whether we have now finally reached and gone beyond a turning point, remains to be seen.

Appendix A:
Organizations (and Number of Individuals) Interviewed, February–August 2007

Acambis Inc. (1)

American Academy of Pediatrics, Massachusetts Chapter (1)

Biotechnology Industry Organization (1)

Blue Cross Blue Shield of Massachusetts (1)

Boston Medical Center (1)

Centers for Disease Control and Prevention (6)

School of Public Health, Emory University (1)

GlaxoSmithKline (2)

Kennedy School of Government, Harvard University (1)

Merck & Co. Inc (6)

Novartis (5)

Sanofi Pasteur (5)

VaxInnate (2)

Wyeth (2)

    Total number of organizations interviewed: 14

    Total number of individuals interviewed: 35

Appendix B:
The Three Traditional Phases of Clinical Development for Vaccines: A Summary

Preapproval human clinical studies for vaccines are typically (but not always) divided into three phases. The first phase, following preclinical studies, generally involves twenty to eighty vaccinees, and focuses on patient safety and preliminary immunogenicity issues at various dosages. It usually begins with adults and then moves to groups likely to be the ultimate target population for the vaccine, such as young children.[1] If results of both the preclinical and phase I studies are promising, development continues on to phase II.

Phase II trials involve up to several hundred vaccinees, and typically take one of two forms. If preliminary safety and immunogenicity have been demonstrated in the phase I analyses, a larger phase IIa study can be undertaken to gain further information. At this point in the development process, the vaccine product must be defined, manufacturing processes must be determined, assays (such as laboratory studies) for release of a satisfactory product must be specified, and the most appropriate immunological assays for clinical specimens must be defined and agreed upon. Already at this stage considerable interactions are occurring among the vaccine developer, the U.S. Food and Drug Administration, public health authorities such as the Centers for Disease Control and Prevention, payers, and physician groups. Larger phase IIb trials can then be conducted to obtain more data on dose and dose interval and on the safety and immunogenicity among the subjects for whom the vaccine is likely to be targeted. In most cases, these trials are not large enough to establish precise measures of efficacy, and for that reason larger and more definitive trials are typically required.

If results from the phase II studies continue to be promising, demonstrating both safety and immunogenicity, development can proceed to the pivotal phase III studies required for FDA product license approval. The "gold standard" phase III trial is a large, randomized, double-blind, placebo-controlled trial, enrolling up to tens of thousands of individuals. Usually these trials assess efficacy by measuring the reduction in incidence of clinical disease among vaccine recipients, compared with placebo recipients, after an appropriate period of time. Many of these trials also attempt to determine an immunologic response, such as a serum antibody level, that correlates with protection from contracting the disease. A benefit of using such a surrogate marker of disease protection is that it allows subsequent studies to measure just the immune response, rather than protection from disease, thereby facilitating testing of the vaccine in various population subgroups in a more rapid and cost-effective manner. These phase III trials also allow for a methodologically rigorous evaluation of vaccine safety for common adverse events and side effects by comparing health status histories for vaccine and placebo recipients. If such events are very rare, however, they may not be identified and measured precisely, even when the trial has tens of thousands of participants.

Different types of phase III trials, called noninferiority or equivalence trials, are designed to compare a treatment group not to a placebo but instead to some other active treatment group. For example, to assess the efficacy of a new combination vaccine to prevent simultaneously the onset of, say, three distinct diseases, three separate trials may be necessary, each comparing the combination vaccine with a different noncombination (singleton) vaccine targeted to only one of the three diseases. Here the goal is to assess whether the combination vaccine is equivalent or not inferior to each of the singleton vaccines. Many variations on equivalence and noninferiority trials are possible, raising a variety of statistical and interpretive issues beyond the scope of this summary.[2]

Before either of these types of phase III trials can commence (and often before the phase IIb studies begin), technology must be transferred from a research laboratory making small lots of vaccine doses to the final site for manufacturing full-scale lots (ten thousand to twenty thousand doses or more) in a facility certified ("qualified") by the FDA to be in compliance with current good manufacturing practice regulations. This technology transfer, called "bridging our scale-up," includes extensive documentation of process and procedure, along with analytical details. To be able to market a vaccine in the United States, licensure of both the manufacturing establishment and of the product is required. The establishment license application and the PLA are reviewed by the Center for Biologics Evaluation and Research at the FDA.

Once approved by the FDA as safe and efficacious, a new vaccine also needs to obtain reimbursement approval to be commercially successful.[3] In the United States, this typically involves the CDC, the Advisory Committee on Immunization Practices, and private payers. Although much coordination with these agencies and payers occurs prior to gaining FDA approval, it is not uncommon for the time interval between FDA approval and vaccine product launch to take three to six months. In Europe this time period between approval as safe and efficacious by medical authorities and reimbursement approval by government payers is called the registration period; in these countries negotiations between vaccine manufacturers and government reimbursement authorities can be lengthier.

Finally, while industry traditionally has taken on most of the clinical development costs of vaccines in the United States, government entities such as the National Institutes of Health, the Veterans Administration, the CDC, and the Department of Defense, as well as academic centers and foundations, all play major roles in funding and/or carrying out a substantial portion of basic and preclinical research for vaccines.[4] In one recent case, religious organizations even played an important role, as Catholic nuns volunteered to participate in a trial involving a vaccine to prevent cervical cancer.[5] An increasingly common occurrence is that small biotech companies undertake some of the very early development steps, and then license to, merge with, or are acquired by established vaccine manufacturers.[6]

Appendix C:
Advisory Committee on Immunization Practices Recommended Immunization Schedules, 2009

Table AC-1

Recommended Immunization Schedule for Persons Aged 0 Through 6 Years—United States • 2009

For those who fall behind or start late, see the catch-up schedule

Vaccine ▼ Age ►	Birth	1 month	2 months	4 months	6 months	12 months	15 months	18 months	19–23 months	2–3 years	4–6 years
Hepatitis B[1]	HepB	HepB		see footnote 1	HepB						
Rotavirus[2]			RV	RV	RV[2]						
Diphtheria, Tetanus, Pertussis[3]			DTaP	DTaP	DTaP	see footnote 3	DTaP				DTaP
Haemophilus influenzae type b[4]			Hib	Hib	Hib[4]	Hib					
Pneumococcal[5]			PCV	PCV	PCV	PCV				PPSV	
Inactivated Poliovirus			IPV	IPV	IPV						IPV
Influenza[6]					Influenza (Yearly)						
Measles, Mumps, Rubella[7]						MMR			see footnote 7		MMR
Varicella[8]						Varicella			see footnote 8		Varicella
Hepatitis A[9]						HepA (2 doses)				HepA Series	
Meningococcal[10]										MCV	

Legend:
▢ Range of recommended ages
■ Certain high-risk groups

This schedule indicates the recommended ages for routine administration of currently licensed vaccines, as of December 1, 2008, for children aged 0 through 6 years. Any dose not administered at the recommended age should be administered at a subsequent visit, when indicated and feasible. Licensed combination vaccines may be used whenever any component of the combination is indicated and other components are not contraindicated and if approved by the Food and Drug Administration for that dose of the series. Providers should consult the relevant Advisory Committee on Immunization Practices statement for detailed recommendations, including high-risk conditions: http://www.cdc.gov/vaccines/pubs/acip-list.htm. Clinically significant adverse events that follow immunization should be reported to the Vaccine Adverse Event Reporting System (VAERS). Guidance about how to obtain and complete a VAERS form is available at http://www.vaers.hhs.gov or by telephone, 800-822-7967.

1. Hepatitis B vaccine (HepB). *(Minimum age: birth)*
At birth:
• Administer monovalent HepB to all newborns before hospital discharge.
• If mother is hepatitis B surface antigen (HBsAg)-positive, administer HepB and 0.5 mL of hepatitis B immune globulin (HBIG) within 12 hours of birth.

• Administer PPSV to children aged 2 years or older with certain underlying medical conditions (see *MMWR* 2000;49[No. RR-9]), including a cochlear implant.

6. Influenza vaccine. *(Minimum age: 6 months for trivalent inactivated influenza vaccine [TIV]; 2 years for live, attenuated influenza vaccine [LAIV])*

- If mother's HBsAg status is unknown, administer HepB within 12 hours of birth. Determine mother's HBsAg status as soon as possible and, if HBsAg-positive, administer HBIG (no later than age 1 week).

After the birth dose:

- The HepB series should be completed with either monovalent HepB or a combination vaccine containing HepB. The second dose should be administered at age 1 or 2 months. The final dose should be administered no earlier than age 24 weeks.
- Infants born to HBsAg-positive mothers should be tested for HBsAg and antibody to HBsAg (anti-HBs) after completion of at least 3 doses of the HepB series, at age 9 through 18 months (generally at the next well-child visit).

4-month dose:

- Administration of 4 doses of HepB to infants is permissible when combination vaccines containing HepB are administered after the birth dose.

2. Rotavirus vaccine (RV). *(Minimum age: 6 weeks)*

- Administer the first dose at age 6 through 14 weeks (maximum age: 14 weeks 6 days). Vaccination should not be initiated for infants aged 15 weeks or older (i.e., 15 weeks 0 days or older).
- Administer the final dose in the series by age 8 months 0 days.
- If Rotarix® is administered at ages 2 and 4 months, a dose at 6 months is not indicated.

3. Diphtheria and tetanus toxoids and acellular pertussis vaccine (DTaP). *(Minimum age: 6 weeks)*

- The fourth dose may be administered as early as age 12 months, provided at least 6 months have elapsed since the third dose.
- Administer the final dose in the series at age 4 through 6 years.

4. *Haemophilus influenzae* type b conjugate vaccine (Hib). *(Minimum age: 6 weeks)*

- If PRP-OMP (PedvaxHIB® or Comvax® [HepB-Hib]) is administered at ages 2 and 4 months, a dose at age 6 months is not indicated.
- TriHiBit® (DTaP/Hib) should not be used for doses at ages 2, 4, or 6 months but can be used as the final dose in children aged 12 months or older.

5. Pneumococcal vaccine. *(Minimum age: 6 weeks for pneumococcal conjugate vaccine [PCV]; 2 years for pneumococcal polysaccharide vaccine [PPSV])*

- PCV is recommended for all children aged younger than 5 years. Administer 1 dose of PCV to all healthy children aged 24 through 59 months who are not completely vaccinated for their age.

- Administer annually to children aged 6 months through 18 years.
- For healthy nonpregnant persons (i.e., those who do not have underlying medical conditions that predispose them to influenza complications) aged 2 through 49 years, either LAIV or TIV may be used.
- Children receiving TIV should receive 0.25 mL if aged 6 through 35 months or 0.5 mL if aged 3 years or older.
- Administer 2 doses (separated by at least 4 weeks) to children aged younger than 9 years who are receiving influenza vaccine for the first time or who were vaccinated for the first time during the previous influenza season but only received 1 dose.

7. Measles, mumps, and rubella vaccine (MMR). *(Minimum age: 12 months)*

- Administer the second dose at age 4 through 6 years. However, the second dose may be administered before age 4, provided at least 28 days have elapsed since the first dose.

8. Varicella vaccine. *(Minimum age: 12 months)*

- Administer the second dose at age 4 through 6 years. However, the second dose may be administered before age 4, provided at least 3 months have elapsed since the first dose.
- For children aged 12 months through 12 years the minimum interval between doses is 3 months. However, if the second dose was administered at least 28 days after the first dose, it can be accepted as valid.

9. Hepatitis A vaccine (HepA). *(Minimum age: 12 months)*

- Administer to all children aged 1 year (i.e., aged 12 through 23 months). Administer 2 doses at least 6 months apart.
- Children not fully vaccinated by age 2 years can be vaccinated at subsequent visits.
- HepA also is recommended for children older than 1 year who live in areas where vaccination programs target older children or who are at increased risk of infection. See *MMWR* 2006;55(No. RR-7).

10. Meningococcal vaccine. *(Minimum age: 2 years for meningococcal conjugate vaccine [MCV] and for meningococcal polysaccharide vaccine [MPSV])*

- Administer MCV to children aged 2 through 10 years with terminal complement component deficiency, anatomic or functional asplenia, and certain other high-risk groups. See *MMWR* 2005;54(No. RR-7).
- Persons who received MPSV 3 or more years previously and who remain at increased risk for meningococcal disease should be revaccinated with MCV.

The Recommended Immunization Schedules for Persons Aged 0 Through 18 Years are approved by the Advisory Committee on Immunization Practices (www.cdc.gov/vaccines/recs/acip), the American Academy of Pediatrics (http://www.aap.org), and the American Academy of Family Physicians (http://www.aafp.org).

DEPARTMENT OF HEALTH AND HUMAN SERVICES • CENTERS FOR DISEASE CONTROL AND PREVENTION

SOURCE: http://www.cdc.gov/vaccines/recs/schedules/downloads/child/2009/09_0-6yrs_schedule_pss.pdf (accessed February 1, 2009).

Table AC-2

Recommended Immunization Schedule for Persons Aged 7 Through 18 Years—United States • 2009

For those who fall behind or start late, see the schedule below and the catch-up schedule

Vaccine ▼ Age ▶	7–10 years	11–12 years	13–18 years
Tetanus, Diphtheria, Pertussis[1]	see footnote 1	Tdap	Tdap
Human Papillomavirus[2]	see footnote 2	HPV (3 doses)	HPV Series
Meningococcal[3]	MCV	MCV	MCV
Influenza[4]	Influenza (Yearly)		
Pneumococcal[5]	PPSV		
Hepatitis A[6]	HepA Series		
Hepatitis B[7]	HepB Series		
Inactivated Poliovirus[8]	IPV Series		
Measles, Mumps, Rubella[9]	MMR Series		
Varicella[10]	Varicella Series		

Legend:
- Range of recommended ages
- Catch-up immunization
- Certain high-risk groups

This schedule indicates the recommended ages for routine administration of currently licensed vaccines, as of December 1, 2008, for children aged 7 through 18 years. Any dose not administered at the recommended age should be administered at a subsequent visit, when indicated and feasible. Licensed combination vaccines may be used whenever any component of the combination is indicated and other components are not contraindicated and if approved by the Food and Drug Administration for that dose of the series. Providers should consult the relevant Advisory Committee on Immunization Practices statement for detailed recommendations, including high-risk conditions: http://www.cdc.gov/vaccines/pubs/acip-list.htm. Clinically significant adverse events that follow immunization should be reported to the Vaccine Adverse Event Reporting System (VAERS). Guidance about how to obtain and complete a VAERS form is available at http://www.vaers.hhs.gov or by telephone, 800-822-7967.

1. Tetanus and diphtheria toxoids and acellular pertussis vaccine (Tdap). *(Minimum age: 10 years for BOOSTRIX® and 11 years for ADACEL®)*
- Administer at age 11 or 12 years for those who have completed the recommended childhood DTP/DTaP vaccination series and have not received a tetanus and diphtheria toxoid (Td) booster dose.
- Persons aged 13 through 18 years who have not received Tdap should receive a dose.
- A 5-year interval from the last Td dose is encouraged when Tdap is used as a booster dose; however, a shorter interval may be used if pertussis immunity is needed.

2. Human papillomavirus vaccine (HPV). *(Minimum age: 9 years)*
- Administer the first dose to females at age 11 or 12 years.
- Administer the second dose 2 months after the first dose and the third dose 6 months after the first dose (at least 24 weeks after the first dose).
- Administer the series to females at age 13 through 18 years if not previously vaccinated.

3. Meningococcal conjugate vaccine (MCV).
- Administer at age 11 or 12 years, or at age 13 through 18 years if not previously vaccinated.
- Administer to previously unvaccinated college freshmen living in a dormitory.
- MCV is recommended for children aged 2 through 10 years with terminal complement component deficiency, anatomic or functional asplenia, and certain other groups at high risk. See *MMWR* 2005;54(No. RR-7).
- Persons who received MPSV 5 or more years previously and remain at increased risk for meningococcal disease should be revaccinated with MCV.

4. Influenza vaccine.
- Administer annually to children aged 6 months through 18 years.
- For healthy nonpregnant persons (i.e., those who do not have underlying medical conditions that predispose them to influenza complications) aged 2 through 49 years, either LAIV or TIV may be used.
- Administer 2 doses (separated by at least 4 weeks) to children aged younger than 9 years who are receiving influenza vaccine for the first time or who were vaccinated for the first time during the previous influenza season but only received 1 dose.

5. Pneumococcal polysaccharide vaccine (PPSV).
- Administer to children with certain underlying medical conditions (see *MMWR* 1997;46[No. RR-8]), including a cochlear implant. A single revaccination should be administered to children with functional or anatomic asplenia or other immunocompromising condition after 5 years.

6. Hepatitis A vaccine (HepA).
- Administer 2 doses at least 6 months apart.
- HepA is recommended for children older than 1 year who live in areas where vaccination programs target older children or who are at increased risk of infection. See *MMWR* 2006;55(No. RR-7).

7. Hepatitis B vaccine (HepB).
- Administer the 3-dose series to those not previously vaccinated.
- A 2-dose series (separated by at least 4 months) of adult formulation Recombivax HB® is licensed for children aged 11 through 15 years.

8. Inactivated poliovirus vaccine (IPV).
- For children who received an all-IPV or all-oral poliovirus (OPV) series, a fourth dose is not necessary if the third dose was administered at age 4 years or older.
- If both OPV and IPV were administered as part of a series, a total of 4 doses should be administered, regardless of the child's current age.

9. Measles, mumps, and rubella vaccine (MMR).
- If not previously vaccinated, administer 2 doses or the second dose for those who have received only 1 dose, with at least 28 days between doses.

10. Varicella vaccine.
- For persons aged 7 through 18 years without evidence of immunity (see *MMWR* 2007;56[No. RR-4]), administer 2 doses if not previously vaccinated or the second dose if they have received only 1 dose.
- For persons aged 7 through 12 years, the minimum interval between doses is 3 months. However, if the second dose was administered at least 28 days after the first dose, it can be accepted as valid.
- For persons aged 13 years and older, the minimum interval between doses is 28 days.

The Recommended Immunization Schedules for Persons Aged 0 Through 18 Years are approved by the Advisory Committee on Immunization Practices (www.cdc.gov/vaccines/recs/acip), the American Academy of Pediatrics (http://www.aap.org), and the American Academy of Family Physicians (http://www.aafp.org).
DEPARTMENT OF HEALTH AND HUMAN SERVICES • CENTERS FOR DISEASE CONTROL AND PREVENTION

Table AC-3

Catch-up Immunization Schedule for Persons Aged 4 Months Through 18 Years Who Start Late or Who Are More Than 1 Month Behind—United States • 2009

The table below provides catch-up schedules and minimum intervals between doses for children whose vaccinations have been delayed. A vaccine series does not need to be restarted, regardless of the time that has elapsed between doses. Use the section appropriate for the child's age.

Vaccine	Minimum Age for Dose 1	Minimum Interval Between Doses			
		Dose 1 to Dose 2	Dose 2 to Dose 3	Dose 3 to Dose 4	Dose 4 to Dose 5
CATCH-UP SCHEDULE FOR PERSONS AGED 4 MONTHS THROUGH 6 YEARS					
Hepatitis B[1]	Birth	**4 weeks**	**8 weeks** (and at least 16 weeks after first dose)		
Rotavirus[2]	6 wks	**4 weeks**	**4 weeks**[2]		
Diphtheria, Tetanus, Pertussis[3]	6 wks	**4 weeks**	**4 weeks**	**6 months**	**6 months**[3]
Haemophilus influenzae type b[4]	6 wks	**4 weeks** if first dose administered at younger than age 12 months / **8 weeks (as final dose)** if first dose administered at age 12-14 months / **No further doses needed** if first dose administered at age 15 months or older	**4 weeks**[4] if current age is younger than 12 months / **8 weeks (as final dose)**[4] if current age is 12 months or older and second dose administered at younger than age 15 months / **No further doses needed** if previous dose administered at age 15 months or older	**8 weeks (as final dose)** This dose only necessary for children aged 12 months through 59 months who received 3 doses before age 12 months	
Pneumococcal[5]	6 wks	**4 weeks** if first dose administered at younger than age 12 months / **8 weeks (as final dose for healthy children)** if first dose administered at age 12 months or older or current age 24 through 59 months / **No further doses needed** for healthy children if first dose administered at age 24 months or older	**4 weeks** if current age is younger than 12 months / **8 weeks (as final dose for healthy children)** if current age is 12 months or older / **No further doses needed** for healthy children if previous dose administered at age 24 months or older	**8 weeks (as final dose)** This dose only necessary for children aged 12 months through 59 months who received 3 doses before age 12 months or for high-risk children who received 3 doses at any age	
Inactivated Poliovirus[6]	6 wks	**4 weeks**	**4 weeks**	**4 weeks**[6]	
Measles, Mumps, Rubella[7]	12 mos	**4 weeks**			
Varicella[8]	12 mos	**3 months**			
Hepatitis A[9]	12 mos	**6 months**			
CATCH-UP SCHEDULE FOR PERSONS AGED 7 THROUGH 18 YEARS					
Tetanus, Diphtheria/ Tetanus, Diphtheria, Pertussis[10]	7 yrs[10]	**4 weeks**	**4 weeks** if first dose administered at younger than age 12 months / **6 months** if first dose administered at age 12 months or older	**6 months** if first dose administered at younger than age 12 months	

CS113897

		Routine dosing intervals are recommended[11]		
Human Papillomavirus[11]	9 yrs			
Hepatitis A[9]	12 months			
Hepatitis B[1]	Birth	6 months	8 weeks (and at least 16 weeks after first dose)	4 weeks[6]
Inactivated Poliovirus[6]	6 wks	4 weeks	4 weeks	
Measles, Mumps, Rubella[7]	12 mos	4 weeks		
Varicella[8]	12 mos	3 months if the person is younger than age 13 years		
		4 weeks if the person is aged 13 years or older		

1. **Hepatitis B vaccine (HepB).**
 • Administer the 3-dose series to those not previously vaccinated.
 • A 2-dose series (separated by at least 4 months) of adult formulation Recombivax HB® is licensed for children aged 11 through 15 years.

2. **Rotavirus vaccine (RV).**
 • The maximum age for the first dose is 14 weeks 6 days. Vaccination should not be initiated for infants aged 15 weeks or older (i.e., 15 weeks 0 days or older).
 • Administer the final dose in the series by age 8 months 0 days.
 • If Rotarix® was administered for the first and second doses, a third dose is not indicated.

3. **Diphtheria and tetanus toxoids and acellular pertussis vaccine (DTaP).**
 • The fifth dose is not necessary if the fourth dose was administered at age 4 years or older.

4. **Haemophilus influenzae type b conjugate vaccine (Hib).**
 • Hib vaccine is not generally recommended for persons aged 5 years or older. No efficacy data are available on which to base a recommendation concerning use of Hib vaccine for older children and adults. However, studies suggest good immunogenicity in persons who have sickle cell disease, leukemia, or HIV infection, or who have had a splenectomy; administering 1 dose of Hib vaccine to these persons is not contraindicated.
 • If the first 2 doses were PRP-OMP (PedvaxHIB® or Comvax®), and administered at age 11 months or younger, the third (and final) dose should be administered at age 12 through 15 months and at least 8 weeks after the second dose.
 • If the first dose was administered at age 7 through 11 months, administer 2 doses separated by 4 weeks and a final dose at age 12 through 15 months.

5. **Pneumococcal vaccine.**
 • Administer 1 dose of pneumococcal conjugate vaccine (PCV) to all healthy children aged 24 through 59 months who have not received at least 1 dose of PCV on or after age 12 months.
 • For children aged 24 through 59 months with underlying medical conditions, administer 1 dose of PCV if 3 doses were received previously or administer 2 doses of PCV at least 8 weeks apart if fewer than 3 doses were received previously.
 • Administer pneumococcal polysaccharide vaccine (PPSV) to children aged 2 years or older with certain underlying medical conditions (see MMWR 2000;49[No. RR-9]), including a cochlear implant, at least 8 weeks after the last dose of PCV.

6. **Inactivated poliovirus vaccine (IPV).**
 • For children who received an all-IPV or all-oral poliovirus (OPV) series, a fourth dose is not necessary if the third dose was administered at age 4 years or older.
 • If both OPV and IPV were administered as part of a series, a total of 4 doses should be administered, regardless of the child's current age.

7. **Measles, mumps, and rubella vaccine (MMR).**
 • Administer the second dose at age 4 through 6 years. However, the second dose may be administered before age 4, provided at least 28 days have elapsed since the first dose.
 • If not previously vaccinated, administer 2 doses with at least 28 days between doses.

8. **Varicella vaccine.**
 • Administer the second dose at age 4 through 6 years. However, the second dose may be administered before age 4, provided at least 3 months have elapsed since the first dose.
 • For persons aged 12 months through 12 years, the minimum interval between doses is 3 months. However, if the second dose was administered at least 28 days after the first dose, it can be accepted as valid.
 • For persons aged 13 years and older, the minimum interval between doses is 28 days.

9. **Hepatitis A vaccine (HepA).**
 • HepA is recommended for children older than 1 year who live in areas where vaccination programs target older children or who are at increased risk of infection. See MMWR 2006;55(No. RR-7).

10. **Tetanus and diphtheria toxoids vaccine (Td) and tetanus and diphtheria toxoids and acellular pertussis vaccine (Tdap).**
 • Doses of DTaP are counted as part of the Td/Tdap series
 • Tdap should be substituted for a single dose of Td in the catch-up series or as a booster for children aged 10 through 18 years; use Td for other doses.

11. **Human papillomavirus vaccine (HPV).**
 • Administer the series to females aged 13 through 18 years if not previously vaccinated.
 • Use recommended routine dosing intervals for series catch-up (i.e., the second and third doses should be administered at 2 and 6 months after the first dose). However, the minimum interval between the first and second doses is 4 weeks. The minimum interval between the second and third doses is 12 weeks, and the third dose should be given at least 24 weeks after the first dose.

Information about reporting reactions after immunization is available online at http://www.vaers.hhs.gov or by telephone, 800-822-7967. Suspected cases of vaccine-preventable diseases should be reported to the state or local health department. Additional information, including precautions and contraindications for immunization, is available from the National Center for Immunization and Respiratory Diseases at http://www.cdc.gov/vaccines or telephone, 800-CDC-INFO (800-232-4636).

DEPARTMENT OF HEALTH AND HUMAN SERVICES • CENTERS FOR DISEASE CONTROL AND PREVENTION

SOURCE: http://www.cdc.gov/vaccines/recs/schedules/downloads/child/2008_08_catch-up_schedule_pr.pdf (accessed February 1, 2009).

Table AC-4

Recommended Adult Immunization Schedule
UNITED STATES · 2009

Note: These recommendations *must* be read with the footnotes that follow
containing number of doses, intervals between doses, and other important information.

Figure 1. Recommended adult immunization schedule, by vaccine and age group

VACCINE ▼	AGE GROUP ▶	19–26 years	27–49 years	50–59 years	60–64 years	≥65 years
Tetanus, diphtheria, pertussis (Td/Tdap)[1],*		Substitute 1-time dose of Tdap for Td booster; then boost with Td every 10 yr				Td booster every 10 yrs
Human papillomavirus (HPV)[2],*		3 doses (females)				
Varicella[3],*		2 doses				
Zoster[4]					1 dose	
Measles, mumps, rubella (MMR)[5],*		1 or 2 doses			1 dose	
Influenza[6],*		1 dose annually				
Pneumococcal (polysaccharide)[7,8]		1 or 2 doses				1 dose
Hepatitis A[9],*		2 doses				
Hepatitis B[10],*		3 doses				
Meningococcal[11],*		1 or more doses				

*Covered by the Vaccine Injury Compensation Program.

For all persons in this category who meet the age requirements and who lack evidence of immunity (e.g., lack documentation of vaccination or have no evidence of prior infection)

Recommended if some other risk factor is present (e.g., on the basis of medical, occupational, lifestyle, or other indications)

No recommendation

Report all clinically significant postvaccination reactions to the Vaccine Adverse Event Reporting System (VAERS). Reporting forms and instructions on filing a VAERS report are available at www.vaers.hhs.gov or by telephone, 800-822-7967.

Information on how to file a Vaccine Injury Compensation Program claim is available at www.hrsa.gov/vaccinecompensation or by telephone, 800-338-2382. To file a claim for vaccine injury, contact the U.S. Court of Federal Claims, 717 Madison Place, N.W., Washington, D.C. 20005; telephone, 202-357-6400.

Additional information about the vaccines in this schedule, extent of available data, and contraindications for vaccination is also available at www.cdc.gov/vaccines or from the CDC-INFO Contact Center at 800-CDC-INFO (800-232-4636) in English and Spanish, 24 hours a day, 7 days a week.

Use of trade names and commercial sources is for identification only and does not imply endorsement by the U.S. Department of Health and Human Services.

Figure 2. Vaccines that might be indicated for adults based on medical and other indications

INDICATION ▶ / VACCINE ▼	Pregnancy	Immuno-compromising conditions (excluding human immunodeficiency virus [HIV])[13]	HIV infection[12,13] CD4+ T lymphocyte count <200 cells/μL	HIV infection[12,13] CD4+ T lymphocyte count ≥200 cells/μL	Diabetes, heart disease, chronic lung disease, chronic alcoholism	Asplenia[12] (including elective splenectomy and terminal complement component deficiencies)	Chronic liver disease	Kidney failure, end-stage renal disease, receipt of hemodialysis	Health-care personnel
Tetanus, diphtheria, pertussis (Td/Tdap)[1],*	Td	Substitute 1-time dose of Tdap for Td booster; then boost with Td every 10 yrs							
Human papillomavirus(HPV)[2],*		3 doses for females through age 26 yrs							
Varicella[3],*	Contraindicated	Contraindicated			2 doses				
Zoster[4]	Contraindicated	Contraindicated			1 dose				
Measles, mumps, rubella (MMR)[5],*	Contraindicated	Contraindicated			1 or 2 doses				
Influenza[6],*	1 dose TIV annually								1 dose TIV or LAIV annually
Pneumococcal (polysaccharide)[7,8]		1 or 2 doses							
Hepatitis A[9],*		2 doses							
Hepatitis B[10],*		3 doses							
Meningococcal[11],*		1 or more doses							

* Covered by the Vaccine Injury Compensation Program.

For all persons in this category who meet the age requirements and who lack evidence of immunity (e.g., lack documentation of vaccination or have no evidence of prior infection)

Recommended if some other risk factor is present (e.g., on the basis of medical, occupational, lifestyle, or other indications)

No recommendation

These schedules indicate the recommended age groups and medical indications for which administration of currently licensed vaccines is commonly indicated for adults ages 19 years and older, as of January 1, 2009. Licensed combination vaccines may be used whenever any components of the combination are indicated and when the vaccine's other components are not contraindicated. For detailed recommendations on all vaccines, including those used primarily for travelers or that are issued during the year, consult the manufacturers' package inserts and the complete statements from the Advisory Committee on Immunization Practices (www.cdc.gov/vaccines/pubs/acip-list.htm).

The recommendations in this schedule were approved by the Centers for Disease Control and Prevention's (CDC) Advisory Committee on Immunization Practices (ACIP), the American Academy of Family Physicians (AAFP), the American College of Obstetricians and Gynecologists (ACOG), and the American College of Physicians (ACP).

DEPARTMENT OF HEALTH AND HUMAN SERVICES
CENTERS FOR DISEASE CONTROL AND PREVENTION

CS122051

(continued on the next page)

Table AC-4 (continued)

Footnotes

Recommended Adult Immunization Schedule—UNITED STATES · 2009

For complete statements by the Advisory Committee on Immunization Practices (ACIP), visit www.cdc.gov/vaccines/pubs/ACIP-list.htm.

1. Tetanus, diphtheria, and acellular pertussis (Td/Tdap) vaccination

Tdap should replace a single dose of Td for adults aged 19 through 64 years who have not received a dose of Tdap previously.

Adults with uncertain or incomplete history of primary vaccination series with tetanus and diphtheria toxoid-containing vaccines should begin or complete a primary vaccination series. A primary series for adults is 3 doses of tetanus and diphtheria toxoid-containing vaccines; administer the first 2 doses at least 4 weeks apart and the third dose 6–12 months after the second. However, Tdap can substitute for any one of the doses of Td in the 3-dose primary series. The booster dose of tetanus and diphtheria toxoid-containing vaccine should be administered to adults who have completed a primary series and if the last vaccination was received 10 or more years previously. Tdap or Td vaccine may be used, as indicated.

If a woman is pregnant and received the last Td vaccination 10 or more years previously, administer Td during the second or third trimester. If the woman received the last Td vaccination less than 10 years previously, administer Tdap during the immediate postpartum period. A dose of Tdap is recommended for postpartum women, close contacts of infants aged less than 12 months, and all health-care personnel with direct patient contact if they have not previously received Tdap. An interval as short as 2 years from the last Td is suggested; shorter intervals can be used. Td may be deferred during pregnancy and Tdap substituted in the immediate postpartum period, or Tdap may be administered instead of Td to a pregnant woman after an informed discussion with the woman.

Consult the ACIP statement for recommendations for administering Td as prophylaxis in wound management.

2. Human papillomavirus (HPV) vaccination

HPV vaccination is recommended for all females aged 11 through 26 years (and may begin at 9 years) who have not completed the vaccine series. History of genital warts, abnormal Papanicolaou test, or positive HPV DNA test is not evidence of prior infection with all vaccine HPV types; HPV vaccination is recommended for persons with such histories.

Ideally, vaccine should be administered before potential exposure to HPV through sexual activity; however, females who are sexually active should still be vaccinated consistent with age-based recommendations. Sexually active females who have not been infected with any of the four HPV vaccine types receive the full benefit of the vaccination. Vaccination is less beneficial for females who have already been infected with one or more of the HPV vaccine types.

A complete series consists of 3 doses. The second dose should be administered 2 months after the first dose; the third dose should be administered 6 months after the first dose.

HPV vaccination is not specifically recommended for females with the medical indications described in Figure 2. "Vaccines that might be indicated for adults based on medical and other indications." Because HPV vaccine is not a live-virus vaccine, it may be administered to persons with the medical indications described in Figure 2. However, the immune response and vaccine efficacy might be less for persons with the medical indications described in Figure 2 than in persons who do not have the medical indications described or who are immunocompetent. Health-care personnel are not at increased risk because of occupational exposure, and should be vaccinated consistent with age-based recommendations.

3. Varicella vaccination

All adults without evidence of immunity to varicella should receive 2 doses of single-antigen varicella vaccine if not previously vaccinated or the second dose if they have received only one dose unless they have a medical contraindication. Special consideration should be given to those who 1) have close contact with persons at high risk for severe disease (e.g., health-care personnel and family contacts

disease among persons with asplenia; however, influenza is a risk factor for secondary bacterial infections that can cause severe disease among persons with asplenia.

Occupational indications: All health-care personnel, including those employed by long-term care and assisted-living facilities, and caregivers of children less than 5 years old.

Other indications: Residents of nursing homes and other long-term care and assisted-living facilities; persons likely to transmit influenza to persons at high risk (e.g., in-home household contacts and caregivers of children aged less than 5 years old, persons 65 years old and older and persons of all ages with high-risk condition[s]); and anyone who would like to decrease their risk of getting influenza. Healthy, nonpregnant adults aged less than 50 years without high-risk medical conditions who are not contacts of severely immunocompromised persons in special care units can receive either intranasally administered live, attenuated influenza vaccine (FluMist®) or inactivated vaccine. Other persons should receive the inactivated vaccine.

7. Pneumococcal polysaccharide (PPSV) vaccination

Medical indications: Chronic lung disease (including asthma); chronic cardiovascular diseases; diabetes mellitus; chronic liver diseases, cirrhosis; chronic alcoholism; chronic renal failure or nephrotic syndrome; functional or anatomic asplenia (e.g., sickle cell disease or splenectomy [if elective splenectomy is planned, vaccinate at least 2 weeks before surgery]); immunocompromising conditions; and cochlear implants and cerebrospinal fluid leaks. Vaccinate as close to HIV diagnosis as possible.

Other indications: Residents of nursing homes or long-term care facilities and persons who smoke cigarettes. Routine use of PPSV is not recommended for Alaska Native or American Indian persons younger than 65 years unless they have underlying medical conditions that are PPSV indications. However, public health authorities may consider recommending PPSV for Alaska Natives and American Indians aged 50 through 64 years who are living in areas in which the risk of invasive pneumococcal disease is increased.

8. Revaccination with PPSV

One-time revaccination after 5 years for persons with chronic renal failure or nephrotic syndrome; functional or anatomic asplenia (e.g., sickle cell disease or splenectomy); and for persons with immunocompromising conditions. For persons aged 65 years and older, one-time revaccination if they were vaccinated 5 or more years previously and were aged less than 65 years at the time of primary vaccination.

9. Hepatitis A vaccination

Medical indications: Persons with chronic liver disease and persons who receive clotting factor concentrates.

Behavioral indications: Men who have sex with men and persons who use illegal drugs.

Occupational indications: Persons working with hepatitis A virus (HAV)-infected primates or with HAV in a research laboratory setting.

Other indications: Persons traveling to or working in countries that have high or intermediate endemicity of hepatitis A (a list of countries is available at www.cdc.gov/travel/contentdiseases.aspx) and any person seeking protection from HAV infection.

Single-antigen vaccine formulations should be administered in a 2-dose schedule at either 0 and 6 months (Havrix®), or 0 and 6 through 18 months (Vaqta®). If the combined hepatitis A and hepatitis B vaccine (Twinrix®) is used, administer 3 doses at 0, 1, and 6 months; alternatively, a 4-dose schedule, administered on days 0, 7 and 21 to 30 followed by a booster dose at month 12 may be used.

of persons with immunocompromising conditions) or 2) are at high risk for exposure or transmission (e.g., teachers; child care employees; residents and staff members of institutional settings, including correctional institutions; college students; military personnel; adolescents and adults living in households with children; nonpregnant women of childbearing age; and international travelers).

Evidence of immunity to varicella in adults includes any of the following: 1) documentation of 2 doses of varicella vaccine at least 4 weeks apart; 2) U.S.-born before 1980 (although for health-care personnel and pregnant women birth before 1980 should not be considered evidence of immunity); 3) history of varicella based on diagnosis or verification of varicella by a health-care provider (for a patient reporting a history of or presenting with an atypical case, a mild case, or both, health-care providers should seek either an epidemiologic link with a typical varicella case or to a laboratory-confirmed case or evidence of laboratory confirmation, if it was performed at the time of acute disease); 4) history of herpes zoster based on health-care provider diagnosis or verification of herpes zoster by a health-care provider; or 5) laboratory evidence of immunity or laboratory confirmation of disease.

Pregnant women should be assessed for evidence of varicella immunity. Women who do not have evidence of immunity should receive the first dose of varicella vaccine upon completion or termination of pregnancy and before discharge from the health-care facility. The second dose should be administered 4 through 8 weeks after the first dose.

4. Herpes zoster vaccination

A single dose of zoster vaccine is recommended for adults aged 60 years and older regardless of whether they report a prior episode of herpes zoster. Persons with chronic medical conditions may be vaccinated unless their condition constitutes a contraindication.

5. Measles, mumps, rubella (MMR) vaccination

Measles component: Adults born before 1957 generally are considered immune to measles. Adults born during or after 1957 should receive 1 or more doses of MMR unless they have a medical contraindication, documentation of 1 or more doses, history of measles based on health-care provider diagnosis, or laboratory evidence of immunity.

A second dose of MMR is recommended for adults who 1) have been recently exposed to measles or are in an outbreak setting; 2) have been vaccinated previously with killed measles vaccine; 3) have been vaccinated with an unknown type of measles vaccine during 1963 through 1967; 4) are students in postsecondary educational institutions; 5) work in a health-care facility; or 6) plan to travel internationally. Adults born during or after 1957 should receive 1 dose of MMR unless they have a medical contraindication, history of mumps based on health-care provider diagnosis, or laboratory evidence of immunity.

Mumps component: Adults born before 1957 generally are considered immune to mumps. Adults born during or after 1957 should receive 1 dose of MMR unless they have a medical contraindication, history of mumps based on health-care provider diagnosis, or laboratory evidence of immunity.

A second dose of MMR is recommended for adults who 1) live in a community experiencing a mumps outbreak and are in an affected age group; 2) are students in postsecondary educational institutions; 3) work in a health-care facility; or 4) plan to travel internationally. For unvaccinated health-care personnel born before 1957 who do not have other evidence of mumps immunity, administering 1 dose on a routine basis should be considered and administering a second dose during an outbreak should be strongly considered.

Rubella component: 1 dose of MMR vaccine is recommended for women whose rubella vaccination history is unreliable or who lack laboratory evidence of immunity. For women of childbearing age, regardless of birth year, rubella immunity should be determined and women should be counseled regarding congenital rubella syndrome. Women who do not have evidence of immunity should receive MMR upon completion or termination of pregnancy and before discharge from the health-care facility.

6. Influenza vaccination

Medical indications: Chronic disorders of the cardiovascular or pulmonary systems, including asthma; chronic metabolic diseases, including diabetes mellitus, renal or hepatic dysfunction, hemoglobinopathies, or immunocompromising conditions (including immunocompromising conditions caused by medications or human immunodeficiency virus [HIV]); any condition that compromises respiratory function or the handling of respiratory secretions or that can increase the risk of aspiration (e.g., cognitive dysfunction, spinal cord injury, or seizure disorder or other neuromuscular disorder); and pregnancy during the influenza season. No data exist on the risk for severe or complicated influenza

10. Hepatitis B vaccination

Medical indications: Persons with end-stage renal disease, including patients receiving hemodialysis; persons with HIV infection; and persons with chronic liver disease.

Occupational indications: Health-care personnel and public-safety workers who are exposed to blood or other potentially infectious body fluids.

Behavioral indications: Sexually active persons who are not in a long-term, mutually monogamous relationship (e.g., persons with more than 1 sex partner during the previous 6 months); persons seeking evaluation or treatment for a sexually transmitted disease; current or recent injection-drug users; and men who have sex with men.

Other indications: Household contacts and sex partners of persons with chronic hepatitis B virus (HBV) infection; clients and staff members of institutions for persons with developmental disabilities; international travelers to countries with high or intermediate prevalence of chronic HBV infection (a list of countries is available at www.cdc.gov/travel/contentdiseases.aspx); and any adult seeking protection from HBV infection.

Hepatitis B vaccination is recommended for all adults in the following settings: STD treatment facilities; HIV testing and treatment facilities; facilities providing drug-abuse treatment and prevention services; health-care settings targeting services to injection-drug users or men who have sex with men; correctional facilities; end-stage renal disease programs and facilities for chronic hemodialysis patients; and institutions and nonresidential daycare facilities for persons with developmental disabilities.

If the combined hepatitis A and hepatitis B vaccine (Twinrix®) is used, administer 3 doses at 0, 1, and 6 months; alternatively, a 4-dose schedule, administered on days 0, 7 and 21 to 30 followed by a booster dose at month 12 may be used.

Special formulation indications: For adult patients receiving hemodialysis or with other immunocompromising conditions, 1 dose of 40 μg/mL (Recombivax HB®) administered in a 3-dose schedule or 2 doses of 20 μg/mL (Engerix-B®) administered simultaneously on a 4-dose schedule at 0, 1, 2 and 6 months.

11. Meningococcal vaccination

Medical indications: Adults with anatomic or functional asplenia, or complement component deficiencies.

Other indications: First-year college students living in dormitories; microbiologists who are routinely exposed to isolates of Neisseria meningitidis; military recruits; and persons who travel to or live in countries in which meningococcal disease is hyperendemic or epidemic (e.g., the "meningitis belt" of sub-Saharan Africa during the dry season [December–June]), particularly if their contact with local populations will be prolonged. Vaccination is required by the government of Saudi Arabia for all travelers to Mecca during the annual Hajj.

Meningococcal conjugate (MCV) vaccine is preferred for adults with any of the preceding indications who are aged 55 years or younger, although meningococcal polysaccharide vaccine (MPSV) is an acceptable alternative. Revaccination with MCV after 5 years might be indicated for adults previously vaccinated with MPSV who remain at increased risk for infection (e.g., persons residing in areas in which disease is epidemic).

12. Selected conditions for which *Haemophilus influenzae* type b (Hib) vaccine may be used

Hib vaccine generally is not recommended for persons aged 5 years and older. No efficacy data are available on which to base a recommendation concerning use of Hib vaccine for older children and adults. However, studies suggest good immunogenicity in persons who have sickle cell disease, leukemia, or HIV infection or who have had a splenectomy; administering 1 dose of vaccine to these persons is not contraindicated.

13. Immunocompromising conditions

Inactivated vaccines generally are acceptable (e.g., pneumococcal, meningococcal, and influenza [trivalent inactivated influenza vaccine]), and live vaccines generally are avoided in persons with immune deficiencies or immunocompromising conditions. Information on specific conditions is available at www. cdc.gov/vaccines/pubs/acip-list.htm.

SOURCE: http://www.aafp.org/online/etc/medialib/aafp_org/documents/clinical/immunization/adultsched07-08.Par.0001.File.tmp/adult schedule.pdf

Appendix D:
CDC Pediatric, Adult, and
Influenza Vaccine Price Lists, 2008

TABLE AD-1

PEDIATRIC/VFC VACCINE PRICE LIST, NOVEMBER 5, 2008

Vaccine	Brandname/ Tradename	Packaging	CDC Cost/Dose	Private Sector Cost/Dose	Contract End Date	Manufacturer
DTaP[1]	Tripedia® DAPTACEL®	10 pack—1 dose vials 10 pack—1 dose vials	$12.65 $13.25	$21.40 $22.04	03/31/2009	Sanofi Pasteur
DTaP[1]	Infanrix®	10 pack—1 dose vials 5 pack—1 dose T-L syringes. No needle	$13.75 $13.75	$20.96 $21.44	03/31/2009	GlaxoSmithKline
DTaP-IPV[2]	Kinrix®	10 pack—1 dose vials 5 pack—1 dose T-L syringes	$32.25 $32.25	$48.00 $48.00	03/31/2009	GlaxoSmithKline
DTaP-Hep B-IPV[4]	Pediarix®	10 pack—1 dose vials 5 pack—1 dose T-L syringes. No needle	$48.75 $48.75	$70.72 $70.72	03/31/2009	GlaxoSmithKline
DTaP-IP-HI[4]	Pentacel®	5 pack—1 dose vials	$50.10	$72.91	03/31/2009	Sanofi Pasteur
DTaP-Hib[2]	TriHIBit®	5 pack—1 dose vials	$26.88	$42.89	03/31/2009	Sanofi Pasteur
e-IPV[5]	IPOL®	10 dose vials 10-pack—1 dose syringes. No needle	$11.48 $11.48	$22.80 $26.34	03/31/2009	Sanofi Pasteur

continued on the next page

TABLE AD-1 (CONTINUED)
PEDIATRIC/VFC VACCINE PRICE LIST, NOVEMBER 5, 2008

Vaccine	Brandname/ Tradename	Packaging	CDC Cost/Dose	Private Sector Cost/Dose	Contract End Date	Manufacturer
Hepatitis B-Hib[3]	COMVAX®	10 pack—1 dose vials	$28.80	$43.56	03/31/2009	Merck
Hepatitis A Pediatric[5]	VAQTA®	10 pack—1 dose vials	$12.75	$30.37	03/31/2009	Merck
Hepatitis A Pediatric[5]	Havrix®	10 pack—1 dose vials 5 pack—1 dose T-L syringes. No needle	$12.25 $12.25	$27.41 $27.41	03/31/2009	GlaxoSmithKline
Hepatitis A-Hepatitis B 18 only[3]	Twinrix®	10 pack—1 dose vials 5 pack—1 dose T-L syringes. No needle	$38.64 $38.64	$78.16 $78.42	03/31/2009	GlaxoSmithKline
Hepatitis B[5] Pediatric/Adolescent	ENGERIX B®	10 pack—1 dose vials 5 pack—1 dose T-L syringes. No needle	$9.50 $9.50	$21.37 $21.37	03/31/2009	GlaxoSmithKline
Hepatitis B[5] Pediatric/Adolescent	RECOMBIVAX HB®	10 pack—1 dose vials	$9.75	$23.20	03/31/2009	Merck

NOTES: 1. Vaccine cost includes $2.25 dose Federal Excise Tax. 2. Vaccine cost includes $3.00 per dose Federal Excise Tax. 3. Vaccine cost includes $1.50 per dose Federal Excise Tax. 4. Vaccine cost includes $3.75 per dose Federal Excise Tax. 5. Vaccine cost includes $0.75 per dose Federal Excise Tax. 6. Vaccines which contain Thimerosal as a preservative.

TABLE AD-2

ADULT VACCINE PRICE LIST, NOVEMBER 5, 2008

Vaccine	Brandname/ Tradename	Packaging	CDC Cost/Dose	Private Sector Cost/Dose	Contract End Date	Manufacturer
Hepatitis A Adult[5]	VAQTA®	1 dose vials 10 pack—1 dose vials	$20.00 $19.75	$63.51 $59.99	6/30/09	Merck
Hepatitis A Adult[5]	Havrix®	10 pack—1 dose vials 5 pack—1 dose T-L syringes. No needle	$18.99 $18.99	$60.69 $60.69	6/30/09	GlaxoSmithKline
Hepatitis A-Hepatitis B Adult[3]	Twinrix®	10 pack—1 dose vials 5 pack—1 dose T-L syringes. No needle	$38.64 $38.64	$86.44 $86.44	6/30/09	GlaxoSmithKline
Hepatitis B-Adult[5]	RECOMBIVAX HB®	1 dose vials 10 pack—1 dose vials 6 pack—1 dose prefilled syringe	$23.78 $23.372 $25.30	$59.70 $59.09 $61.22	6/30/09	Merck
Hepatitis B-Adult[5]	ENGERIX-B®	10 pack—1 dose vials 5 pack—1 dose T-L syringes. No needle	$24.90 $24.90	$52.50 $52.50	6/30/09	GlaxoSmithKline
Pneumococcal Polysaccharide (23 Valent)	Pneumovax®	1 pack—5 dose vials 10 pack – single dose 0.5 mL vials	$16.26 $18.93	$28.69 $32.20	6/30/09	Merck

continued on the next page

TABLE AD-2 (CONTINUED)
ADULT VACCINE PRICE LIST, NOVEMBER 5, 2008

Vaccine	Brandname/ Tradename	Packaging	CDC Cost/Dose	Private Sector Cost/Dose	Contract End Date	Manufacturer
Tetanus & Diphtheria Toxoids[6,3]	Tetanus & Diphtheria Toxoids Adsorbed for adults No preservative	10 pack—1 dose vials	$13.50	$18.23	6/30/09	MassBioLogics (Akorn, Inc)
Zoster Vaccine Live	Zostavax®	10 pack—1 dose vial 1 pack-single dose 0.65mL vials	$107.67 $113.16	$153.93 $161.50	6/30/09	Merck

NOTES: 3. Vaccine cost includes $1.50 per dose Federal Excise Tax. 5. Vaccine cost includes $0.75 per dose Federal Excise Tax. 6. Vaccines which contain Thimerosal as a preservative.

Table AD-3
Influenza Vaccine Price List, November 5, 2008

Vaccine	Brandname/ Tradename	Packaging	CDC Cost/Dose	Private Sector Cost/Dose	Contract End Date	Manufacturer
Influenza[6,5] (Age 6 months and older)	Fluzone®	10 dose vials	$9.965	$11.72	2/28/09	Sanofi Pasteur
Influenza[5] (Age 6–35 months)	Fluzone® Pediatric dose No preservative	10 pack—1 dose syringes	$13.087	$14.93	2/28/09	Sanofi Pasteur
Influenza[5] (Age 36 months and older)	Fluzone® No preservative	10 pack—1 dose syringes 10 pack – 1 dose vials	$14.247 $14.247	$16.09 $16.09	2/28/09	Sanofi Pasteur
Influenza[6,5] (Age 4 years and older)	Fluvirin® Fluvirin® Preservative-free	10 dose vials 10 pack—1 dose syringes	$9.25 $10.40	$12.48 $15.54	2/28/09 2/28/09	Novartis Novartis
Influenza[5] (Age 18 years and older)	Fluarix™ Preservative-free FluLaval™	5 pack—1 dose syringes 10 dose vials	$10.25 $6.70	$13.25 $11.10	2/28/09	GlaxoSmithKline
Influenza[5] Live, Intranasal (Age 2–49 years)	FluMist® No preservative	10 pack—1 dose sprayers	$18.50	$19.70	2/28/09	MedImmune

Source: http://www.cdc.gov/vaccines/programs/vfc/cdc-vac-price_list_htm (accessed November 22, 2008).
Notes: 5. Vaccine cost includes $0.75 per dose Federal Excise Tax. 6. Vaccines which contain Thimerosal as a preservative.

Notes

Introduction

1. For further discussion, see Phelps 2003, 470–74.

2. We use the words "vaccine markets" rather than "vaccine market," since the various vaccines are heterogeneous, distinct, and nonsubstitutable. Specifically, a vaccine targeted to prevent one disease is typically not therapeutically interchangeable for the prevention of others. On the demand side, a polio vaccine, for instance, cannot be substituted for a smallpox vaccine for the prevention of smallpox (Arnould and DeBrock 1996, 105). Moreover, on the supply side, for regulatory and manufacturing reasons, a firm cannot easily switch from producing one vaccine to another whose price has increased, as will be discussed in detail in chapter 2.

Introduction to Part I

1. Anderson 1998, 194.

2. Quoted from a U.S. Advisory Committee on Immunization Practices 2002 document in Stern and Markel 2005, 613.

3. Kenneth Kaitin (director, Tufts Center for the Study of Drug Development), in correspondence with the authors, April 2008.

4. BioSignpost 2007.

5. For further discussion on the economics of vaccines compared to pharmaceuticals, see Kremer and Snyder 2003, 2007 and Kremer and Glennerster 2004. A reviewer has also pointed out to us that vaccines are unique in having a well-organized political and ideological opposition to their utilization.

6. Datamonitor 2005b, 91–92.

7. Murray Aitken (senior vice president, corporate strategy, IMS Health), personal communication with the authors, June 20, 2007, and November 11, 2008. According to Aitken, IMS defines "other biologics" as "pharmaceuticals that have been manufactured via recombinant DNA technology."

8. See chapter 6 for a detailed discussion.

9. In a June 30, 2005, presentation to investors and analysts, GlaxoSmithKline officials estimated U.S. vaccine sales in 2004 at $4.03 billion (£2.2 billion, at a $1.83 exchange rate), which comprised 42.3 percent of the $9.52 billion global vaccine market. See the sixth slide (numbered 40) in the presentation by David Stout, president of pharmaceutical operations at GlaxoSmithKline (Stout 2005).

10. Moreover, even with no imports or exports, dollar values of production and consumption could differ due to wholesaler and distributor margins, as well as shipping costs.

11. For further discussion, see Berndt et al. 2000, 153.

12. U.S. Census Bureau 2004a, 2004b. Pharmaceutical preparations are based on product shipments in industry number 325412, as designated by the Census Bureau, vaccines on shipments in industry 3254144 (vaccines, toxoids, and antigens, excluding allergens, for human use), and other biologics on shipments in industry 325414 (biological product, excluding diagnostic, manufacturing), minus vaccine shipments in industry 3254144.

Chapter 1: Envisaging and Developing a Vaccine

1. Scherer 2000, 1316–19.

2. On this, see Demaine and Fellmeth 2003 and the references cited therein.

3. Scherer 2006.

4. See page 3 and appendix A.

5. A reviewer pointed out to us that one exception is the hepatitis B vaccine, for which intellectual property protection was originally owned by the University of California and Genentech, which then transferred it to Merck and GlaxoSmithKline. In large part because of this patent protection, Merck and GlaxoSmithKline are the sole producers, and to date no other hepatitis B entry has occurred.

6. "Scale economies" refers to average or unit costs decreasing as volume of output increases. In the context of vaccine production, as liters of vaccine production capacity increase, the manufacturing cost per liter declines.

7. Datamonitor 2005b, 48. For results of a recent clinical study highlighting the role of adjuvants, see Giannini, Hanon, Van Mechelen, et al. 2006.

8. Werble 2006.

9. World Intellectual Property Organization 2006.

10. Van Gelder 2005.

11. World Intellectual Property Organization 2006.

12. Whalen 2007.

13. Danzon, Pereira, and Tejwani 2005, 706.

14. In the text that follows, we will make frequent reference to the various phases or stages of clinical development. We assume readers are generally familiar with the traditional distinctions among phases I, II, and III in clinical trials, but for completeness we include a brief discussion of these trial phases in appendix B; we recommend

that those not familiar with the phases of clinical trial development review appendix B before proceeding further.

15. Orenstein et al. 2005, 608.

16. Offit 2005, 626.

17. For further discussion of noninferiority trials, see, among others, Kaul and Diamond 2006; Piaggio et al. 2006; Gotzsche 2006; and Snapinn 2000.

18. Also see a third study, Grabowski and Vernon 1997, whose findings are summarized in DiMasi and Grabowski 2008.

19. See discussion on pages 16–21.

20. Struck (1994) states, "The products surveyed were all biologicals; however, I did not restrict coverage to products made through hybridoma or recombinant DNA technology: nonrecombinant production methods were also included. The main product groups in this analysis were antibodies, vaccines, interferons, interleukins, recombinant growth factors and hormones, and therapeutic proteins such as superoxide dismutase, α-1-antitrypsin, Factor VIII, and Factor IX" (674). Struck (1994) appeared to indicate that about forty-six vaccine projects were included in the statistical analysis, comprising about 10 percent of his entire biopharmaceutical sample (figure 1, 675).

21. The p-value for the hypothesis of no difference is 0.12 for phase I to phase II, and 0.07 for phase III to preregistration. Preregistration refers to the time period between submission of data to national health authorities following completion of phase III trials and marketing approval from them.

22. Struck 1996, 582.

23. Ibid.

24. Ibid.

25. For chickenpox; see chapter 7.

26. See, for example, Finkelstein 2004 and Kremer and Glennerster 2004.

27. One interviewee with many years of industry experience explained that any vaccine development project needed to surmount three hurdles to proceed: first, to establish clinical efficacy and safety; second, to have technical manufacturing feasibility (reliability, scalability and reproducibility, and consistency); and, third, to be commercially viable.

28. Exclusion of preclinical measures is preferable, since identification of precisely when preclinical development begins is inherently ambiguous.

29. The incidence rate refers to the number of new cases of a particular disease that develop during a specified time interval. The prevalence (which is not strictly a rate, since no time period is specified) refers to the number of cases of disease that exist at a particular point in time. See Campbell and Machin 1993, 117.

30. See chapter 6.

31. Comprising 278 recombinant proteins and 244 monoclonal antibodies.

32. Like PharmaProjects, R&D Focus and iDDb3 track the progress of thousands of drugs through research and development.

33. DiMasi, Hansen, and Grabowski 2003.

34. Another recent study (Federal Trade Commission 2007), using PharmaProjects data on 3,181 compounds (primarily pharmaceuticals) that went into human clinical trials for the first time between 1989 and 2002, reported a mean transition probability from phase I to phase II of 0.74, and from phase II to phase III of 0.46, very similar to the 0.710 and 0.442 probabilities reported in DiMasi and Grabowski 2008.

35. Computed from table 1-2 by summing the times from phase I, phase II, and phase III to registration.

36. RotaShield was withdrawn from the U.S. market after 13.5 months, while LymeRx was voluntarily withdrawn after being on the U.S. market for about 39 months. LymeRx and RotaShield are discussed in more detail in chapters 3 and 6, respectively.

37. See, for example, Adams and Brantner 2006; DiMasi et al. 1995; and DiMasi, Grabowski, and Vernon 2004.

38. DiMasi and Grabowski 2008, 469.

39. See presentation of H. Bogaerts 2005, vice president, Worldwide Medical Affairs, HPV Vaccines, GlaxoSmithKline.

Chapter 2: Planning for Vaccine Launch

1. For a recent example of the FDA's withholding approval of an orphan drug—a drug treating a rare disease—due to manufacturing problems involving scale-up from clinical trial to commercial levels, see Armstrong and Anand 2007.

2. See Scherer 2007 for a more detailed discussion of this distinction.

3. Although data are proprietary, several interviewees stated that investment in a new vaccine facility ranged from $50 million to $75 million.

4. Some vaccines are given orally, including FluMist (discussed below in chapter 5), and the new rotavirus vaccines, such as RotaTeq.

5. One interviewee compared ambient environmental controls to those used for the production of silicon microprocessor chips, and noted that while particulate standards were comparable, the microbial contamination standards for vaccine manufacturing were much higher.

6. Orenstein et al. 2005, 603.

7. Sing and Willian 1996, 55–57; Orenstein et al. 2005, 603.

8. Danzon, Pereira, and Tejwani 2005, 708.

9. Sing and Willian 1996, 66–67.

10. Scherer 2007.

11. Institute of Medicine 2004a, 114.

12. Scherer 2007.

13. On this, also see Danzon and Pereira 2005.

14. Stratton, Durch, and Lawrence 2000 extensively discuss cost-effectiveness analyses for vaccines; for a more general discussion on the role of cost-effectiveness

analyses in U.S. public health policy, see Grosse, Teutsch, and Haddix 2007.

15. Much of the material in this section is taken from Morgan Stanley 2005.

16. Morgan Stanley 2005, 6–8.

17. The 2009 Recommended Adult and Pediatric Immunization Schedules are reproduced in appendix C.

18. An example of this last case is the ACIP's tepid recommendation in 1999 of SmithKline's LymeRx vaccine to prevent Lyme disease (Morgan Stanley 2005, 8). The recommendation was cited by numerous interviewees as being in large part responsible for the vaccine's eventual exit from the U.S. market; we discuss LymeRx in greater detail in chapter 3 below.

19. Morgan Stanley 2005, 8. Italics in the original.

20. Sing and Willian 1996, 72.

21. In 2002, national wholesalers accounted for 46 percent of prescription drug shipments from manufacturers. Chain warehouses accounted for 32 percent, regional and specialty wholesalers, 9 percent, and providers and pharmacies, 13 percent. See Schondelmeyer and Wrobel 2004, 10.

22. Vaccine distribution channels are, however, beginning to change. See appendix D for current packaging variations.

23. A vial is a glass container with a metal-enclosed rubber seal from which the vaccine is drawn. Multidose vials pose challenges not faced in pharmaceutical distribution, since multiple draws of a syringe from a vial raise the possibility of contamination, calling for the use of preservatives such as thimerosal. See "Syringe" in Anderson 1998, 1581. We discuss the use of thimerosal in chapter 8, with reference to product liability issues.

24. Centers for Disease Control and Prevention 2007i, chapter 11.

25. Many of these transport temperature issues also emerge in distribution channels in the food industries.

26. See discussion on pages 20–21.

27. McKesson Specialty 2006. Another large distributor of vaccines is Henry Schein Inc.

28. For discussion of specialty pharmacies, see Namovicz-Peat 2003.

29. Orenstein et al. 2005, 605.

30. The "high-touch, high-cost" characterization of biologics refers to the fact that biologics frequently require administration and close monitoring by professional health-care providers (rather than being self-administered capsules or tablets), and are very costly on a per-unit administration basis.

31. Because of reimbursement to providers, ultimate payers such as the CDC or employers can differ from the initial purchasers, such as physicians' practices.

32. This legislation also established the ACIP, discussed above.

33. Pauly et al. 1996, 21. Private providers are not obliged to accept patients into their practices simply because they are eligible for the VFC program.

34. Robinson and Sepe 1996, 38–39.

35. Ibid., 39.

36. Coleman et al. 2005, 638.

37. U.S. Department of Health and Human Services 2007b.

38. Orenstein et al. 2005, 604; Robinson and Sepe 1996, 39.

39. Lee et al. 2007.

40. See, for example, the editorial by Davis (2007) in the *Journal of the American Medical Association*.

41. Hinman 2005, 702.

42. Orenstein et al. 2005, 605.

43. Based in part on favorable cost-offset analyses, Medicare has reimbursed providers for influenza vaccinations since the 1980s under Medicare Part B. Data on payment allowance limits for Medicare Part B vaccine acquisition, on a quarterly basis, are publicly available. For the third quarter 2008 (based on the average sales price methodology), these data are publicly available at http://www.cms.hhs.gov/McrPartBDrugAvgSalesPrice/01a_2008aspfiles.asp (accessed November 15, 2008). We are grateful to a reviewer for pointing this out to us.

44. Physicians then bill using coding schemes, such as the widely used CPT (Current Procedures and Therapies) codes.

45. *Infectious Diseases in Children Round Table* 2007a, 2007b. Capitation is when the physician is paid a fixed amount per patient per month, regardless of the amount of services provided by the physician.

46. Pollack 2007.

47. American Academy of Pediatrics Task Force on Immunization 2007, figure 1.

48. Ibid., figure 2.

49. National Immunization Congress 2007.

50. American Academy of Pediatrics Task Force on Immunization 2007, 9; the CPT codes for the first injection are 90465 and 90471, while those for each additional injection are 90466 and 90472. Also see Orenstein et al. 2005, 605.

Chapter 3: Rolling Out the New Vaccine

1. Product liability issues are discussed in greater detail in chapters 4 and 8.

2. Orenstein et al. 2005, 599–600.

3. Baker 2003; Colgrove and Bayer 2005.

4. Manning 1994, table 1, 254. By comparison with this $155.42 price increase for the DTP vaccine, over the same time period the wholesale price of the DT combination vaccine (not containing the pertussis component) increased by only $2.84, from $3.81 to $6.65.

5. Offit 2005, 627.

6. Sing and Willian 1996, 52.

7. National Childhood Vaccine Injury Act of 1986 (42 U.S.C. §§ 300aa-1–300aa-34).

8. Orenstein et al. 2005, 607.

9. National Vaccine Injury Compensation Program 2007.

10. Ibid. For further discussion of the controversy associated with vaccines and autism, see chapter 8, below.

11. In late June 2007, a much-publicized VICP court began considering claims on behalf of 4,800 children stating that the thimerosal preservative in pertussis and certain combination vaccines causes autism. As indicated above, preservatives are compounds that kill or prevent the growth of microorganisms, particularly bacteria and fungi. They are used in vaccines to prevent microbial growth in the event that the vaccine is accidentally contaminated, as might occur with repeated puncture of multidose vials. See Offit 2007a, 2007b. For additional discussion, see Epstein 2005, 742–43.

12. Offit 2005, 627. Thimerosal has been removed from or reduced to trace amounts in all vaccines routinely recommended for children six years of age and younger, with the exception of inactivated influenza vaccine, for which only a limited supply is currently available for use in infants, children, and pregnant women. For a list of current vaccines containing thimerosal, see appendix D. For details and discussion of thimerosal in vaccines, see U.S. Food and Drug Administration 2008a. For further discussion of the thimerosal controversy, see chapter 8, below.

13. Reichert 2006, table 2, 297; Offit 2005, 628. A third flaw in the VICP noted by Offit is that the program does not include the unborn child of a pregnant woman who is immunized, thereby discouraging manufacturers from developing a vaccine for pregnant women that would work to protect newborns. Currently, the earliest that most vaccines are administered to infants is at two months.

14. For discussions of the pricing of pharmaceuticals, see Berndt 2001, 2002 and Frank 2001; for biologics, see Calfee, Villareal, and DuPre 2007.

15. See appendix D. Issues concerning FDA regulation of "biosimilars" or "follow-on biologics" for biologics other than vaccines subsequent to loss of patent protection are currently being debated, but further discussion of them is beyond the scope of this research. See Grabowski 2007 and the references cited therein, as well as Mac-Neil and Douglas 2007, for further discussion of follow-on or biosimilar biologics.

16. Grabowski and Vernon 1992; Berndt 2002; Reiffen and Ward 2005.

17. See chapter 2.

18. Reiffen and Ward 2005.

19. For further discussion of price discrimination, see chapters 6 and 7, below, and Berndt 2002.

20. Danzon, Pereira, and Tejwani 2005, 708.

21. For a discussion of game theory and Bertrand price competition among homogeneous products, see Pindyck and Rubinfeld 2005, 449–50.

22. See appendix D.

23. Although the lower public-sector prices likely reflect the greater bargaining power of the federal government, the literature suggests that demand for vaccines is less price-responsive in the private sector, and that the higher prices charged there

reflect traditional third-degree price discrimination. See, for example, Arnould and DeBrock 1996, Salkever and Frank 1996, and Pauly 2005.

24. See chapter 4.

25. See appendix D.

26. See the introductory chapter.

27. Kremer and Snyder 2003, 2007; Kremer and Glennerster 2004.

28. A price–cost margin is the percentage surplus of sales revenues over materials purchases and total payroll expenses—an estimate of the cash flow available after paying variable in-plant production costs to cover fixed plant, R&D, and corporate overhead costs, along with a contribution to profits.

29. Scherer 2007. The industry segments are 3254144 (vaccines, toxoids, and antigens, for human use), 3254147 (other biologics, excluding diagnostics, for human use), and pharmaceutical preparations. By comparison, the average for all manufacturing industries in 2001 was 28 percent.

30. For a review of the cost-effectiveness literature, see Garber 2000; the role of cost-effectiveness in U.S. public health policy, including that for vaccines, is discussed in Grosse, Teutsch, and Haddix 2007. Cost-effectiveness studies of vaccines in developing countries are discussed in Global Alliance for Vaccines and Immunization (GAVI) 2004.

31. For further discussion, see, among others, Salkever and Frank 1996.

32. A standard reference in this context is the National Institutes of Health–sponsored "cost-effectiveness bible," by Gold et al. (1996).

33. Zhou et al. 2005, 1136.

34. Even Avorn, a strong critic of the pharmaceutical industry, is laudatory in his evaluation of the value of vaccines, stating, "Vaccines are one of the clearest examples of slam-dunk benefit–risk relationships. Vaccinate 100,000 kids against measles, for example, and a few will develop complications, sometimes severe ones. This is tragic when it occurs, but children as a whole are far better off because measles vaccine is available" (Avorn 2004, 141). For a review of vaccine cost-benefit and cost-effectiveness studies, see, among others, Lieu, McGuire, and Hinman 2005.

35. For a discussion on the economics of importing lower-priced pharmaceuticals into the United States, see Berndt 2007a. Calfee, Villareal, and DuPre 2006 compare prices of biologics in the United States with those in a number of other countries.

36. See chapter 2, above, "Coordination with Public Health Officials and Payers."

37. Controversial issues surrounded the efficacy and side effects of LymeRx. See, for example, Drug Store News 1999, Hilts 2001, Offit 2005, and RxList 1998; see also the earlier discussion in this chapter, "Product Liability Issues."

38. For discussion of the role of direct-to-consumer advertising of pharmaceuticals and its impact, see Berndt 2007b, Berndt and Donohue 2008, and Donohue, Cevasco, and Rosenthal 2007.

39. The material in this section is largely taken from Orenstein et al. 2005.

40. Orenstein et al. 2005, 605–6.

41. Ibid., 606.

42. Person-years takes into account the total number of persons observed for a year. If 2,000 individuals were observed during two annual flu seasons, and 1,000 were observed for a single flu season, the total number of person-season observations would be 5,000.

43. Note that with its observational rather than prospective randomized design, the study could examine association but not causality.

44. Nichol et al. 2007, 1373.

45. Brown 2008; see chapter 5.

46. Roush and Murphy 2007.

47. Orenstein et al. 2005, 606–7.

48. See, for example, Avorn 2004, chapter 6; Hass et al. 2006; Lorenzo 2005a, 2005b; Olson 2002.

49. But see U.S. Department of Health and Human Services, Office of Inspector General 2006 and Carpenter 2005.

50. See U.S. Food and Drug Administration 2006b.

51. Toxoids are adsorbed when they are attracted and retained on a surface, such as on a wound.

52. Appendix D, "Adult Vaccine Price List," lists the Massachusetts Biologics (Akorn, Inc) as selling the tetanus and diphtheria toxoid in 10-dose vials for a CDC price of $13.50 per dose. It is possible that this is inventory from previous production. The contract end date is listed as June 30, 2009.

53. Sing and Willian 1996, 68–69.

54. Since 2004, Chiron has been acquired by Novartis (2005) and MedImmune by AstraZeneca (2007). U.S.-based Pfizer acquired the British vaccine manufacturer Posdermed (2006), and GlaxoSmithKline the Canadian firm ID Biomedical (2005).

55. We are grateful to a reviewer who provided us details on the manufacturing locations of vaccines marketed in the United States.

56. Offit 2005; Danzon and Pereira 2005; Danzon, Pereira, and Tejwani 2005; Sing and Willian 1996; Arnould and DeBrock 1996; Pauly 2005.

57. Danzon, Pereira, and Tejwani (2005) document and interpret the greater concentration of suppliers for individual vaccines in the United States as compared to Europe.

58. Three of these are new patented vaccines—for pneumococcal, meningococcal, and varicella, while two are old vaccines—inactivated polio virus, and measles, mumps, and rubella.

59. Sanofi Pasteur is the sole manufacturer; see appendix table AD-3, "Influenza Vaccine Price List."

60. On September 28, 2007, the FDA granted approval to CSL Biotherapies Inc. of King of Prussia, Pennsylvania, to market a trivalent inactivated influenza vaccine, with brand name Afluria. Afluria is approved to be administered intramuscularly in persons eighteen years and older, for any adult influenza vaccine indication. This

brings to five the number of manufacturers of injected influenza vaccines for adults. See Centers for Disease Control and Prevention 2007d. Afluria is manufactured by CSL Limited in dedicated production facilities in Melbourne, Australia, and Marburg, Germany, and is available in two formulations: a preservative-free, thimerosal-free, latex-free, single-use prefilled syringe, and a latex-free multidose vial containing thimerosal as a preservative. For further details, see CSL Biotherapies Inc. 2007. Apparently Afluria is not sold to the CDC, for it does not appear in the CDC Influenza Vaccine Price List (appendix table AD-3).

61. Orenstein, Douglas, Rodewald, and Hinman 2005, 607; also see Plotkin 2005.

62. See chapter 7.

63. Centers for Disease Control and Prevention 2007k.

64. Merck Vaccines 2008; Centers for Disease Control and Prevention 2009b.

65. Centers for Disease Control and Prevention 2007k.

66. Centers for Disease Control and Prevention 2007j, 2007k.

67. Centers for Disease Control and Prevention 2007b.

68. Merck Vaccines 2008.

69. Centers for Disease Control and Prevention 2007j, 2007b.

70. Ibid.

71. See, for example, South Carolina Department of Health and Environmental Control 2008 and Arizona Department of Health Services 2008.

72. See, for example, Arnould and DeBrock 2005; Coleman et al. 2005; Danzon and Pereira 2005; Datamonitor 2005b; Institute of Medicine 2004a; Offit 2005; Pauly 2005; Plotkin 2005; Scherer 2007; and Stern and Markel 2005. According to several observers, liability issues have played a relatively minor role in creating shortages of influenza vaccines, and manufacturers have experienced shortages for other reasons; see Mello and Brennan 2005.

73. Scherer 2007.

Introduction to Part II

1. For a list of the sixty vaccines licensed in the United States as of October 2008, see U.S. Food and Drug Administration 2008b.

Chapter 4: Diphtheria, Tetanus, and Pertussis and Related Combination Vaccines

1. Centers for Disease Control and Prevention 2005b.

2. World Health Organization 2005.

3. Brooks and Clover 2006.

4. See discussion on page 75.

5. Ibid.

6. American Academy of Pediatrics 2007.

7. DTaP is the combination vaccine with an acellular pertussis component.

8. National Institute of Allergy and Infectious Diseases 1999.

9. U.S. Food and Drug Administration 2002a.

10. Centers for Disease Control and Prevention 2003.

11. U.S. Food and Drug Administration 2001.

12. U.S. Food and Drug Administration 2005.

13. Ibid.

14. GlaxoSmithKline 2007b.

15. Centers for Disease Control and Prevention 1996.

16. Sanofi Pasteur Inc. 2007a, 2007b.

17. U.S. Food and Drug Administration 2002b.

18. See chapter 2, above.

19. On this, see Frank 2001 and Berndt 2002.

20. Vaccine Adverse Event Reporting System 2007.

21. Centers for Disease Control and Prevention 2007h.

Chapter 5: Seasonal Influenza Vaccines

1. Centers for Disease Control and Prevention 2006b.

2. Altman 2008.

3. Centers for Disease Control and Prevention 2007d and CSL Biotherapies 2007. A live, attenuated virus is a weakened, less vigorous virus capable of stimulating an immune response and creating immunity, but not causing illness. Inactivated products contain viral strains that have been killed with chemicals (such as betapropiolactone or formaldehyde) to eliminate the virus's ability to infect humans, whereas the live, attenuated influenza vaccine contains a genetic recombinant that splices the hemaglutinin genes from the annual strains into the cold-adapted influenza virus. Immunization with the live, attenuated influenza vaccine is intended to produce a response that would be similar to that which would be mounted against a weakened version of the same viral strains.

4. If and when constraints on production capacity become less of an issue for manufacturers, it is possible that the number of strains may be expanded to provide a greater range of viral protection per vaccine.

5. The 2007–8 trivalent vaccines were, for the A strains, Solomon Islands/3/2006 (H1N1)-like (which was new for the season), and Wisconsin/67/2005 (H3N2)-like; and for the B strain, Malaysia/2506/2004-like viruses. Centers for Disease Control and Prevention 2007a.

6. Centers for Disease Control and Prevention 2007g.

7. Brown 2008.

8. Heavey 2008.

9. For the 2008–9 flu season, the match between actual and predicted A strains was very good, but for the B strain about three-quarters of the circulating virus

strains did not match the predicted Yamagata lineage. For the 2009–10 flu season, based on WHO recommendations, in February 2009 the FDA recommended that the A strains remain the same as those for the 2008–9 flu season, but that the B component be changed to the Victoria lineage variety. Centers for Disease Control and Prevention 2009a.

10. Dooren 2008a.

11. Heavey 2008.

12. See chapter 8, below, for discussion of the implications of thimerosal content.

13. Centers for Disease Control and Prevention 2007d; CSL Biotherapies 2007.

14. We are grateful to a reviewer for providing us with this information.

15. Waknine 2007.

16. Rosenwald 2007.

17. Smith 2007.

18. Rosenwald 2007.

19. Rosenwald 2005; Centers for Disease Control and Prevention 2007e.

20. See chapter 8, below.

21. U.S. Food and Drug Administration 2008a.

22. In this context a surrogate marker, such as antibody or other immunologic response, is an indirect measure of the body's response to the vaccine, substituting for a clinical endpoint such as the ability to fight off the viral strains and not come down with the illness.

23. Novartis 2006.

24. Novartis 2007b, 2007c.

25. See part I, above.

26. Centers for Disease Control and Prevention 2006a.

27. As discussed earlier, for the 2008–9 flu season, all three strains differ from those of the previous year.

28. It is worth noting, incidentally, that all vaccines manufactured through this process are contraindicated for people with egg allergies, so a segment of the general population remains underserved by it.

29. Novartis 2007c; Edwin Valeriano (Director, Investor Relations, Novartis Corporation), personal telephone call with the authors, December 8, 2008.

30. Macdonald 2009.

31. Others, however, believe that recombinant DNA technologies may ultimately leapfrog both the egg- and cell-based manufacturing processes; see, for example, Lauerman 2007. We discuss one such promising new technology below.

32. VaxInnate is a privately held, Connecticut-based biotechnology company partnered in collaboration with academic centers, with additional financial support from the Bill and Melinda Gates Foundation and the National Institute of Allergy and Infectious Diseases at the National Institutes of Health.

33. Lewcock 2007.

34. Ibid.

35. PharmaLive.com 2007.

36. VaxInnate 2008b.

37. VaxInnate 2008a.

38. LaFee 2009.

39. For the definition of a surrogate marker, see this chapter, note 21, above.

40. U.S. House of Representatives 2005.

41. U.S. Department of Health and Human Services 2007a.

42. The 2006 ACIP recommendations included, among other expansions, administering two doses of vaccine to all children ages six months to eight years if they had not been vaccinated previously at any time with either the intranasal or injectable flu vaccines. See Advisory Committee on Immunization Practices 2006c.

43. Centers for Disease Control and Prevention 2007c, 2008b.

44. Centers for Disease Control and Prevention 2006c.

45. Advisory Committee on Immunization Practices 2006c.

46. The Medicare Part B benefit covering flu vaccinations with zero copay has been in effect since the 1980s, according to officials we interviewed.

47. Centers for Disease Control and Prevention 2008b.

48. Centers for Disease Control and Prevention 2005a. Since the vaccines are specific for each year and cannot be sold in subsequent years, any reimbursed return to the manufacturer represents an unrecoverable loss in sales and profits. Thus, in making their annual manufacturing, pricing, and return-policy decisions, manufacturers must carefully evaluate the risks of substantial losses from less-than-anticipated demand resulting in an unanticipated return of large numbers of unused vaccine doses.

49. Centers for Disease Control and Prevention 2007g.

50. Ibid.; Nichol et al. 2007, 1374.

51. Person-year observations take into account the total number of persons observed for a year. If 2,000 individuals were observed during two annual flu seasons, and 1,000 were observed for a single flu season, the total number of person-season observations would be 5,000.

52. Congressional Budget Office 2006.

53. U.S. Food and Drug Administration 2007a.

54. After winning a $221 million grant from the U.S. government supporting clinical trials based on a cell-based process, Novartis invested $600 million in building a plant in Holly Springs, North Carolina; similarly, after being awarded $275 million from the U.S. government, Glaxo acquired an old manufacturing facility site from Wyeth in 2005, and is now retrofitting it. See Lauerman 2007.

55. ClinicalTrials.gov 2008.

56. For a discussion of the great 1918 influenza pandemic and its economic and epidemiological impacts, see Garrett 2008.

57. Novartis 2007a.

58. Whalen 2008; GlaxoSmithKline 2008.

Chapter 6: Prevnar—The Seven-Valent
Pneumococcal Conjugate Vaccine

1. Prevnar is indicated for the prevention of invasive disease caused by *Streptococcus pneumoniae* due to the capsular serotypes included in the vaccine (types 4, 6B, 9V, 14, 18C, 19F and 23F).

2. Brouwer et al. 2005.

3. As stated in Pharmaceutical Research and Manufacturers of America 2004, 18.

4. Henrichsen 1995.

5. A polysaccharide vaccine is made from complex chains of simple sugar molecules that form the outer coat of many bacteria.

6. Clarke 2006.

7. Williams 1998.

8. *Drug Facts and Comparisons* 2006, 1962–63.

9. See appendix C.

10. Robbins and Schneerson were cited as outstanding scientists at NIH for "conceptualizing, developing, testing and bringing into universal use, a conjugate vaccine to prevent meningitis caused by Haemophilus influenza type b (Hib), eliminating this condition as the leading cause of acquired mental retardation in the United States, and ending the scourge of this disease for children everywhere." See National Institute of Child Health and Human Development 2003.

11. University of Rochester Medical Center 2003.

12. Ibid.

13. U.S. Food and Drug Administration 2007b.

14. Butler et al. 1995.

15. Eby, Madore, and Puvanesarajah n.d.

16. Kaiser Permanente 2007.

17. Gordon 2000.

18. Stoller 2001.

19. Shinefield 1999.

20. Chan and Ahnn 2005.

21. U.S. House of Representatives 2004.

22. Rios 2006.

23. Datamonitor 2006.

24. Zimmerman 2001.

25. Ibid.

26. U.S. sales of Prevnar are estimated to have been about $700 million in 2006; data kindly made available by Murray Aitken 2007.

27. Carey 2002.

28. Datamonitor 2004.

29. Whitney et al. 2003.

30. See the discussion of consumption externalities at the beginning of the introductory chapter to this book.

31. Ibid.

32. Lexau et al. 2005.

33. U.S. Patent and Trademark Office 2007. The original expiration date for patent number 5,360,897 covering Prevnar expired on June 16, 2004, but under terms of the 35 USC §156 patent extension provisions, 1,086 days were added so that the extended expiration date was January 7, 2007.

34. Congressional Budget Office 2005; Danzon and Pereira 2005; Grabowski, Cockburn, and Long 2006; and Reiffen and Ward 2005. See also chapter 3, above.

35. Fast Track designation is designed to facilitate review of products that address serious or potentially life-threatening conditions for which there is an unmet medical need.

36. Wyeth 2008; but also see Hirschler 2009.

37. Breuer 2005. This slide set refers both to eleven-valent and ten-valent versions of Streptorix. As noted in the text above, the ten-valent version is now given the trade name of Synflorix.

38. PharmaLive 2008.

39. Datamonitor 2006.

40. Ibid.

41. According to some experts, however, extensive replacement has not happened with other widely used vaccines, likely because many other bacteria exist in only a small number of disease-causing varieties. Kyaw et al. 2006.

42. Hochman 2005.

43. World Health Organization 2006.

44. Ibid.

45. Ibid.

46. Ibid.

47. For further discussions, see Berndt and Hurvitz 2005; Berndt et al. 2007; Kremer and Glennerster 2004; and Levine, Kremer, and Albright 2005.

48. Global Alliance for Vaccines and Immunization 2007. The Global Alliance for Vaccines and Immunization is an alliance among different stakeholders in both the private and public sectors, as well as other nongovernmental organizations, committed to the mission of saving children's lives and protecting people's health through the worldwide expansion of childhood vaccination programs.

49. GlaxoSmithKline 2007a. See the above discussion on the nine-valent Synflorix as a possible competitor to Wyeth's seven-valent Prevnar.

Chapter 7: Varicella Zoster Vaccines

1. Centers for Disease Control and Prevention n.d.

2. World Health Organization 1998, 2003.

3. Preblud 1986.

4. Advisory Committee on Immunization Practices 1996.

5. Merck & Co. Inc. 2005.

6. This decision demonstrates the practical implications of the concepts of vaccine consumption externalities and herd immunity; see the book introduction.

7. Gershon 1999.

8. White 1999.

9. U.S. Food and Drug Administration 1995.

10. Chan and Ahnn 2005.

11. Advisory Committee on Immunization Practices 2006b.

12. U.S. Department of Veterans Affairs 2005.

13. Oxman et al. 2005.

14. See, for example, Galambos 1995.

15. U.S. Department of Veterans Affairs 2006.

16. Buckland 2005.

17. Advisory Committee on Immunization Practices 2002.

18. Advisory Committee on Immunization Practices 2007a and Centers for Disease Control and Prevention 2007f.

19. Lieu et al. 1994.

20. The CDC maintains annual lists of nationally notifiable diseases, through its National Notifiable Diseases Surveillance System. See "Post-Launch Surveillance" in chapter 3, above, for further discussion; for a list of the 2008 nationally notifiable infectious diseases, see Centers for Disease Control and Prevention 2008a.

21. Seward et al. 2002.

22. Li et al. 2002.

23. Chaves et al. 2007.

24. Advisory Committee on Immunization Practices 2006a.

25. Advisory Committee on Immunization Practices 2007b. See appendix C, below.

26. Datamonitor 2005a.

27. Advisory Committee on Immunization Practices 2006b, 2007a, 2007b, and Centers for Disease Control and Prevention 2007f.

28. Centers for Disease Control and Prevention 2007k, Loftus 2008.

29. Vazquez and Shapiro 2005.

Chapter 8: Challenges in Maintaining Public Trust in Vaccine Safety

1. Offit 2007c, 178.

2. Baker 2008, 6, referencing Tanner 1943.

3. Ibid.

4. Ibid., 6–7.

5. Ibid., 7.

6. Ibid.

7. Offit 2007c, 174.

8. Offit 2007b, 1278.

9. Ibid.

10. Gever 2008.

11. Baker 2008, 7–9.

12. Ibid., 159. Why it took seventeen years for Merck to introduce MMR into the United Kingdom is unclear. According to Dr. Andrew Wakefield, a central figure in the controversy there, MMR was introduced to save the Department of Health money. Campbell 2007, 5.

13. Wakefield et al. 1998.

14. Deer 2007c, 2.

15. Wakefield et al. 1998, 639.

16. Campbell 2007, 3.

17. Offit 2007c, 160.

18. Deer 2007c, 12.

19. Campbell 2007, 3.

20. Wakefield et al. 1998, 640.

21. Ibid., 638.

22. Campbell 2007, 3.

23. Offit 2007c, 159–62.

24. As quoted in Offit 2007c, 162.

25. Offit 2007c, 162.

26. Ibid.; Campbell 2007, 7.

27. Campbell 2007, 8.

28. Ibid., 7.

29. Offit 2007c, 163.

30. As quoted in Deer 2007c, 2.

31. Offit 2007c, 167.

32. Deer 2007c, 2.

33. Ibid., 3. In the British legal system, a solicitor is a lawyer who advises and represents clients outside of courts, while a barrister acts on litigation within the courtroom setting.

34. Ibid., 6.

35. Ibid., 8.

36. Ibid., 9.

37. Ibid., 11–13.

38. Deer 2007b, 3.

39. Horton 2004, 821. The editors' statement was followed by three separate statements from coauthors Simon Murch, John Walker-Smith, and Andrew Wakefield, and a joint one by the Royal Free and University College Medical School and the Royal Free Hampstead National Health Service Trust.

40. Murch et al. 2004, 750.

41. Deer 2007c, 13.

42. Campbell 2007, 4; Offit 2007c, 169. Dr. Wakefield's short biography is available at http://www.thoughtfulhouse.org/bio_awakefield.htm (accessed December 28, 2007).

43. Deer 2007c, 18; Deer 2007b, 5.

44. Offit 2007c, 169.

45. As quoted in Offit 2007c, 170.

46. Laurance 2007; Deer 2007c, 16; Deer 2007a.

47. Campbell 2007, 4.

48. Deer 2007a.

49. Emling 2008.

50. National Autistic Society 2008.

51. Deer 2007c, 17.

52. Brian Deer, personal email communication with the authors, November 14, 2008.

53. Deer 2009.

54. Histories of the vaccine controversies in the United Kingdom and United States are found in Baker 2003 and Baker 2008, respectively.

55. Much of the material in this and the following paragraphs is taken from Baker 2008.

56. Baker 2008, 5.

57. Prescription Drug User Fee Act (PDUFA) of 1992, PL 102-571 (October 29, 1992).

58. Offit 2007b, 1278.

59. Baker 2008, 4.

60. Baker 2008, 8.

61. Offit 2007c, 175.

62. Offit 2007b, 1278. For recent evidence on the pharmacokinetics of thimerosal-containing vaccines in infants, see Pichichero et al. 2008.

63. Offit 2007b, 1278.

64. Ibid.

65. As quoted in ibid.

66. See chapter 5 and table 5-1.

67. Baker 2008, 8.

68. Offit 2007b, 1278.

69. Baker 2008, 8.

70. Offit 2007b, 1278.

71. Baker 2008, 8–9; Offit 2007c, 174.

72. Kirby 2005.

73. Offit 2007c, 174.

74. Baker 2008, 9.

75. As quoted in Offit 2007c, 163.

76. Ibid, 164–66.

77. National Vaccine Information Center 2000.

78. As quoted in Offit 2007c, 166.

79. The eight reports can be accessed at www.iom.edu/–ID=4705 (accessed January 14, 2008).

80. Institute of Medicine 2001, 2004b.

81. As quoted in Kennedy 2005, 2.

82. Palta 2004, 2. Earlier that year, Congressman Burton attended opening ceremonies at the Christian Sarkine Autism Treatment Center in Indianapolis, named after his grandson and supported with funding from the National Institute of Mental Health, the CDC, and private foundations. See Burton 2003 and Christian Sarkine Autism Treatment Center 2008. In early January 2008, Burton secured for the center an additional $2 million in federal funding (coming in part from the U.S. Department of Defense and in part from the Omnibus Spending Bill). See Riley Children's Hospital 2008.

83. Offit 2007c, 172–73.

84. Palta 2004, 2.

85. Fuentes 2004.

86. Offit 2007b, 1279.

87. Offit 2007c, 173b.

88. For a list of states that have banned mercury, or introduced legislation banning mercury that was not enacted, see Advocates for Children's Health Affected by Mercury Poisoning 2007.

89. Kennedy 2005, 2. According to Offit (2007c, 173), Kennedy's article "was supported by plaintiff lawyers."

90. Kennedy 2005, 4. Italics in original version.

91. Ibid., 6.

92. See chapter 2.

93. Sugarman 2007.

94. Ibid.

95. Wallis 2008. The amount of damages awarded was not disclosed.

96. Ibid.

97. Giles 2008.

98. Wallis 2008

99. As quoted in Offitt 2008.

100. Ibid.

101. Harris 2008; Fallik 2008.

102. Mehigh 2008.

103. Harris 2008.

104. Carey 2008.

105. National Vaccine Injury Compensation Program 2007.

106. Sugarman 2007.

107. Special Masters are appointed by the U.S. Court of Federal Claims, which has jurisdiction over vaccine and death cases, for four-year terms, subject to reappointment. The Special Masters have substantial legal experience and technical knowledge relevant to the cases they try, and in the current context function as trial judges in the vaccine cases. See U.S. Court of Federal Claims 2008b.

108. Associated Press 2007.

109. U.S. Court of Federal Claims 2008a.

110. Ibid.

111. Ibid.

112. U.S. Court of Federal Claims 2009.

113. Sugarman 2007.

114. National Autism Association 2007, 1.

115. Sugarman 2007. On the historical role of Eli Lilly in manufacturing thimerosal, see Baker 2008.

116. Thompson et al. 2007, 1281.

117. SafeMinds 2007; Sataline 2007.

118. Sataline 2007.

119. Offit 2007b, 1279.

Conclusion

1. See table 1-1, above.

2. Revenues from Varivax more than doubled in 2007 relative to 2006, reaching a level of $855 million. See Loftus 2008.

3. Dooren 2008b.

4. Ibid.

5. Loftus 2008.

6. Hofman 2008.

7. Ibid.

8. Hitti 2008.

9. Ibid.

10. Hofman 2008.

11. Also see Morgan Stanley 2005 and Landry and Heilman 2005.

12. See, for example, Sloan and Eesley 2007.

13. On this, see, for example, Phelps 2003, 488–89, 521–31.

14. Lauerman 2007.

Appendix B

1. Some of the material in this appendix is taken from Orenstein et al. 2005. A much more thorough discussion is found in the various chapters of Plotkin and Orenstein 2004.

2. For a discussion, see Snapinn 2000 and Chan and Ahnn 2005 and the references cited therein.

3. This is discussed in further detail in chapter 2, above, in "Coordination with Public Health Officials and Payers."

4. Arnould and Debrock 2005; Scherer 2007.

5. McNeil 2006.

6. Sing and Willian 1996, 55–56. There is a long tradition of collaboration among industry, academia, and government in developing vaccines; for a historical perspective, see Galambos 1995.

References

Adams, Christopher P., and Van V. Brantner. 2006. Estimating the Cost of New Drug Development: Is It Really $802 Million– *Health Affairs* 25 (2): 420–28.

Advisory Committee on Immunization Practices. 1996. Prevention of Varicella: Recommendations of the Advisory Committee on Immunization Practices. *Morbidity and Mortality Weekly Report (MMWR)* 45 (RR11): 1–25. http://www.cdc.gov/mmwr/preview/mmwrhtml/00042990.htm (accessed July 8, 2008).

———. 2002. Notice to Readers: Shortage of Varicella and Measles, Mumps and Rubella Vaccines and Interim Recommendations from the Advisory Committee on Immunization Practices. *Morbidity and Mortality Weekly Report (MMWR)* 51 (09): 190–97. http://www.cdc.gov/mmwr/preview/mmwrhtml/mm5109a6.htm (accessed July 8, 2008).

———. 2006a. ACIP Provisional Recommendations for Prevention of Varicella. June. http://www.migrantclinician.org/toolsource/resource/acip-provisional-recommendations-prevention-varicella.html (accessed November 27, 2008).

———. 2006b. ACIP Provisional Recommendations for the Use of Zoster Vaccine, October 25. http://www.ncchca.org/files/Clinical/clinical%20resources/immunization/zoster-11-20-06.pdf (accessed November 27, 2008).

———. 2006c. Prevention and Control of Influenza: Recommendations of the Advisory Committee on Immunization Practices. *Morbidity and Mortality Weekly Report (MMWR)* 55 (RR10): 1–42. http://www.cdc.gov/mmwr/preview/mmwrhtml/rr5510a1.htm (accessed July 8, 2008).

———. 2007a. Notice to Readers: Supply of Vaccines Containing Varicella-Zoster Virus. *Morbidity and Mortality Weekly Report (MMWR)* 56 (07): 146–47. http://www.cdc.gov/mmwr/preview/mmwrhtml/mm5607a4.htm (accessed July 8, 2008).

———. 2007b. Prevention of Varicella: Recommendations of the Advisory Committee on Immunization Practices. *Morbidity and Mortality Weekly Report (MMWR)* 56 (RR04): 1–40. http://www.cdc.gov/mmwr/preview/mmwrhtml/rr5604a1.htm (accessed July 8, 2008).

Advocates for Children's Health Affected by Mercury Poisoning (A-CHAMP). 2007. State Legislation to Ban Mercury in Vaccines, February. http://www.a-champ.org/state.html (accessed January 14, 2008).

Aitken, Murray. 2007. Personal email communication with the authors. June 20.

_____. 2008. Personal email communication with the authors. November 11.

Altman, Lawrence K. 2008. Panel Advises Flu Shots for Children Up to Age 18. *New York Times*. February 28, A4.

American Academy of Pediatrics. 2007. Status of Licensure and Recommendations for New Vaccines: Red Book Online Table. *Red Book Online*. http://aapredbook. aappublications.org/news/vaccstatus.shtml (accessed August 24, 2007).

American Academy of Pediatrics Task Force on Immunization. 2007. Immunization Financing: Where is the Breaking Point– Post Immunization Congress Discussion White Paper. February 28. http://www.cispimmunize.org/ImmunizationCongress. htm (accessed June 29, 2007).

Anderson, Kenneth N., ed. 1998. *Mosby's Medical, Nursing, & Allied Health Dictionary*, 5th ed. St. Louis, Mo.: Mosby-Year Book.

Arizona Department of Health Services. 2008. HIV Vaccine Shortage. October 24. www.care1st.com/az/PDF/news/oct2008/HIBVaccineShortage.pdf (accessed November 14, 2008).

Armstrong, David, and Geeta Anand. 2007. Genzyme's Hit Turns Headache—Drug for Rare Disease Has Been in Demand, But FDA Blocks Factory. *Wall Street Journal*. August 9, C1.

Arnould, Richard, and Larry DeBrock. 1996. The Application of Economic Theory to the Vaccine Market. In *Supplying Vaccines: An Economic Analysis of Critical Issues*, ed. Mark V. Pauly, Chester A. Robinson, Stephen J. Sepe, Merrile Sing, and Mary Kaye Willian, 101–31. Amsterdam: IOS Press.

_____. 2005. An Overview of the Market for Vaccines in the United States. Unpublished manuscript. Department of Economics, University of Illinois, Champaign, Ill. January 4.

Associated Press. 2007. Court Investigates Vaccine Link to Autism. June 11. http:// www.msnbc.msn.com/id/19168291/print/1/displaymode/1098/ (accessed December 28, 2007).

Avorn, Jerry. 2004. *Powerful Medicines: The Benefits, Risks, and Costs of Prescription Drugs*. New York: Alfred A. Knopf.

Baker, Jeffrey P. 2003. The Pertussis Vaccine Controversy in Great Britain, 1974–1986. *Vaccine* 21 (25–26): 4003–10.

_____. 2008. Mercury, Vaccines, and Autism: One Controversy, Three Histories. *American Journal of Public Health* 98 (2): 2–11.

Bardiya, N., and J. H. Bae. 2005. Influenza Vaccines: Recent Advances in Production Technologies. *Applied Microbiology and Biotechnology* 67 (3): 299–305.

Berndt, Ernst R. 2001. The U.S. Pharmaceutical Industry: Why Major Growth in Times of Cost Containment– *Health Affairs* 20 (2): 100–114.

_____. 2002. Pharmaceuticals in U.S. Health Care: Determinants of Quantity and Price. *Journal of Economic Perspectives* 16 (4): 45–66.

_____. 2007a. A Primer on the Economics of Re-Importation of Prescription Drugs. *Managerial and Decision Economics* 28: 415–37.

———. 2007b. The United States' Experience with Direct-to-Consumer Advertising of Prescription Drugs: What Have We Learned– *Pharmaceutical Innovation: Incentives, Competition, and Cost-Benefit Analysis in International Perspective*, ed. Frank A. Sloan and Chee-Ruey Hsieh. 174–95. Cambridge: Cambridge University Press.

Berndt, Ernst R., David M. Cutler, Richard G. Frank, Zvi Griliches, Joseph P. Newhouse, and Jack E. Triplett. 2000. Medical Care Prices and Output. In *Handbook of Health Economics*, ed. Anthony J. Culyer and Joseph P. Newhouse, 1A: 119–80. Amsterdam: Elsevier Sciences B.V.

Berndt, Ernst R., and John Hurvitz. 2005. Vaccine Advance-Purchase Agreements for Low-Income Countries: Practical Issues. *Health Affairs* 24 (3): 653–65.

Berndt, Ernst R., and Julie M. Donohue. 2008. Direct-to-Consumer Advertising in Health Care: An Overview of Economic Issues. In *Incentives and Choice in Health and Health Care*, ed. Frank A. Sloan and Hershel Kasper. 131–62. Cambridge, Mass.: MIT Press.

Berndt, Ernst R., Rachel Glennerster, Michael R. Kremer, Jean Lee, Ruth Levine, Georg Weizsacker, and Heidi Williams. 2007. Advance Market Commitments for Vaccines Against Neglected Diseases: Estimating Costs and Effectiveness. *Health Economics* 16 (1): 491–511.

BioSignpost. 2007. New Chemical Entity. http://www.biosignpost.com/GLOSSARY– (accessed June 13, 2007).

Boegaerts, H. 2005. Background to Vaccines. Slide 15 of 29. http://www.gsk.com/investors/presentations_webcast05.htm (accessed June 16, 2007).

Breuer, Thomas (vice president, Worldwide Regulatory, Epidemiology & Safety, GlaxoSmithKline). 2005. *Streptorix—Going Beyond Prevnar.* Slide presentation. http://www.glaxosmithklinepic.net/investors/presentations/vaccines2005/Streptorix.pdf (accessed August 22, 2007).

Brooks, Dennis A., and Richard Clover. 2006. Pertussis Infection in the United States: Role for Vaccination of Adolescents and Adults. *Journal of the American Board of Family Medicine* 19 (6): 603–11.

Brouwer C. N., A. R. Maille, M. M. Rovers, R. H. Veenhoven, D. E. Grobbee, E. A. Sanders, and A. G. Schilder. 2005. Effect of Pneumococcal Vaccination on Quality of Life in Children with Recurrent Acute Otitis Media: A Randomized, Controlled Trial. *Pediatrics* 115 (2): 273–79.

Brown, David. 2008. This Season's Flu Strains Are Not a Good Match for Vaccine. *Washington Post.* February 10, A3.

Buckland, Barry C. 2005. The Process Development Challenge for a New Vaccine. *Nature Medicine* 11: S16–S19.

Butler, Jay C., Robert F. Breiman, Harvey B. Lipman, Jo Hoffman, and Richard R. Facklam. 1995. Serotype Distribution of Streptococcus Pneumoniae Infections among Preschool Children in the United States, 1978–1994: Implications for Development of a Conjugate Vaccine. *Journal of Infectious Diseases* 171 (4): 885–9.

Calfee, John E., Mario Villarreal, and Elizabeth DuPre. 2007. Biotechnology Drugs, Traditional Pharmaceuticals and Price Controls. Working Paper 06-07. AEI-Brookings Joint Center for Regulatory Studies. Washington, D.C. http://www.aei-brookings. org/admin/authorpdfs/page.php–id=1265 (accessed November 23, 2008).

Campbell, Denis. 2007. I Told the Truth All Along, Says Doctor at Heart of Autism Row. *Observer.* July 8. http://observer.guardian.co.uk/uk_news/story/0,,2121522,00.html (accessed December 28, 2007).

Campbell, Michael J., and David Machin. 1993. *Medical Statistics: A Commonsense Approach.* 2d ed. New York: John Wiley & Sons.

Carey, Benedict. 2008. Into the Fray Over the Cause of Autism. *New York Times.* March 4, A18.

Carey, John. 2002. Vaccines Are Getting a Booster Shot. *BusinessWeek.* December 9. http://www.businessweek.com/magazine/content/02_49/b3811060.htm (accessed August 22, 2007).

Carpenter, Daniel. 2005. A Proposal for Financing Postmarketing Drug Safety Studies by Augmenting FDA User Fees. *Health Affairs Web Exclusive* W5-469-480, posted October 18.

Centers for Disease Control and Prevention (n.d.). Varicella. http://www.cdc. gov/vaccines/pubs/pinkbook/downloads/varicella.pdf (accessed August 23, 2007).

———. 1996. Food and Drug Administration Notice to Readers: FDA Approval of a Haemophilus B Conjugate Vaccine Combined by Reconstitution with an Acellular Pertussis Vaccine. *Morbidity and Mortality Weekly Report* 45 (45): 993–95. http://wonder.cdc.gov.woner/PrevGuid/m0044501/m0044501.asp (accessed August 21, 2007).

———. 2003. Notice to Readers: FDA Approval of Diphtheria and Tetanus Toxoids and Acellular Pertussis Vaccine Adsorbed (INFANRIX) for Fifth Consecutive DTaP Vaccine Dose. *Morbidity and Mortality Review* 52 (38): 921–22. http://www. cdc.gov/mmwr/preview/mmwrhtml/mm5238a9.htm (accessed August 21, 2007).

———. 2005a. CDC Announces New Strategies to Promote Continued Influenza Vaccination. Press release. January 27. http://www.cdc.gov/od/oc/media/pressrel/ r050127.htm (last accessed August 21, 2007).

———. 2005b. Pertussis. Division of Bacterial and Mycotic Diseases. October 13. http://www.cdc.gov/ncidod/dbmd/diseaseinfo/pertussis_t.htm (accessed August 21, 2007).

———. 2006a. Questions & Answers: Influenza Vaccine Production, Supply & Distribution in the United States. June 30. http://www.cdc.gov/flu/about/qa/ vaxsupply.htm (accessed August 21, 2007).

———. 2006b. Fact Sheet: Key Facts about Influenza and the Influenza Vaccine. August 30. http://www.cdc.gov/flu/keyfacts.htm (accessed August 21, 2007).

———. 2006c. More than 100 Million Doses of Influenza Vaccine Expected to be Available This Year. Press release. September 6. http://www.cdc.gov/od/oc/media/ pressrel/r060906b/htm (accessed August 21, 2007).

————. 2006d. National Influenza Vaccine Summit Newsletter. No. 4, November 13. http://www.cdc.gov/flu/professionals/bulletin/2006-07/bulletin4_111306.htm (accessed August 21, 2007).

————. 2007a. 2007–08 Influenza Prevention & Control Recommendations: Primary Changes and Updates in the 2007 Recommendations. October 26. http://www.cdc.gov/flu/professionals/acip/primarychanges.htm (accessed December 28, 2007).

————. 2007b. Interim Recommendations for the Use of *Haemophilus influenzae* Type b (Hib) Conjugate Vaccines Related to the Recall of Certain Lots of Hib-Containing Vaccines (PedvaxHIB™ and Comvax™). http://www.cdc.gov/mmwr/preview/mmwrhtml/mm56d1219a1.htm (accessed December 28, 2007).

————. 2007c. Nation's Influenza Vaccine Supplies Continue to Increase; CDC Advises Broadening of Vaccination Efforts. November 9. http://www.cdc.gov/od/oc/media/pressrel/2007/r071109.htm (last accessed December 28, 2007).

————. 2007d. Notice to Readers: Availability of Additional Trivalent Inactivated Influenza Vaccine for Adults (Afluria™). November 23. http://wwww.cdc.gov/mmwr/preview/mmwrhtml/mm5646a5.htm (accessed December 28, 2007).

————. 2007e. Notice to Readers: Expansion of Use of Live Attenuated Influenza Vaccine (FluMist) to Children Aged 2–4 Years and Other FluMist Changes for the 2007–08 Influenza Season. November 23. http://www.cdc.gov/mmwr/preview/mmwrhtml/mm5646a4.htm (accessed December 28, 2007).

————. 2007f. Notice to Readers: Update on Supply of Vaccines Containing Varicella-Zoster Virus. *Journal of the American Medical Association* 298 (7): 736.

————. 2007g. Questions & Answers: The 2007–2008 Flu Season. December 17. http://www.cdc.gov/flu/about/qa/season.htm (accessed December 28, 2007).

————. 2007h. Vaccine Safety Datalink Project (VSD). March 21. http://www.cdc.gov/od/science/iso/research_activities/vsdp.htm (accessed August 21, 2007).

————. 2007i. *Vaccine Storage and Handling Toolkit*. National Immunization Program. http://www2.cdc.gov/nip/isd/shtoolkit/content.html (accessed June 25, 2007).

————. 2007j. Vaccines and Immunizations: Questions and Answers about Hib Recall. December 12. http://www.cdc.gov/vaccines/recs/recalls/hib-recall-faqs-12-12-07.htm (accessed December 12, 2007).

————. 2007k. Vaccines and Preventable Diseases: Current Vaccine Shortages & Delays. December 19. http://www.cdc.gov/vaccines/vac-gen/shortages/default.htm (accessed December 28, 2007).

————. 2008a. Nationally Notifiable Infectious Diseases, United States 2008. Updated November 4, 2008. http://www.cdc.gov.ncphi/disss/nndss/PHS/infdis2008.htm (accessed November 22, 2008).

————. 2008b. Seasonal Influenza Vaccine Supply for the U.S. 2008–09 Influenza Season. October 29. http://www.cdc.gov/flu/about/qa/vaxsupply.htm (accessed November 22, 2008).

————. 2009a. 2008–2009 Influenza Season Week 8 ending February 28, 2009. March 6. http://www.cdc.gov/flu/weekly/ (accessed March 12, 2009).

_____. 2009b. Current Vaccine Shortages & Delays. Last updated March 2, 2009. http://www.cdc.gov/vaccines/vac-gen/shortages/default.htm (accessed March 28, 2009).

Centers for Medicare & Medicaid Services. 2008. 2008 ASP Drug Pricing Files October 2008 Updates. Updated September 23, 2008. http://www.cms.hhs.gov/McrPartBDrugAvgSalesPrice/01a_2008aspfiles.asp (accessed November 15, 2008).

Chan, Ivan S. F., and Sang Ahnn. 2005. Statistical Issues and Challenges in Combination Vaccines. Presentation at 2005 FDA/Industry Statistics Workshop. Washington, D.C., September.

Chaves, Sandra S., Paul Gargiullo, John X. Zhang, Rachel Civen, Dalya Guris, Laurene Mascola, and Jane F. Steward. 2007. Loss of Vaccine-Induced Immunity to Varicella Over Time. *New England Journal of Medicine* 356 (11): 1121–29.

Christian Sarkine Autism Treatment Center. 2008. Welcome. http://www.handsinautism.org (accessed January 13, 2008).

Clarke, Stewart C. 2006. Control of Pneumococcal Disease in the United Kingdom—The Start of a New Era. *Journal of Medical Microbiology.* 55 (8): 975–80.

ClinicalTrials.gov. 2008. Trial to Evaluate the Efficacy of GSK Biologicals' Influenza Vaccine GSK2186877A in Adults 65 Years of Age and Older. November 13, 2008. http://clinicaltrials.gov/ct2/show/NCT00753272 (accessed November 15, 2008).

Coleman, Margaret S., Nalinee Sangrujee, Fangjun Zhou, and Susan Chu. 2005. Factors Affecting US Manufacturers' Decisions to Produce Vaccines. *Health Affairs* 24 (3): 635–42.

Colgrove, James, and Ronald Bayer. 2005. Could It Happen Here– Vaccine Risk Controversies and the Specter of Derailment. *Health Affairs* 24 (3): 729–39.

Congressional Budget Office. 2005. Economic Issues in the Human Vaccine Markets. By Ernst R. Berndt. Presentation to the Advisory Panel Meeting. Washington, D.C., November 18.

———. 2006. A Potential Influenza Pandemic: An Update on Possible Macroeconomic Effects and Policy Issues. Revised July 27. Washington, D.C.: U.S. Government Printing Office.

CSL Biotherapies Inc. 2007. Afluria Influenza Virus Vaccine. http://www.afluria.com/AfluriaInfluenzaVirusVaccine (accessed December 30, 2007).

Danzon, Patricia M., and Nuno Sousa Pereira. 2005. Why Sole-Supplier Vaccine Markets May Be Here to Stay. *Health Affairs* 24 (3): 694–96.

Danzon, Patricia M., Nuno Sousa Pereira, and Sapna S. Tejwani. 2005. Vaccine Supply: A Cross-National Perspective. *Health Affairs* 24 (3): 706–17.

Datamonitor. 2004. *Commercial Perspectives: Vaccines—Nosocomial Pathogens.* London. January 20. http://www.alacrastore.com/storecontent/datamonitor-premium-profiles/DMHC1958 (accessed November 27, 2008).

———. 2005a. *Merck & Co: PharmaVitae Profile.* November 8. http://www.alacrastore.com/storecontent/datamonitor-premium-profiles/CSHC1312 (accessed November 27, 2008).

———. 2005b. *Stakeholder Perspectives: Influenza Vaccines—Flying Back Into Flu.* December 26. http://www.alacrastore.com/storecontent/datamonitor-premium-profiles/DMHC2156 (accessed November 27, 2008.

———. 2006. *Wyeth: PharmaVitae Profile.* December. http://www.plusdetudes.com/p044054/aWyeth-PharmaVitae-Profile.html (accessed November 27, 2008).

Davis, Matthew M. 2007. Reasons and Remedies for Underinsurance for Child and Adolescent Vaccines. *Journal of the American Medical Association* 298 (6): 680–82.

Deer, Brian. 2007a. GMC Announces Wakefield MMR Misconduct Hearing. http://briandeer.com/wakefield/gmc-notice.htm (accessed January 5, 2008).

———. 2007b. How Lawyers Paid for Start of MMR Scare: Letters Refute Andrew Wakefield's Story. http://briandeer.com/wakefield/wakefield-deal.htm (accessed January 7, 2008).

———. 2007c. The MMR-Autism Scare—Our Story So Far. http://briandeer.com/mmr/lancet-sumary.htm (accessed January 7, 2008).

———. 2008. Personal email communication with the authors. November 14, 2008.

———. 2009. Hidden Records Show MMR Truth. *The Sunday Times.* February 8. http://www.timesonline.co.uk/tol/life_and_style/health/article5683643.ece–print =yes&ran (accessed March 12, 2009).

Demaine, Linda J., and Aaron X. Fellmeth. 2003. Natural Substances and Patentable Inventions. *Science* 300 (5624): 1375–76.

DiMasi, Joseph A., and Henry G. Grabowski. 2008. The Cost of Biopharmaceutical R&D: Is Biotech Different– *Managerial and Decision Economics* 28: 469–79.

DiMasi, Joseph A., Henry G. Grabowski, and John M. Vernon. 2004. R&D Costs and Returns by Therapeutic Category. *Drug Information Journal* 38 (3): 211–23.

DiMasi, Joseph A., Ronald W. Hansen, and Henry G. Grabowski. 2003. The Price of Innovation: New Estimates of Drug Development Costs. *Journal of Health Economics* 22 (3): 141–85.

DiMasi, Joseph A., Ronald W. Hansen, Henry G. Grabowski, and Louis C. Lasagna. 1995. Research and Development Costs for New Drugs by Therapeutic Category: A Study of the U.S. Pharmaceutical Industry. *PharmacoEconomics* 7 (2): 152–69.

Donohue, Julie M., Marisa Cevasco, and Meredith B. Rosenthal. 2007. A Decade of Direct-to-Consumer Advertising of Prescription Drugs. *New England Journal of Medicine* 357 (7): 35–43.

Dooren, Jennifer Corbett. 2008a. Flu-Vaccine Change Risks Delivery Delay. *Wall Street Journal.* February 22, B4.

———. 2008b. HPV Vaccine Gaining Acceptance. *Wall Street Journal.* October 10, B5.

Drug Facts and Comparisons. 2006. Pneumococcal Vaccine, Polyvalent. St. Louis: Wolters Kluwer Health, 1962–63.

Drug Store News. 1999. FDA Approves First Lyme Disease Vaccine. January 11. http://findarticles.com/p/articles/mi_m3374/is_1_21/ai_53617529 (accessed September 3, 2007).

Eby, Ronald J., Dace V. Madore, and Velupillai Puvanesarajah. n.d. The Story of Prevnar. Innovation.org. http://www.innovation.org/index.cfm/StoriesofInnovation/InnovatorStories/The_Story_of_Prevnar (accessed August 22, 2007).

Emling, Shelley. 2008. Autism Doctor Faces Disciplinary Hearing. *Austin American-Statesman*. March 28. http://www.statesman.com/news/content/news/stories/world/03/28/0328wakefield.html (accessed April 21, 2008).

Epstein, Richard A. 2005. It Did Happen Here: Fear and Loathing on the Vaccine Trail. *Health Affairs* 24 (3): 740–43.

Fallik, Dawn. 2008. Questions about Links between Mitochondrial Encephalopathies and Autism Raised in National Meeting. *Neurology Today* 8 (16): 33–35.

Federal Trade Commission. 2007. Bureau of Economics. Developing a Vaccine: AIDS versus Malaria. By Christopher P. Adams and Van V. Brantner. Unpublished working paper. Washington, D.C., June 17.

Finkelstein, Amy. 2004. Static and Dynamic Effects of Health Policy: Evidence from the Vaccine Industry. *Quarterly Journal of Economics* 119 (2): 527–64.

Frank, Richard G. 2001. Prescription Drug Prices: Why Do Some Pay More Than Others Do– *Health Affairs* 20 (2): 115–28.

Fuentes, Annette. 2004. A Quiet Victory in Iowa. *In These Times*. June 9. http://www.alternet.org/story/18911/ (accessed January 13, 2008).

Galambos, Louis. 1995. *Networks of Innovation: Vaccine Development at Merck, Sharp & Dohme, and Mulford, 1895–1995*. With Jane Eliot Sewell. Cambridge: Cambridge University Press.

Garber, Alan M. 2000. Advances in CE Analysis. In *Handbook of Health Economics*, ed. Anthony J. Culyer and Joseph P. Newhouse 1A: 181–221. Amsterdam: Elsevier Publishers.

Garrett, Thomas A. 2008. Pandemic Economics: The 1918 Influenza and Its Modern-Day Implications. *Federal Reserve Bank of St. Louis Review*. March/April, 75–93.

Gershon, Anne A. 1999. Varicella Vaccine: Its History and Its Uses. *P&S Medical Review* 6 (1). http://www.cumc.columbia.edu/news/review/medrev_v6n1_0001.html (accessed August 23, 2007).

Gever, John. 2008. NIMH Cancels Autism Chelation Trial. September 19. http://www.printthis.clickability.com/pt/cpt–action=cpt&title=NIMH+Cancels+Autism+C... (accessed November 8, 2008).

Giannini, Sandra L., Emmanuel Hanon, Philippe Moris, Marcelle Van Mechelen, Sandra Morel, Francis Dessy, Marc A. Fourneau, Brigitte Colau, Joann Suzich, Genevieve Losonksy, Marie-Therese Martin, Gary Dubin, and Martine A. Wettendorf. 2006. Enhanced Humoral and Memory B Cellular Immunity Using HPV16/188 L1 VLP Vaccine Formulated with the MPL/Aluminum Salt Combination (AS04) Compared to Aluminum Salt Only. *Vaccine* 24 (33–34): 5937–49.

Giles, Jim. 2008. Autism Payout Reignites Vaccine Controversy. *New Scientist*. March 8. http://www.newscientist.com/channel/health/mg19726464.100-autism-payout-reignites-va (accessed April 21, 2008).

GlaxoSmithKline. 2007a. GlaxoSmithKline Commends $1.5 Billion Advance Market Commitment for Pneumococcal Vaccines. Press release. February 9, 2007. http://us.gsk.com/ControllerServlet–appId=4&pageId=402&newsid=1019 (accessed January 6, 2008).

———. 2007b. PEDIARIX (Dipththeria and Tetanus Toxoids and Acellular Pertussis Adsorbed, Hepatitis B (Recombinant) and Inactivated Poliovirus Vaccine Combined). http://www.us.gsk.com/products/assets/us_pediarix.pdf (accessed August 21, 2007).

———. 2008. New Data for GlaxoSmithKline's Pre-pandemic H5N1 Influenza Vaccine, Prepandrix, Show Administration Flexibility for Pandemic Planning. Press release. September 16, 2008. http://www.gsk.com/media/pressreleases/2008/2008_pressrelease_10106.htm (accessed November 22, 2008).

Global Alliance for Vaccines and Immunization (GAVI). 2004. Research Briefing No. 2: Vaccines are Cost-Effective: A Summary of Recent Research. In *Health, Immunization and Economic Growth.* http://www.gavistg3.elca-services.com/General_Information/Immunization_informa/Economic_Impact/vacc..cost.php (accessed August 23, 2007).

———. 2007. Five Nations and the Bill & Melinda Gates Foundation Launch Advance Market Commitment for Vaccines to Combat Deadly Disease in Poor Nations. Press release. February 9. http://www.gavialliance.org/media_centre/press_releases/2007_02_09_en_pr_amc.php (accessed January 6, 2008).

Gold, Martha R., Joanna E. Siegel, Louise B. Russell, and Milton C. Weinstein, eds. 1996. *Cost-Effectiveness in Health and Medicine.* New York: Oxford University Press.

Gordon, Nancy P. 2000. *Kaiser Permanente Northern California 1999 Adult Member Health Survey: Characteristics of Adult Health Plan Members in the Northern California Region Membership, as Estimated from the 1999 Member Health Survey: Regional and Medical Center Service Area Populations.* Oakland, Calif.: Division of Research, Kaiser Permanente Medical Care Program.

Gotzsche, Peter C. 2006. Lessons from and Cautions about Noninferiority and Equivalence Trials. Editorial, March 8. *Journal of the American Medical Association* 295 (10): 1172–74.

Grabowski, Henry G. 2007. Data Exclusivity for New Biological Entities. Unpublished working paper, Department of Economics, Duke University. June.

Grabowski, Henry G., Iain M. Cockburn, and Genia C. Long. 2006. The Market for Follow-On Biologics: How Will It Evolve– *Health Affairs* 25 (5): 1291–1301.

Grabowski, Henry G., and John M. Vernon. 1992. Brand Loyalty, Entry and Price Competition in Pharmaceuticals after the 1984 Drug Law Act. *Journal of Law and Economics* 35 (October): 331–50.

———. 1997. *The Search for New Vaccines: The Effects of the Vaccines for Children Program.* Washington, D.C.: AEI Press.

Grosse, Scott D., Steven M. Teutsch, and Anne C. Haddix. 2007. Lessons from Cost-Effectiveness Research for United States Public Health Policy. *Annual Review of Public Health* 28 (January 12): 365–91.

Halliday, R. G., S. R. Walker, and C. E. Lumley. 1992. R&D Philosophy and Management in the World's Leading Pharmaceutical Companies. *Journal of Pharmaceutical Medicines* 2: 139–54.

Harris, Gariner. 2008. Experts to Discuss One Puzzling Autism Case, as a Second Case Has Arisen. *New York Times*, national edition. June 28, A15.

Hass, Arthur E., Randall Lutter, John Goldsmith, and Allan Begosh. 2006. Measuring Change in the Effectiveness of FDA's Post-Market Drug Surveillance and Risk Management: Insights from the Timing of Label Warnings. Powerpoint presentation to Joint Productivity and Health Workshop, National Bureau of Economic Research. Cambridge, Mass. July

Heavey, Susan. 2008. U.S. Approves 6 Flu Vaccines for Next Season. *Reuters Business and Finance*. August 5. http://uk.reuters.com/article/healthNews/idUK0534516320080805–feedType=RSS&fee... (accessed November 15, 2008).

Henrichsen, Jorgen. 1995. Six Newly Recognized Types of Streptococcus Pneumoniae. *Journal of Clinical Microbiology* 33 (10): 2759–62.

Hilts, Philip J. 2001. Certainty and Uncertainty in Treatment of Lyme Disease. *New York Times*. July 10. http://query.nytimes.com/gst/fullpage.html–res=9E02E2D71038F933A25754 (accessed September 3, 2007).

Hinman Alan R. 2005. Addressing the Vaccine Financing Conundrum. *Health Affairs* 24 (3): 701–4.

Hirschler, Ben. 2007. Wyeth Says Glaxo Rival Won't Derail Prevnar. Reuters. December 4. http://www.reuters.com/article/reutersEdge/idUSL0472797720071204 (accessed December 28, 2007).

———. 2009. Glaxo May Not Launch Synflorix Vaccine in U.S. February 5. http://www.iht.com/articles/reuters/2009/02/05/business/OUKBS-UK-SYNFLORIX.php (accessed February 9, 2009).

Hitti, Miranda. 2008. HPV Vaccine Gardasil May Help Boys, Men. WebMD HPV/Genital Warts Health Center. November 13. http://www.webmd.com/sexual-conditions/hpv-genital-warts/news/20081113/hpv-vaccin... (accessed November 15, 2008).

Hochman, Michael. 2005. Childhood Vaccine Saves Lives, But May Lead to Other Infections. *Boston Globe*. June 21.

Hofman, Jan. 2008. Vaccinating Boys for Girls' Sake– *New York Times*. February 24.

Horton, Richard. 2004. A Statement by the Editors of the *Lancet*. *Lancet* 363 (March 6): 820–21.

Infectious Diseases in Children Round Table. 2007a. Experts Propose Solutions to the Vaccine Reimbursement Issue. February. http://idinchildren.com/200702/roundtable.asp (accessed July 31, 2008).

———. 2007b. Pediatric Practitioners Feeling the Squeeze. January. http://idinchildren.com/200701/roundtable.asp (accessed July 31, 2008).

Institute of Medicine. 2001. *Immunization Safety Review: Thimerosal-Containing Vaccines and Neurodevelopmental Disorders.* Washington, D.C.: National Academies Press.

———. 2004a. *Financing Vaccines in the 21st Century: Assuring Access and Availability.* Washington, D.C.: National Academies Press.

———. 2004b. *Immunization Safety Review: Vaccines and Autism.* Washington, D.C.: National Academies Press.

Kaiser Permanente. 2007. Kaiser Permanente: Facts and Statistics National. https://newsmedia. kaiserpermanente.org/kpweb/fastfactsmedia/entrypage2.do (accessed July 4, 2007).

Kaitin, Kenneth. 2008. Personal communications with the authors. April.

Kaul, Sanjay, and George A. Diamond. 2006. Good Enough: A Primer on the Analysis and Interpretation of Noninferiority Trials. *Annals of Internal Medicine* 145 (63): 62–69.

Kennedy, Robert F. Jr. 2005. Deadly Immunity: Robert F. Kennedy Jr. Investigates the Government Coverup of a Mercury/Autism Scandal. *Rolling Stone.* June 20. http://www.rollingstone.com/politics/story/7395411/deadly_immunity/print (accessed January 13, 2008).

Kirby, David. 2005. *Evidence of Harm: Mercury in Vaccines and the Autism Epidemic: A Medical Controversy.* New York: St. Martin's Press.

Kremer, Michael, and Christopher M. Snyder. 2003. Why Are Drugs More Profitable Than Vaccines– Working Paper No. 9833. July. Cambridge, Mass.: National Bureau of Economic Research.

———. 2007. Why Is There No AIDS Vaccine– Unpublished paper, Department of Economics, Dartmouth College, Hanover, N.H.

Kremer, Michael, and Rachel Glennerster. 2004. *Strong Medicine: Creating Incentives for Pharmaceutical Research on Neglected Diseases.* Princeton N.J.: Princeton University Press.

Kyaw, Moe H., Ruth Lynfield, William Schaffner, Allen S. Craig, James Hadler, Arthur Reingold, Ann R. Thomas, Lee H. Harrison, Nancy M. Bennett, Monica M. Farley, Richard R. Facklam, James H. Jorgensen, John Besser, Elizabeth R. Zell, Ann Schuchat, and Cynthia G. Whitney (Active Bacterial Core Surveillance of the Emerging Infections Program Network). 2006. Effect of Introduction of the Pneumococcal Conjugate Vaccine on Drug-Resistant *Streptococcus pneumoniae. New England Journal of Medicine* 354 (14): 1455–63.

LaFee, Scott. 2009. More Local Scientists Identify Flu Antibody. February 26. http://www3.signonsandiego.com/stories/2009/feb/26/bn26flu-antibody-cure/–zIndex=58998 (accessed Feburary 27, 2009).

Landry, Sarah, and Carole Heilman. 2005. Future Directions in Vaccines: The Payoffs Of Basic Research. *Health Affairs* 24 (3): 758–69.

Lauerman, John. 2007. Glaxo, Novartis May Have Bet Wrong on Flu-Shot Race (Update2). August 23. Bloomberg.com. http://www.bloomberg.com/apps/news–pid=20601109&sid=akQiRFCOu32k&refer=home (accessed August 24, 2007).

Laurance, Jeremy. 2007. MMR Scare Doctor 'Paid Children £5 for Blood Samples.' *Independent News.* July 17. http://news.independent.co.uk/health/article2776140.ece (accessed December 28, 2007).

Lee, Grace M., Jeanne M. Santoli, Claire Hannan, Mark L. Messonnier, James E. Sabin, Donna Rusinak, Charlene Gay, Susan M. Lett, and Tracy A. Lieu. 2007. Gaps in Vaccine Financing for Underinsured Children in the United States. *Journal of the American Medical Association* 298 (6): 638–43.

Levine, Ruth, Michael Kremer, and Alice Albright. 2005. *Making Markets for Vaccines: Ideas to Action.* Report of the Center for Global Development. Advance Market Commitment Working Group. Washington, D.C. http://www.cgdev.org/vaccine (accessed July 31, 2008).

Lewcock, Anna. 2007. VaxInnate's Universal Flu Shot Enters Trials. *In-Pharma Technologist.* September 26. http://www.in-pharmatechnologist.com/news/ng.asp–n= 80106-vaxinnate-universal-vaccin (accessed September 29, 2007).

Lexau, Catherine A., Ruth Lynfield, Richard Danila, Tamara Pilishvili, Richard Facklam, Monia M. Farley, Lee H. Harrison, William Schaffner, Arthur Reingold, Nancy M. Bennett, James Hadler, Paul R. Cieslak, Cynthia G. Whitney (Active Bacterial Core Surveillance of the Emerging Infections Program Network). 2005. Changing Epidemiology of Invasive Pneumococcal Disease Among Older Adults in the Era of Pediatric Pneumococcal Conjugate Vaccine. *Journal of the American Medical Association* 294 (16): 2043–51.

Li, S., I. S. Chan, H. Matthews, J. F. Heyse, C. Y. Chan, B. J. Kuter, K. M. Kaplan, S. J. Vessey, and J. C. Sadoff. 2002. Inverse Relationship Between Six Week Postvaccination Varicella Antibody Response to Vaccine and Likelihood of Long Term Breakthrough Infection. *Pediatric Infectious Disease Journal* 21 (4): 337–42.

Lieu, Tracy A., Stephen L. Cochi, Steven B. Black, M. Elizabeth Halloran, Henry R. Shinefield, Sandra J. Holmes, Melinda Wharton, and A. Eugene Washington. 1994. Cost-Effectiveness of a Routine Varicella Vaccination Program for U.S. Children. *Journal of the American Medical Association* 271 (5): 375–81.

Lieu, Tracy A., Thomas G. McGuire, and Alan R. Hinman. 2005. Overcoming Economic Barriers to the Optimal Use of Vaccines. *Health Affairs* 24 (3): 666–77.

Loftus, Peter. 2008. Merck Signals Delays For Its Shingles Vaccine. *Wall Street Journal.* June 26, D2.

Lorenzo, Aaron. 2005a. Crawford: Safety Issues at FDA Require Better Communication. *BioWorld Today* 16 (81): 1, 4.

———. 2005b. What's Wrong at the FDA– The System, Says One Critic. *BioWorld Today* 16 (1): 1, 5.

Macdonald, Gareth. 2009. Novartis Gets $487m for US Cell Culture Flu Vac Plant. January 19. http://www.in-pharmatechnologist.com/content/view/print/233298 (accessed January 19, 2009).

MacNeil, John S., and Frank L. Douglas. 2007. Challenges to Establishing a Regulatory Framework for Approving Follow-on Biologics: A Background Paper. Unpublished manuscript. Center for Biomedical Innovation, Massachusetts Institute of Technology. September 2007.

Manning, Richard L. 1994. Changing Rules in Tort Law and the Market for Child-hood Vaccines. *Journal of Law and Economics* 37 (1): 247–75.

McKesson Specialty. 2006. McKesson Corporation Selected by CDC for National Vaccine Distribution Program. Press release. September 18. http://www.redorbit.com/news/health/660573/mckesson_corporation_selected_by_cdc_fo… (accessed November 27, 2008).

McNeil, Donald G. Jr. 2006. How a Vaccine Search Ended in Triumph. *New York Times*. August 29, D1, D6.

Mehigh, Christine. 2008. New Possible Cause Identified for Autism. *Biotech Files*. July 10. http://biotechfiles.com/2008/07/new-possible-cause-identified-for-autism/ (accessed November 15, 2008).

Mello, Michelle M., and Troyen A. Brennan. 2005. Legal Concerns and the Influenza Vaccine Shortage. *Journal of the American Medical Association* 294 (14): 1817–20.

Merck & Co. Inc. 2005. FDA Approves PROQUAD(R), the First and Only Vaccine in the U.S. to Help Protect Children against Measles, Mumps, Rubella and Chickenpox in One Shot. Press release. September 6. http://goliath.ecnext.com/coms2/gi_0199-4660492/FDA-Approves-PROQUAD-R-the.html (accessed August 23, 2007).

Merck Vaccines. 2008. Vaccine Supply Status Updates. Posted November 7, 2008. https://www.merckvaccines.com/srv/gw/home/desktop.jsp–in-frame=yes (accessed November 14, 2008).

Morgan Stanley. 2005. *Highlighting a New Generation of Promising Vaccines*. Morgan Stanley Equity Research, North America, Pharmaceuticals, Major: Industry Overview. June 6. www.morganstanley.com/equityresearch.

Murch, Simon H., Andrew Anthony, David H. Casson, Mohsin Malik, Mark Berelowitz, Amar P. Dhillon, Michael A. Thomson, Alan Valentine, Susan E. Davies, and John A. Walker-Smith. 2004. Retraction of an Interpretation. *Lancet* 363: 750.

Namovicz-Peat, Susan, ed. 2003. *Specialty Pharmacy: Stakeholders, Strategies and Markets*. Washington, D.C.: Atlantic Information Services.

National Autism Association. 2007. Autism Families Keep Close Watch as First Test Case Goes to Vaccine Court. June 4. http://www.vaclib/org/news/2007/naatestcase.htm (accessed January 15, 2008).

National Autistic Society. 2008. General Medical Council Hearing against Dr. Andrew Wakefield. Statement. http://www.nas.org.uk/nas/jsp/polopoly.jsp–d=459&a=13952 (accessed April 21, 2008).

National Immunization Congress. 2007. Adult and Adolescent Immunization Summary. February 28–March 1.

National Institute of Allergy and Infectious Diseases. 1999. Improved Pertussis Vaccines: Enhancing Protection. Stories of Discovery. http://www.niaid.nih.gov/publications/discovery/pertus.htm (accessed August 21, 2007).

National Institute of Child Health and Human Development. 2003. NICHD Honors Outstanding Scientists During 40th Anniversary Year. http://www.nichd.nih.gov/news/releases/40th_anniversary.cfm (accessed August 14, 2007).

National Vaccine Information Center. 2000. Parents and Researchers Call for Action to End Gaps in Knowledge about Autism and the Vaccine Connection. April 6. http://www.nvic.org/PressReleases/pr040600autism.htm (accessed January 13, 2008).

National Vaccine Injury Compensation Program. 2007. Post-1988 statistics report, as of June 1, 2007. http://www.hrsa.gov/vaccinecompensation/statistics_report.htm (accessed June 24, 2007).

Nichol, Kristin L., James D. Nordin, David B. Nelson, John P. Mullooly, and Eelko Hak. 2007. Effectiveness of Influenza Vaccine in the Community-Dwelling Elderly. *New England Journal of Medicine* 357 (14): 1373–81.

Novartis. 2006. Pivotal Phase III Trial Results Show Novartis Cell Culture–Derived Influenza Vaccine Well-Tolerated and Efficacious. Press release. October 19. http://novartisvaccines.com/press-room/news/20061019-fcc.shtml (accessed August 21, 2007).

———. 2007a. Focetria, the Novartis Pandemic Influenza Vaccine, Receives European Union Approval. Press release. May 8. http://novartisvaccines.com/press-room/news/20070508_Focetria.shtml (accessed August 21, 2007).

———. 2007b. Novartis Gains European Approval for Its Innovative Flu Vaccine Optaflu. Press release. June 13. http://novartisvaccines.com/press-room/news/20070613_Optaflu_approved.shtml (accessed August 21, 2007).

———. 2007c. Optaflu, the Novartis Cell Culture-Derived Influenza Vaccine, Receives Positive Opinion Supporting European Union Regulatory Approval. Press release. April 27. http://www.novartisvaccines.com/press-room/news/20070427_Optaflu.shtml (accessed August 21, 2007).

Offit, Paul A. 2005. Why Are Pharmaceutical Companies Gradually Abandoning Vaccines–*Health Affairs* 24 (3): 622–30.

———. 2007a. At Risk: Vaccines. *Boston Globe*. June 3, C1, C10.

———. 2007b. Thimerosal and Vaccines—A Cautionary Tale. *New England Journal of Medicine* 357: 1278–79.

———. 2007c. *Vaccinated: One Man's Quest to Defeat the World's Deadliest Diseases.* New York: HarperCollins Publishers Inc.

———. 2008. Inoculated against Facts. *New York Times*. Opinion. March 31. http://www.nytimes.com/2008/03/31/opinion/31offit.html-_r=1&oref-slogin (accessed April 21, 2008).

Olson, Mary K. 2002. Pharmaceutical Policy and the Safety of New Drugs. *Journal of Law and Economics* 45 (2): 615–42.

Orenstein, Walter A., R. Gordon Douglas, Lance E. Rodewald, and Alan R. Hinman. 2005. U.S. Vaccines: Success, Structure and Stress. *Health Affairs* 24 (3): 599–610.

Oxman, M. N., M. J. Levin, G. R. Johnson, K. E. Schmader, S. E. Straus, L. D. Gelb, R. D. Arbeit, M. S. Simberkoff, A. A. Gershon, L. E. Davis, A. Weinberg, K. D. Boardman, H. M. Williams, J. Hongyuan Zhang, P. N. Peduzzi, C. E. Beisel, V. A. Morrison, J. C. Guatelli, P. A. Brooks, C. A. Kauffman, C. T. Pachucki,

K. M. Neuzil, R. F. Betts, P. F. Wright, M. R. Griffin, P. Brunell, N. E. Soto, A. R. Marques, S. K. Keay, R. P. Goodman, D. J. Cotton, J. W. Gnann Jr., J. Loutit, M. Holodniy, W. A. Keitel, G. E. Crawford, S. S. Yeh, Z. Lobo, J. F. Toney, R. N. Greenberg, P. M. Keller, R. Harbecke, A. R. Hayward, M. R. Irwin, T. C. Kyriakides, C. Y. Chan, I. S. F. Chan, W.W. B. Wang, P. W. Annunziato, and J. L. Silber for the Shingles Prevention Study Group. 2005. A Vaccine to Prevent Herpes Zoster and Postherpetic Neuralgia in Older Adults. *New England Journal of Medicine* 352 (22): 2271–84.

Palta, Rina. 2004. A Timeline of the Thimerosal Controversy. *Mother Jones*. March 1. http://www.motherjones.com/news/featurex/2004/03/ttp_timeline.html (accessed January 13, 2008).

Pauly, Mark V. 2005. Improving Vaccine Supply and Development: Who Needs What– *Health Affairs* 24 (3): 680–89.

Pauly, Mark V., Chester A. Robinson, Stephen J. Sepe, Merrile Sing, and Mary Kaye Willian, eds. 1996. *Supplying Vaccines: An Economic Analysis of Critical Issues*. Amsterdam: IOS Press.

Pharmaceutical Research and Manufacturers of America. 2004. 2004 Survey: Medicines in Development for Infectious Diseases. hhttp://www.phrma.org/files/infectious%20disease%20survey.pdf (accessed August 22, 2007).

PharmaLive.com. 2007. Vaxinnate Initiates Phase I Clinical Study of M2e Universal Influenza Vaccine. http://www.pharmalive.com/News/Index.cfm–articleid=478248 (accessed September 29, 2007).

———. 2008. GlaxoSmithKline Files Pneumococcal Paediatric Vaccine in the EU. http://www.pharmalive.com/news/Print.cfm–articleid=510384 (accessed February 1, 2008).

Phelps, Charles E. 2003. *Health Economics*. 3d ed. Boston: Addison-Wesley.

Piaggio, Gilda, Diana R. Elbourne, Douglas G. Altman, Stuart J. Pocock, and Stephen J. W. Evans for the CONSORT Group. 2006. Reporting of Noninferiority and Equivalence Randomized Trials: An Extension of the Consort Statement. Special Communication. March 8. *Journal of the American Medical Association* 295 (10): 1152–60.

Pichichero, Michael E., Angela Gentile, Norberto Giglio, Veronica Umide, Thomas Clarkson, Elsa Cernichiari, Grazyna Zareba, Carlos Gotelli, Mariano Gotelli, Lihan Yan, and John Treanor. 2008. Mercury Levels in Newborns and Infants after Receipt of Thimerosal-Containing Vaccines. *Pediatrics* 121: e208–e214, DOI: 10.1542/peds.2006-3363.

Pindyck, Robert S., and Daniel L. Rubinfeld. 2005. *Microeconomics*. 6th ed. Upper Saddle River, N.J.: Pearson Prentice Hall.

Plotkin, Stanley A. 2005. Why Certain Vaccines Have Been Delayed or Not Developed at All. *Health Affairs* 24 (3): 631–34.

Plotkin, Stanley A., and Walter A. Orenstein. 2004. *Vaccines*. 4th ed. Amsterdam: Elsevier.

Pollack, Andrew. 2007. In Need of a Booster Shot: Rising Costs Making Doctors Balk at Giving Vaccines. *New York Times*. March 24.

Preblud, Stephen R. 1986. Varicella: Complications and Costs. *Pediatrics* 78 (Supp.): 728–35.

Reichert, Janice M. 2006. Trends in US Approvals: New Biopharmaceuticals and Vaccines. *Trends in Biotechnology* 24 (7): 293–98.

Reiffen, David A., and Michael R. Ward. 2005. Generic Drug Industry Dynamics. *Review of Economics and Statistics* 87 (1): 37–49.

Reuters. 2007. FDA Delays Decision on Sanofi's Pentacel to Nov. 2. June 11. http://investing.reuters.co.uk/news/articleinvesting.aspx–type=health&storyID=2006-06-1 (accessed August 21, 2007).

Riley Children's Hospital. 2008. Congressman Burton Secures an Additional $2 Million in Federal Funds to Enhance Clinical Care and Research for Autism at Riley. Press release. January 3. http://rileychildrenshospital.com/information-desk/media-center/article.jsp–id=311 (accessed January 13, 2008).

Rios, Maribel. 2006. Wrap Up: AAPS National Biotech Conference. *PharmTech*. June 22. http://www.pharmtech.com/pharmtech/article/articleDetail.jsp–id=338157.

Robinson, Chester A., and Stephen J. Sepe. 1996. Immunization Policies for the 1990s and Beyond. In *Supplying Vaccines: An Economic Analysis of Critical Issues,* ed. Mark V. Pauly, Chester A. Robinson, Stephen J. Sepe, Merrile Sing, and Mary Kaye Willian. Amsterdam: IOS Press.

Rosenwald, Michael S. 2005. FluMist Sales Falling Short, Survey Finds—Maryland Company Increased Vaccine Production at U.S. Government's Request. *Washington Post*. January 6, E05.

———. 2007. FDA Panel Supports Expanded FluMist Use, Safety for Children Under 2 Still Debated. http://www.washingtonpost.com/wp-dyn/content/article/2007/05/16/AR2007051602693.htm (accessed August 14, 2007).

Roush, Sandra W., and Trudy V. Murphy. 2007. Historical Comparisons of Morbidity and Mortality for Vaccine-Preventable Diseases in the United States. *Journal of the American Medical Association* 298: 2155–63.

RxList. 1998. Lymerix: Side Effects & Drug Interactions. http://www.rxlist.com/cgi/generic/lymerix_ad.htm (accessed September 3, 2007).

SafeMinds. 2007. Vaccine Study in *New England Journal of Medicine* Wrong in Concluding Mercury Exposures Are Harmless. State Safeminds. Press release. September 26. http://www.autismspeaks.org/science/science_news/safeminds_nejm_study.php (accessed December 28, 2007).

Salkever, David, and Richard G. Frank. 1996. Economic Issues in Vaccine Purchase Arrangements. In *Supplying Vaccines: An Economic Analysis of Critical Issues,* ed. Mark V. Pauly, Chester A. Robinson, Stephen J. Sepe, Merrile Sing, and Mary Kaye Willian. Amsterdam: IOS Press.

Sanofi Pasteur. 2007a. FDA Advisory Committee Recommends Licensure of New Pediatric Combination Vaccine. http://198.73.159.217/sanofi-pasteur/

ImageServlet–imageCode=18840&siteCode=AVPI_US (accessed August 21, 2007).

———. 2007b. Sanofi Pasteur US Products. http://www.vaccineplace.com/products/ (accessed August 21, 2007).

Sataline, Suzanne. 2007. No Vaccine Link to Behavior; CDC Study Finds Kids' Mental Acuity Not Hurt by Mercury. *Wall Street Journal.* September 27, D7.

Scherer, F. Michael. 2000. The Pharmaceutical Industry. In *Handbook of Health Economics*, ed. Anthony J. Culyer and Joseph P. Newhouse 1B: 1297–1336. Amsterdam: Elsevier Science B.V.

———. 2006. The Political Economy of Patent Policy Reform in the United States. Unpublished manuscript. John F. Kennedy School of Government, Harvard University. December.

———. 2007. An Industrial Organization Perspective on the Influenza Vaccine Shortage. *Managerial and Decision Economics* 28: 393–405.

Schondelmeyer, Stephen W., and Marian V. Wrobel. 2004. *Medicaid and Medicare Drug Pricing: Strategy to Determine Market Prices.* Introduction and Final Report, Contract #500-00-0049, Task Order 1. Prepared for Centers for Medicare and Medicaid Services by Abt Associates Inc., Cambridge, Mass. August 30. www.abtassociates.com/reports/20040830_500__00_0049.pdf.

Seward, Jane F., Barbara M. Watson, Carol L. Peterson, Laurene Mascola, Jan W. Pelosi, John X. Zhang, Teresa J. Maupin, Gary S. Goldman, Laura J. Tabony, Kimberly G. Brodovicz, Aisha O. Jumaan, and Melinda Wharton. 2002. Varicella Disease after Introduction of Varicella Vaccine in the United States, 1995–2000. *Journal of the American Medical Association* 287: 606–11.

Shinefield, Henry. 1999. Pneumococcal Vaccine and Ongoing Lessons, Kaiser-Permanente Trial: Invasive Disease. Slide presentation. http:www/medscape.com/viewarticle/413056_28 (accessed August 22, 2007).

Sing, Merrile, and Mary Kaye Willian. 1996. Supplying Vaccines: An Overview of the Market and Regulatory Context. In *Supplying Vaccines: An Economic Analysis of Critical Issues*, ed. Mark V. Pauly, Chester A. Robinson, Stephen J. Sepe, Merrile Sing, and Mary Kaye Willian. Amsterdam: IOS Press.

Sloan, Frank A., and Charles E. Eesley. 2007. Implementing a Public Subsidy for Vaccines. In *Pharmaceutical Innovation: Incentives, Competition, and Cost-Benefit Analysis in International Perspective*, ed. Frank A. Sloan and Chee-Ruey Hsieh. 107–26. Cambridge: Cambridge University Press.

Smith, Aaron. 2007. FDA Slaps MedImmune with FluMist Warning Letter. http://money.cnn.com/2007/05/29/news/companies/medimmune/index.htm (accessed August 14, 2007).

Snapinn, Steven M. 2000. Noninferiority Trials. *Current Controlled Trials in Cardiovascular Medicine* 1: 19–21.

South Carolina Department of Health and Environmental Control. 2008. Hib Vaccine Supply Crisis, Vaccine Shortage Extended, Compliance is Mandatory! October 24.

www.scdhec.net/health/disease/immunization/docs/Critical%20HIB%20 Messaging_10_22_08.pdf (accessed November 14, 2008).

Stern, Alexandra Minna, and Howard Markel. 2005. The History of Vaccines and Immunizations: Familiar Patterns, New Challenges. *Health Affairs* 24 (3): 611–21.

Stoller, Steve. 2001. Financing Clinical Trials Research at Kaiser Permanente. *Permanente Journal* 5 (2). http://xnet.kp.org/permanentejournal/Spring01/ClinTrials.html (accessed September 10, 2008).

Stout, David. 2005. Introduction. Slide presentation to investors. GSK Vaccines Seminar. June 30. http://www.gsk.com/investors/presentations_webcasts05.htm (accessed June 16, 2007).

Stratton, Kathleen R., Jane S. Durch, and Robert S. Lawrence, eds. 2000. *Vaccines for the 21st Century: A Tool for Decisionmaking.* Washington, D.C.: National Academies Press for the Institute of Medicine.

Struck, Mark-M. 1994. Biopharmaceutical R&D Success Rates and Development Times. *Biotechnology* 12 (July): 674–77.

———. 1996. Vaccine R&D Success Rates and Development Times. *Nature Biotechnology* 14 (May): 581–83.

Sugarman, Stephen D. 2007. Cases in Vaccine Court—Legal Battles Over Vaccines and Autism. *New England Journal of Medicine* 357 (13): 1275–77.

Tanner, Leo. 1943. Autistic Disturbances of Affective Contact. *Nervous Child* 2: 217–250.

Thompson, William W., Cristofer Price, Barbara Goodson, David K. Shay, Patti Benson, Virginia L. Hinrichsen, Edwin Lewis, Eileen Eriksen, Paula Ray, Michael Marcy, John Dunn, Lisa Jackson, Tracy A. Lieu, Steve Black, Gerrie Stewart, Eric S. Weintraub, Robert L. Davis, and Frank DeStefano for the Vaccine Safety Datalink Team. 2007. Early Thimerosal Exposure and Neuropsychological Outcomes at 7 to 10 Years. *New England Journal of Medicine* 357 (13): 1281–92.

U.S. Census Bureau. 2004a. *Biological Product (Except Diagnostic) Manufacturing: 2002.* 2002 Economic Census, Manufacturing, Industry Series, ECO2-311-325414 (RV), December. http://www.census.gov/econ/census02/data/comparative/USCS_31.HTM (accessed August 23, 2007).

———. 2004b. *Pharmaceutical Preparation Manufacturing: 2002.* 2002 Economic Census, Manufacturing, Industry Series, ECO2-311-325412 (RV), December. http://www.census.gov/econ/census02/data/comparative/USCS_31.HTM (accessed August 23, 2007).

U.S. Court of Federal Claims. 2008a. Autism Update—September 29, 2008. http://www.uscfc.uscourts.gov/sites/default/files/autism/autism_update_9_29_08.pdf (accessed November 15, 2008).

———. 2008b. U.S. Court of Federal Claims Vacancy Announcement, Position of Special Master. http://www.uscfc.uscourts.gov/print/4708 (accessed November 15, 2008).

U.S. Court of Federal Claims. 2009. Autism Decisions and Background Information. February 12. http://www.uscfc.uscourts.gov/autism-decisions-and-background-information (accessed March 12, 2009).

U.S. Department of Health and Human Services. Office of Inspector General. 2006. FDA's Monitoring of Postmarketing Study Commitments. Report OEI-01-04-00390. June. http://oig.hhs.gov.

———. 2007a. HHS Awards Two Contracts to Expand Domestic Vaccine Manufacturing Capacity for a Potential Influenza Pandemic. Press release. June 14. http://www.hhs.gov/news/pres/06/pr20070614a.html (accessed August 21, 2007).

———. 2007b. Immunization Grant Program (Section 317). Program in Brief. February. www.cdc.gov/NCIR/progbriefs/downloads/grant-317.pdf (accessed November 10, 2008).

U.S. Department of Veterans Affairs. 2005. Shingles Vaccine Shows Promise in Clinical Trial. Research Highlights. June 2. http://www.research.va.gov/news/research_highlights/shingles-060205.cfm (accessed August 23, 2007).

———. 2006. VA's Cooperative Studies Program Cited for Impact on Clinical Practice. May 25. http://www.research.va.gov/news/press_releases/csp-052506.cfm (accessed August 23, 2007).

U.S. Food and Drug Administration. 1995. Varicella: Summary for Basis of Approval. http://www.fda.gov/cber/sba/varmer031795sba.pdf (accessed August 23, 2007).

———. 2001. Tripedia Product Approval Information. http://www.fda.gov/ccber/products/tripedia.htm (accessed August 21, 2007).

———. 2002a. Daptacel Product Approval Information—Licensing Action. Letter dated May 14. http://www.fda.gov/cber/approvltr/dtapave051402L.htm (accessed August 21, 2007).

———. 2002b. Vaccine Shortages: An Update. http://www.fda.gov/fdac/features/2002/502_vacc.html (accessed August 21, 2007).

———. 2005. Boostrix Product Approval Information. http://www.fda.gov/cber/products/boostrix.htm (accessed August 21, 2007).

———. 2006a. Adacel Product Approval Information. http://www.fda.gov/cber/products/adacel.htm (accessed August 21, 2007).

———. 2006b. Vaccines Licensed for Immunization and Distribution in the US. Updated October 11, 2006. http://www.fda.gov/cber/vaccine/licvacc.htm (accessed February 8, 2007).

———. 2007a. Influenza Virus Vaccine, H5N1 Product Approval Information. April 17. http://www.fda.gov/cber/products/h5n1.htm (accessed August 21, 2007).

———. 2007b. Menactra Product Approval Information. http://www.fda.gov/cber/products/menactra.htm (accessed August 22, 2007).

———. 2008a. Thimerosal in Vaccines. http://www.fda.gov/cber/vaccine/thimerosal.htm (accessed November 15, 2008).

_____. 2008b. Vaccines Licensed for Immunization and Distribution in the US. Updated October 7, 2008. http://www.fda/gov/Cber/vaccine/licvacc.htm (accessed November 22, 2008).

U.S. House of Representatives. 2004. Subcommittee on Health, Committee on Energy and Commerce. Flu Vaccine: Protecting High-Risk Individuals and Strengthening the Market. Peter Paradiso, witness testimony. November 18, 2004. http://energycommerce.house.gov/reparchives/108/Hearings/11182004 hearing1404/Paradiso2258.htm.

————. 2005. Committee on Energy and Commerce. Statement of Jesse L. Goodman, M.D., M.P.H., director, Center for Biologics Evaluation and Research. May 4. http://www.fda.gov/ola/2005/influenza0504.html (accessed June 23, 2007).

U.S. Patent and Trademark Office. 2007. Patent Terms Extended Under 35 USC § 156. Last modified April 4. http://www.uspto.gov/web/offices/pac/dapp/opla/term/156.html (accessed August 22, 2007).

University of Rochester Medical Center. 2003. Vaccine with University of Rochester Roots Saves Thousands from Illness. News archives. April 30. http://www.urmc/rochester.edu/pr/news/story.cfm–id=241 (accessed August 22, 2007).

Vaccine Adverse Event Reporting System. 2007. Introduction. http://vaers.hhs.gov (accessed August 21, 2007).

Valeriano, Edwin. 2008. Telephone conversation with the authors. December 8.

Van Gelder, Alex. 2005. Patent Nonsense on Avian Flu. *Boston Globe*. Editorial. October 31. http://www.boston.com/news/globe/editorial_opinion/oped/articles/2005/10/31/patent_no (accessed December 28, 2007).

VaxInnate. 2008a. VaxInnate's Second Flu Vaccine Candidate Enters Clinical Development; Results Expected in Early 2009. September 30. Press release. http://biz.yahoo.com/bw/080930/20080930005068.html–.vv=1&printer=1 (accessed November 22, 2008).

————. 2008b. VaxInnate's Universal Flu Vaccine Candiate Shown Safe and Immunogenic in Phase I Clinical Study. October 28. Press release. http://www.medicalnewstoday.com/articles/126992.php (accessed November 19, 2008).

Vazquez, Marietta, and Eugene D. Shapiro. 2005. Varicella Vaccine and Infection with Varicella-Zoster Virus. *New England Journal of Medicine* 352: 439–40.

Wakefield Andrew J., Simon H. Murch, Andrew Anthony, John Linnell, David H. Casson, Mohsin Malik, Mark Berelowitz, Amar P. Dhillon, Michael A. Thomson, P. Harvey, Alan Valentine, Susan E. Davies, and John A. Walker-Smith. 1998. Ileal-Lymphoid-Nodular Hyperplasia, Non-specific Colitis, and Pervasive Developmental Disorder in Children. *Lancet* 351 (9103): 637–41.

Waknine, Yael. 2007. FDA Approvals: FluMist and Alaway. http://www.medscape.com/viewarticle/550649 (accessed August 14, 2007).

Wallis, Claudia. 2008. Case Study: Autism and Vaccines. *Time*. March 10. http://www.time.com/time/printout/0,8816,1721109,00.html (accessed April 21, 2008).

Werble, Cole. 2006. Vaccines Enter the New Age of Adjuvants. *RPM Report* 1 (9): 13–24. www.theRPMreport.com (accessed June 8, 2007).

Whalen, Jeanne. 2007. Roche Encounters Dilemma as Bird-Flu Fears Fade. *Wall Street Journal.* December 21. http://online.wsj.com/article/SB119820184702543895.html (accessed December 28, 2007).

———. 2008. European Regulators Back Bird-Flu Vaccine. *Wall Street Journal* February 22, B4.

White, C. Jo. 1999. Varicella-Zoster Virus Vaccine. *Clinical Investigations of Infectious Diseases* 24: 753–63.

Whitney, Cynthia G., Monica M. Farley, James Hadler, Lee H. Harrison, Nancy M. Bennett, Ruth Lynfield, Arthur Reingold, Paul R. Cieslak, Tamra Pilishvili, Delois Jackson, Richard R. Facklam, James H. Jorgensen, and Ann Schuchat for the Active Bacterial Core Surveillance of the Emerging Infections Program Network. 2003. Decline in Invasive Pneumococcal Disease after the Introduction of Protein-Polysaccharide Conjugate Vaccine. *New England Journal of Medicine* 348 (18): 1737–46.

Williams Robert M. 1998. Pneumococcal Vaccination. *Lippincott's Primary Care Practice* 2 (6): 625–33.

World Health Organization (WHO). 1998. Varicella Vaccines: WHO Position Paper. *Weekly Epidemiological Record* 73: 241–48.

———. 2002. Vaccines, Immunizations, and Biologicals: Statistics and Graphs. http://www.who.int/vaccines-surveillance/StatsAndGraphs.htm.

———. 2003. Varicella Vaccine. Immunization, Vaccines and Biologicals. May. http://archives.who.int/vaccines/en/varicella.shtml (accessed November 27, 2008).

———. 2005. Pertussis: Introduction. http://www.who.int/immunization/topics/pertussis/en/index.html (accessed August 21, 2007).

———. 2006. Development of New Vaccines. Revised December. http://www.who.int/mediacentre/factsheets/fs289/en/index.html (accessed August 22, 2007).

World Intellectual Property Organization. 2006. Avian Flu Drugs: Patent Questions. *WIPO Magazine.* No. 2/2006. http://www.wipo.int/wipo_magazine/en/2006/02/article_0005.html (accessed December 28, 2007).

Wyeth. 2007. Research Pipeline. http://www.wyeth.com/research/pipeline (accessed January 6, 2008).

———. 2008. Wyeth Receives FDA Fast Track Designation for its 13-valent Pneumococcal Conjugate Vaccine for Infants and Toddlers. Press release. May 29. http://www.wyeth.com/news–nav=display&navTo=/wyeth_html/home/news/pressrelease (accessed November 27, 2008).

Zhou, Fangjun, Jeanne Santoli, Mark L. Messonnier, Hussain R. Yusuf, Abigail Shefer, Susan Chu, Lance Rodewald, and Rafael Harpaz. 2005. Economic Evaluation of the 7-Vaccine Routine Childhood Immunization Schedule in the United States, 2001. *Archives of Pediatric and Adolescent Medicine* 159 (December): 1136–44.

Zimmerman, Richard K. 2001. Vaccine Policy Decisions: Tension Between Science, Cost-Effectiveness and Consensus——Editorial. *American Family Physician*. May 15. http://findarticles.com/p/articles/mi_m3225/is_10_63/ai_74335212/print (accessed August 22, 2007).

About the Authors

Ernst R. Berndt is the Louis E. Seley Professor in Applied Economics at the MIT Sloan School of Management, and is a member of the affiliated faculty of the Harvard-MIT Division of Health Sciences and Technology. He serves as director of the Program on Technological Progress and Productivity Measurement at the National Bureau of Economic Research, and is co-director of the Harvard-MIT Biomedical Enterprise Program. Prior to coming to MIT in 1980, Berndt was on the faculty of the Department of Economics at the University of British Columbia. He is an elected Fellow of the Econometric Society, holds a BA degree from Valparaiso University, a PhD degree in economics from the University of Wisconsin, and an honorary doctorate from Uppsala University in Sweden. Among other awards and citations, Berndt was named in 1989 as the most cited economist in the United States under the age of forty. The major focus of his research over the last decade has been on the health-care industries, particularly the pharmaceutical, biotechnology, and vaccine industries.

Rena N. Denoncourt is currently a program manager at Alnylam Pharmaceuticals, a biopharmaceutical company developing novel therapeutics based on RNA interference, in Cambridge, Massachusetts. Prior to joining Alnylam, Denoncourt was a patent and licensing associate at the Whitehead Institute for Biomedical Research, where her responsibilities included patent portfolio strategy and commercial assessment in collaboration with the MIT Technology Licensing Office. Prior to taking this position, Denoncourt was an analyst at Decision Resources, where she focused on market research and pharmaceutical consulting. Denoncourt earned a bachelor of science degree from MIT in 2001 and an MBA from MIT's Alfred P. Sloan School of Management in 2007.

Anjli C. Warner is currently the lead market forecaster for the anemia drug Aranesp, at Amgen in Thousand Oaks, California. Prior to joining Amgen in 2007, Warner was a manager at Elan Pharmaceuticals in its Corporate Strategy group, where she analyzed licensing and acquisition opportunities by conducting market assessments, benchmarking competitors, and forecasting financials. Previously, she was a senior analyst in the Strategy & Analysis group at Digitas, where she developed and recommended cross-channel marketing strategies for General Motors. Prior to Digitas, Warner worked at Morgan Stanley within the Equity Capital Markets group, conducting worldwide equity offering business development and execution in the health-care, energy, and consumer products industries. She earned a bachelor of science degree in biology from MIT in 2000, as well as an MBA degree from MIT's Alfred P. Sloan School of Management in 2007.

Index

ACIP, *see* Advisory Committee on
    Immunization Practices
ActHIB (Sanofi Pasteur), 45, 73
Active Bacterial Core surveillance,
    111–12
Adacel (Sanofi Pasteur), 45, 71, 77, 156
Administration of vaccines, cost of,
    34–38, 46
Adult vaccines
    ACIP recommended, 173–75
    clinical trial (Zostavax), 122
    payers and purchasers different from
        child vaccine, 34–38
    programs, 37–38
    See also Varicella zoster, for shingles
Advanced Market Commitment, 116
Advertising, 51
Advisory Committee on Immunization
    Practices (ACIP), 46, 51, 56, 58,
    74, 80, 97, 105, 107, 121,
    125–26, 146, 164
    process of recommendation, 30–32
    recommendation of Prevnar,
        109–10
    recommended immunization
        schedules (2009), 166–75
Advocacy groups, 141, 147
Afluria (CSL Biotherapies), 80, 83
Agency for Toxic Substances and Disease
    Registry (DHHS), 86, 145
Allergy-Induced Autism, 141

American Academy of Family Physicians,
    15, 59, 109
American Academy of Pediatrics, 15,
    59, 107, 151
    Report of the Committee on
        Infectious Diseases, 31
    Task Force on Immunization, 38
    and thimerosal, 145–48
Approval times (FDA), 20–24
Arnould, Richard, 29
AstraZeneca, 55, 80, 96
Australia, 83
Autism
    and MMR vaccine linkage in United
        Kingdom, 135–43, 147–55
    overview and treatment of, 132–35
    and petitions of adverse effects of
        vaccine, 40–42, 158
    and thimerosal-containing vaccines
        (USA), 143–55
Autism Research Institute, 134
Aventis Pasteur Ltd., 70, 111

Bacteremia, 104
Baker, Jeffrey P., 133, 135
Barr, Richard, 139–40
Behavioral Risk Factor Surveillance
    System, 53
Biken Institute (Japan), 120
Biologic, defined, 7–8
Bird flu (H5N1 virus), 13, 101–3

Blair, Tony, 138
Blockbuster vaccines, 9, 156
Boostrix (GlaxoSmithKline), 45, 71, 156
Bradley, Ed, 141, 148
Bundled products, 46–47, 72–73
Burton, Dan, 147–49

California, 149
Canada, 49
CDC, *see* Centers for Disease Control
    and Prevention
Cell-based manufacturing process, 79,
    159
    North Carolina facility, 91–92
    versus egg-based flu vaccine
        production, 87–94
Center for Biologics Evaluation and
    Research (FDA), 55, 108
Centers for Disease Control and
    Prevention (CDC), 15, 33, 52,
        77, 110, 156
    coordination with vaccine manufac-
        turers, 30–32
    economic evaluation of childhood
        immunization, 48–49
    and flu vaccines, 8, 81, 87, 88, 95,
        97, 99–100
    and phases of clinical development,
        162–64
    and post-launch surveillance, 52–54
    and Prevnar, 111–12
    price lists for influenza vaccines
        (2008), 177–81
    and pricing of vaccines, 43–47
    recommendation for varicella
        vaccine, 126
    and shortages, 56–59
    and thimerosal, 145–48, 151,
        154–55
Cervarix (GlaxoSmithKline), 158
Chelating and autism, 134–35
Chemical entity, new, defined, 7–8

Chickenpox, 46, 47
    See also Varicella disease
Chiron, 86
Clinical and preclinical development of
    vaccines, 14–25
    three phases of, 17–24, 162–64
ClinicalTrials.gov, 74
Clinical trials I, II, and III, 162–64,
    184n14
"Cold-chain" refrigeration and minimal
    light conditions, 33
Collaboration, benefits of, 64, 88, 122
Combination vaccines, 46–47, 68–73
Comvax (Merck), 58
Conjugate vaccines, 15, 105–6, 112
Connaught Laboratories, 40, 71
Cooperative Studies Program (VA),
    122–23
Cost-effectiveness and cost-benefit, of
    immunization, 48–49
CSL Biotherapies, 80, 83, 96, 98
CSL Limited (Australian), 80, 83
Current good manufacturing regulations
    (FDA), 75
Current Procedural Terminology
    physician coding system, 83
Czech Republic, 113

Daptacel (Sanofi Pasteur), 45, 70, 71, 73
DeBrock, Larry, 29
Deer, Brian, 139, 143
Delivery channels of vaccines and
    payers, 34–38
Department of Health and Human
    Services, 30–32, 96
Department of Veterans Affairs, 122–23
Developing countries and *S. pneumoniae*,
    115–17
Development timelines, 19–24
DiMasi, Joseph A., 17t, 19–23, 25
Diphtheria, overview of disease and
    treatments, 66–67

Diphtheria, tetanus, and acellular pertussis (DTaP) vaccine, *see* Diphtheria, tetanus, and pertussis (DTP) vaccine
Diphtheria, tetanus, and pertussis (DTP) vaccine, 40, 45, 63
    convenient combination formulations, 72–73
    formulations, 68–71
    history of, 68, 70–73
    long-term outlook, 77–78
    pricing and marketing, 76
Distribution, three ways, 32–34
DTaP and DTP, *see* Diphtheria, tetanus, and pertussis vaccine

Earache, *see* Otitis media
Egg-based versus cell-based flu vaccine production, 87–94
Elderly
    and flu vaccine, 100–101
    and shingles, 118, 127
    and vaccination, 53
Eli Lilly, 154
Emerging Infections Program (CDC), 111–12
Engerix-B (GlaxoSmithKline), 44
Environmental Protection Agency, 86, 145
Eocetria (Novartis), 102
Equivalence trials, 15, 163
Establishment licensure approval, 28, 164
Ethylmercury, 145–46
European Union, 104, 164
    Committee for Medicinal Products for Human Use, 87, 91
    European Medicines Agency, 101, 102, 113
Evaluation process for vaccine approval, 30–32
Evidence of Harm, 147

FDA, *see* Food and Drug Administration
Federal government
    importance of recommendation by, 32
    and purchase of vaccines, 35–36
    role in flu vaccine supply and demand, 95–97
Flu, *see* Influenza
Fluarix (GlaxoSmithKline), 80, 82
FluLaval (GlaxoSmithKline), 80, 82
FluMist (MedImmune)(AstraZeneca), 55, 80, 151, 155
    problems with nasal administration, 83–84
Fluvirin (Novartis), 45, 80, 82–83
Fluzone (Sanofi Pasteur), 45, 80, 82
Food and Drug Administration (FDA), 13, 16, 21, 28, 43, 49, 50, 51, 53, 55, 77, 157, 158
    and approval time, 22–24
    and flu vaccines, 81–84, 86, 88, 95–97, 101
    Modernization Act of 1997, 145
    and phases of clinical development, 162–64
    and Prevnar, 105, 108, 113–14
    and thimerosal, 144–46

Gambia, The, 115–16
Gardasil (Merck), 9, 46, 50, 51, 156
    for both boys and girls, 157–58
Gates, Bill and Melinda, Foundation, 117
Gerberding, Julie, 151
Germany, 83
Gilead, 13
GlaxoSmithKline, 15, 25, 42, 44, 45, 46, 49, 51, 55, 66, 112–13, 126, 156, 157
    and combination (DTP, DTaP) vaccines, 68, 69t, 71–73
    and DTP market, 75, 77

and flu vaccines, 80, 82, 98, 102
and multiple (bundled) products,
73–75
and vaccine shortages, 57–58
and vaccines for developing
countries, 117
Global Alliance for Vaccines and Immunization, 116–17
Grabowski, Henry G., 17t, 19–23, 25
Great Britain, *see* United Kingdom

Haemophilus influenzae type b (Hib), 45,
58–59, 73, 105
vaccine, 58–59
Halliday, R. G. and others, 21
Hastings, George L. Jr., 152–53
Havrix (GlaxoSmithKline), 44, 57
"Healthy People 2010, A," 52
Hepatitus-A and -B project (Merck), 18,
44
-B immunization suspended,
146–47
Hib, *see Haemophilus influenzae* type b
Hilleman, Maurice, 135
HIV vaccine projects, 18
Holly Springs, NC, 91–92
Horton, Richard, 139

ID Biomedical Corporation (Canadian-
based), 82, 96
Immunization
ACIP recommended schedules,
2009, 166–75
for children (DTP), 74
mass, 40
scheduling issues, 73–75
Immunization Action Coalition, 125
Importation of vaccines, 49–50
IMS Health, 9–10
Imus, Don, 147
Infanrix (GlaxoSmithKline), 45, 71
Influenza disease

overview and treatments, 79–80
pandemic issues, 101–2
Influenza vaccines, 63–64
clinical development and testing,
86–87
cross-reactivity, 81–82, 100
distribution issues, 94–95
future issues and challenges, 102–3
manufacturing developments, 87–94
marketing, pricing, and nonprice
competition, 97, 99
post-launch surveillance of, 99–101
price lists, pediatric and adult, 177–81
role of government in supply and
demand, 95–97
and thimerosal issues, 84–8
2008–9 season manufacturers, 98t
"universal" flu vaccine, 93–94, 159
updated annually for changing viral
strains, 79, 80–84
Innovation, 64
Institute of Medicine, 29, 148
Intellectual property protection, 12–14
Iowa, 149
Iraq, 144

Japan, 119, 120, 144
Justice Awareness and Basic Support, 141

Kaiser Permanente in Northern Califor-
nia, 106, 117
Kanner, Leo, 132
Kennedy, Robert F. Jr., 149
Kinrix (GlaxoSmithKline), 72
Kirby, David, 147, 149
Korea, 120

Lancet article linking MMR vaccine and
autism, 136, 139, 140–41, 146
Lawsuits and petitions, over adverse
effects of vaccines, 40, 41–42,
150–54

Lederle Laboratories, 40, 109
Liability issues, 39–42
    See also Autism, Lawsuits
London *Sunday Times*, 139, 140
LymeRx, 23, 42, 51

Manufacturers of vaccines, 39
    industry structure and concentration, 54–57
    numbers of, 55, 57t, 160
    revenues of, 8–10, 35, 156–57
Manufacturing procedures
    consistency and sterility, 27–28
    facility complexity, 26–29, 64
    future, 159–60
    scaled-up facilities, 16, 26
    within the USA, 55–57
Marketing efforts, 50–51
Massachusetts, 55
    Public Health Biologic Lab, 55
McCain, John, 152
McKesson Specialty (McKesson Corporation), 33, 34
Measles, mumps, and rubella vaccine (MMR)(Merck), 45, 47, 50
    and autism, panic in United Kingdom, 135–43
    MMR II in ProQuad, 120, 123–24
    possible link to autism, in USA, 147–55
    "three-in-one jab," 135–43
Medicare/Medicaid, 34, 36, 37, 38, 97
MedImmune, 55, 80, 84, 96, 98
"Mega-shot," 159
Menactra (Sanofi Pasteur), 23, 46, 50, 106, 157
Meningitis, 45, 104–5, 115
Mercer Management Consulting Company, 29
Merck, 15, 18, 44, 45, 46, 50, 55, 64, 96, 105, 135, 156, 157
    and vaccine shortages, 56–58

Merck and varicella zoster vaccines, 119
    challenges, 126–27
    clinical development, 121–23
    manufacturing issues, 123–24
    post-launch surveillance, 125–26
    preclinical research, 120
    pricing and marketing, 124–25
Mercury and vaccines, 143–55
Methylmercury environmental pollution, 143–45
Mexico, 49
Michigan, 55
MMR vaccine, *see* Measles, mumps, and rubella vaccine
Morgan Stanley, 31
M2 ectodomain portion of flu virus, 93–94
Multiple vaccines, *see* Combination vaccines
Mumps, *see* Measles, mumps, and rubella vaccine

National Autistic Society, 142–43
National Childhood Vaccine Injury Act of 1986, 40
National Health Interview Survey, 52–53
National Institute of Allergy and Infectious Diseases, 105, 122
National Institutes of Health, 64, 74, 101, 159, 164
National Notifiable Disease Surveillance System, 126
National population registries (recording childhood immunization), 52
National Vaccine Injury Compensation program, 40–42
New England Journal of Medicine, 114, 126, 154–55
New York Times, 151
Noninferiority trials, 15, 163
North Carolina, 91–92
Novartis, 45

and flu vaccine, 80, 82–83, 87, 91–92, 96, 98, 102
Novartis/Chiron, 49, 55

Offit, Paul, 151
Oka strain varicella virus, 120, 121
Omnibus Autism Proceeding, 152–53
Omnibus Budget Reconciliation Act of 1993, 34
Optaflu (Novartis), 87, 91
Orenstein, Walter A. and others, 40–41
Osaka University, 119–20
Otitis media (earache), 104, 113
    ear infections, 115
Over-the-counter remedies, 80

Pallon, Frank, 144
Patent protection, 12–14
Payers and purchasers, 15–16
    and delivery channels, 34–38
    different for child and adult vaccines, 34–38
    and distribution, 32–34
    and recommendation process, 30–32
Pediarix (GlaxoSmithKline), 68, 72–73
Pediatricians, 38
PedvaxHIB (Merck), 45, 58
Pentacel (Sanofi Pasteur), 68, 72, 73
Pertussis, 40
    overview of disease and treatments, 67–68
Pertussis vaccine
    formulation, whole-organism and acellular, 67–68, 70
    See also Diphtheria, tetanus, and pertussis vaccine
Pharmaceuticals
    clinical development timelines, 14–25
    defined, 7–8
    distribution, 32
    generic, 42–43

profitability, relative to vaccines, 8–10, 47–48
PharmaProjects, 16
Phases of clinical development for vaccines, 17–22, 77, 162–64
Physicians, role in selection of vaccines, 83–84
Plotkin, Stanley, 111
Poling, Hannah, 150–51, 152
Polio, 45, 73
Polysaccharide vaccines, 104–5, 113–14
Pneumococcus, 104, 105, 114–15
    in developing countries, 115–17
Pneumonia, 104
Pneumovax 23 (Merck), 50, 105, 108, 113–14
Praxis, 105
Prepandrix (GlaxoSmithKline), 102–3
Prevnar (Wyeth), 9, 23, 36, 46, 50, 64, 104, 156
    for adults, 113–14
    clinical development, 106–7
    competition for, 112–14
    manufacturing issues, 107–9
    post-launch surveillance, 111–12
    preclinical research, 105–6
    pricing and marketing, 110–11, 116–17
    securing listing on ACIP recommended schedules, 109–10
Pricing of vaccines, 43–50
    CDC price lists, 2008, 177–81
Product liability issues, 39–42
Product license approval, 28, 164
Production, see Manufacturing procedures
Profitability, of vaccines relative to pharmaceuticals, 8–10, 47–48
ProQuad (Merck), 46–47, 56
    challenges, 126–27
    clinical development, 121–23
    manufacturing issues, 123–24

preclinical research, 120
research and development, 120–23
Puerto Rico, 10
Public health officials, 30–32

Recombivax HB (Merck), 44
Recommendation process (ACIP), 30–32
"Red Book," 31
Reichert, Janice M., 21–23
Replacement phenomenon, 114–15
Research and development, 28–29
efforts for new DTP vaccines, 74–75
and future markets, 158–60
Revenues for vaccine manufacturers,
8–10, 35, 156–57
Roche, 13–14
Rolling Stone, 149
Rotarix (GlaxoSmithKline), 46
RotaShield (Wyeth), 23, 110
RotaTeq (Merck), 46, 50
Royal Free Hospital and School of
Medicine, 136, 137, 140, 141
Rubella, *see* Measles, mumps, and
rubella vaccine
Russert, Tim, 147

Safety concerns, 14–15, 54
See also Surveillance
SafeMinds, 147
Sanofi Pasteur, 45, 46, 50, 55, 58, 66,
75, 77, 98, 126, 156
and DTaP vaccine, 70–73
and flu vaccines, 80, 82, 96, 101
and multiple (bundled) products,
73–75
Scale economies, 28–29
Scherer, F. Michael, 29, 47–48, 59
Schwarzenegger, Arnold, 149
Sclavo, 40
Seasonal influenza vaccines, *see*
Influenza vaccines
Section 317 grant program, 36

Seven-valent conjugate vaccine, 104–6
Shingles, *see* Varicella zoster disease and
vaccine
Shortages, 56–59, 108
Sinusitis, 104
60 Minutes (Wakefield interview), 141
Smith, W. Eugene, 144
South Africa, 116
States
and ACIP recommendation, 31
and purchase of vaccines, 35
Streptococcus pneumoniae, see Pneumo-
coccus
Struck, Mark-M., 16–23
Success probabilities, 17–21, 24
Surveillance, post-launch, 52–54, 65
of DTaP vaccines, 76–77
of influenza vaccines, 99–101
Synflorix (GlaxoSmithKline), 112–13

Tamiflu (Roche), 13–14
Tetanus, 68
See also Diphtheria, tetanus, and
pertussis vaccine
Thimerosal preservative (ethylmercury),
41–42, 45, 84–86, 145–47
possible link with autism, 147–55
Thoughtful House Center for Children
(Austin), 141
Three-in-one-jab panic in the United
Kingdom, 135–43
TriHIBit (Sanofi Pasteur), 73
Tripedia (Sanofi Pasteur), 45, 71, 73
Twinrix (GlaxoSmithKline), 57

United Kingdom, 40, 86, 105
British General Medical Council Fit
to Practise Panel, 142
and MMR and autism panic,
135–43, 158
U.S. Court of Federal Claims, 152–54
"Universal" influenza vaccine, 159

University of Rochester, 105

Vaccines
    defined, 7–8
    inherent characteristics of, 14–15
    no generic, 42–43
Vaccine Adverse Event Reporting
        System, 53, 54, 77
Vaccine Injury Compensation Program,
        149–54
Vaccine Safety Data Link Project, 54, 77
Vaccines for Children program, 31, 33,
        34–37, 44, 76, 97, 110, 158
Vaqta (Merck), 44, 57
Varicella Vaccine Collaboration Study
        Group, 121
Varicella zoster disease, 118–20, 127
Varicella zoster vaccine, 56–57, 64
    challenges, 126–27
    clinical development, 121–23
    development of, 118–20
    manufacturing issues, 123–24
    post-launch surveillance, 125–26
    preclinical research, 120
    pricing and marketing, 124–25
Varicelle Merieux (Sanofi Pasteur), 126
Varilrix (GlaxoSmithKline), 126
Varivax (Merck), 46, 47, 50, 120, 156
    challenges, 126–27
    clinical development, 121–23
    manufacturing issues, 123–24

post-launch surveillance, 125–26
preclinical research, 120
pricing and marketing, 124–2
II and III, 18
VaxInnate, 93–94
Veterans Administration, 64, 122, 164
Veterans Health Administration, 123
Vilsack, Thomas J., 149

Wakefield, Andrew (linked MMR
        vaccine and autism), 135–43,
        146–48, 158
Whooping cough, see Pertussis
"Winner-take-all" price-bidding system,
        44, 55
World Health Organization, 67
    and flu vaccines, 81, 82, 86, 88, 95
Wyeth Pharmaceuticals, 40, 46, 50, 55,
        105,156
    exited DTP market, 68, 75
    and vaccines for developing
        countries, 116
Wyeth and Prevnar, 104
    ACIP recommendation, 109–10
    clinical development, 106–7
    future developments, 112–13
    manufacturing issues, 107–9
    post-launch surveillance, 111–12
    pricing and marketing, 110–11

Zostavax (Merck), 50, 64, 122, 124, 127